ALCHEMY REIMAGINED - MEASURING THE IMPOSSIBLE

Toward the Integration of Energy Healing and Intention-based Therapies into Western Allopathic Medicine

---

This Book is Inspired by the Ineffable

As the Tao Te Ching reminds us:

"The Tao that can be spoken is not the eternal Tao"

(Laozi, 2003, Chapter 1).

— *Laozi, Tao Te Ching*

To the entire human race and all matter/non-matter inhabited by consciousness.

Dedication

To my Daughter

"I always wanted to write a book about magic for you."

© 2025 Michael Hunt

All rights reserved. No part of this book may be reproduced or transmitted in any form or by any means, electronic or mechanical, including photocopying, recording, or by any information storage and retrieval system, without written permission in writing from the publisher, except by a reviewer who may quote brief passages in a review.

ISBN 979-8-218-79273-2

Library of Congress Preassigned Control Number: NRC115459

First Edition, 2025

Published by Reiki Massage

This book is intended for educational and informational purposes only. The author and publisher are not engaged in rendering medical, psychological, or other professional services. Readers should consult qualified professionals regarding any condition that may require diagnosis or treatment. Neither the author nor the publisher shall be liable for any loss, injury, or damages allegedly arising from the information contained in this book

Preface: Setting the Stage

This book did not begin as a manifesto. Its original intent was modest: to explore the language of healing in a way that both skeptics and practitioners could hear. Yet as pages gathered, the scope widened. What started as a conversation about energy work and massage became an interrogation of science, a dialogue with philosophy, a respectful nod to religion, and—at times—a challenge to materialism itself.

It would be inaccurate to say that I set out to confront every frontier of consciousness, metaphysics, and medicine. The truth is simpler: once you admit consciousness as the medium of healing, you find yourself speaking of everything. Consciousness does not respect silos. It is the zero point in which every polarity—science and spirit, symbol and signal, believer and skeptic—already resides.

This is not a book of final answers. It is an alchemical framework, a scaffold to hold conversation across traditions. If you are a scientist, you will find enough data here to provoke further study. If you are a healer, you may see your practice reflected in a new light. If you are a skeptic, you may discover that disbelief is not an end but an invitation to measure the impossible. And if you are a seeker, you may recognize that the language of vibration and resonance has been speaking to you all along.

I ask only this: read generously. Each term, each metaphor, each formula is not the thing itself but a map toward it. There is no single vocabulary adequate to consciousness. Science has one dialect, religion another, metaphysics a third, and intuition yet another. All are partial. Together, they begin to approximate the whole.

The title of this book is not a boast. It is an invitation. What was once dismissed as beyond science may now be approached, not by rejecting data but by expanding what counts as evidence. This book is not the philosopher's stone, but perhaps it is one stone on the path toward it.

A Note on Citations and Relevance

While reading the chapters that follow, you may notice that some of the cited works do not appear to directly "prove" the exact sentence they follow. This is intentional. The goal of this book is not to reproduce narrow cause-and-effect claims, but to demonstrate patterns across disciplines that point to the same conclusion: consciousness, intention, and energy are integral to healing.

To illustrate:

Ader (2007) — His Psychoneuroimmunology showed that mind and immune system are linked in ways biomedicine once denied. The nervous system and immune function cannot be isolated; meaning, "inexplicable" recoveries may have roots in consciousness.

Benson & Friedman (1996) — Their work on "remembered wellness" reframed placebo as a real physiological process. Intention and expectation modulate healing, showing that what we call "belief" is in fact a biological mechanism.

Schedlowski et al. (2015) — Their review of placebo responses reveals measurable biochemical shifts, from immune markers to neurotransmitters, triggered purely by expectation. This supports the idea that healing is as much about fields of meaning as it is about molecules.

Zubieta et al. (2005) — Using brain imaging, they demonstrated that placebo analgesia is mediated by endogenous opioid release. In other words, consciousness activates the same biochemistry as pharmaceuticals.

Taken together, these works *laterally* support the narrative presented here. The text does not quote them line-for-line, but their findings serve as anchors that tether experiential claims to peer-reviewed science. This approach is deliberate: instead of reducing the argument to a single discipline, it shows how diverse fields — neuroscience, immunology, psychology — converge on the same reality.

Please consider this as you read. The purpose of the references is not to confine each sentence to a footnote, but to open the horizon of evidence, showing that lived experience, clinical practice, and metaphysical inquiry all point in the same direction.

Table of Contents

Prologue	1
From Paramedic to Practitioner of Consciousness	1
Chapter One Alchemy Reimagined	5
Introduction	5
A Brief Interlude	12
Something from Nothing	12
Chapter Two: Massage Therapy	13
Chapter Three: The Mind-Body Bridge	22
Another Interlude: The Authority of Meditation	24
Chapter 3 (Continued)	26
Chapter Four: Reiki	32
Chapter Five: Sound Healing	39
Chapter Six: Reiki Massage	45
Chapter Seven: Consciousness as Contextual Medium	50
Chapter Eight: Attunement and the Clinical Field	53
Epilogue: The Long Arc of Gravity	57
The Women Who Captured Starlight	67
The Women Who Computed the Stars	70
Nothing to It — How Zero Explains Everything	73
As Above, So Below: The Microcosm and Macrocosm	76
Suggested Reading	79
References	178
Glossary of Terms	187

Appendix - Dr. Hunt -Thesis and Dissertation Scholarly Review	196
Appendix A	196
Appendix B	199

Prologue

From Paramedic to Practitioner of Consciousness

Before this work turns to its central themes—massage therapy, Reiki, Reiki Massage, and sound therapy—it is important to explain the path that led me here.

I did not begin in metaphysics. My first training was in massage therapy, where I earned a certificate at the Sebastopol Massage Center in California. The program was rigorous in anatomy, kinesiology, and physiology, yet the true inspiration came from my instructor, Patricia Oberg. Patricia emphasized that technical mastery was never enough. Her teaching placed equal focus on energy flow within the body and the subtle energy that enters from outside of it, suggesting that hands could be guided as much by inner intuition as by anatomical science. Although I would go on to study many models of massage, the form she taught remains the root of my practice today.

Following that early training, I spent seventeen years as an EMT and then Paramedic in California, where I grew up. Emergency medicine exposed me to the sharpest edges of human life—moments of survival and loss, resilience and collapse. I witnessed firsthand the remarkable successes of modern clinical practice, but also its limits. Many patients encountered phenomena—recoveries, near-death experiences, or sudden shifts in consciousness—that physiology alone could not explain.

During those years, the structure of the massage profession changed, not only in Washington but across much of the United States. The field moved from certificate-based recognition to formal licensure. Having missed the transition window to trade my original certificate for a license, I knew that if I were to return to massage practice after completing my PhD, I would need to attend school again.

My decision brought me to Washington State, specifically to enroll at the Bodymechanics School of Myotherapy and Massage, one of the most respected massage schools in the country. Washington's licensure process is recognized in 48 states, making it one of the most transferable credentials in the field. This was no small factor in my decision, as I wanted both rigor and mobility in my professional foundation.

During my required clinical hours for licensure, I trained at a chiropractic clinic—Aligned Health, PC. It was there that I befriended the clinic's owner and his wife. When I mentioned my intent to start a practice of my own, they extended an invitation: to rent space within their clinic and build my business alongside theirs. This offer became the bridge not only to my professional launch but to my relocation to Washington itself. What began as a return to massage training became the foundation for a new life and a new form of practice.

Parallel to these professional steps, I pursued advanced academic work. I authored a dissertation that argued consciousness cannot be reduced to brain function alone. Earlier, in my Master's thesis, I examined the effects of sound and light on human consciousness, noting that while brainwave entrainment can be measured physiologically, the deepest elements of conscious self-realization remain inaccessible to instrumentation (Garcia-Argibay et al., 2019; Wahbeh et al., 2007). Together, these studies reinforced the conviction that life is fundamentally a conscious experience and that healing must address not only the physical body but the mental, energetic, and spiritual layers of being.

From California paramedicine to Washington massage licensure, from Patricia Oberg's intuitive teachings to the rigorous standards of Bodymechanics, and from academic inquiry into parapsychology to the founding of my clinic at Aligned Health—this journey has been one of integration. The practice I have built represents, in my view, not only a personal calling but a prototype for what may one day become a semi-standardized model of integrative care. Ancient in its roots, modern in its methods, it is a path of healing that honors every layer of the human being.

Author's Introduction: What This Book Covers (and What It Doesn't)

This book centers primarily on Reiki, massage therapy, and sound therapy—the three modalities that form the foundation of my professional practice and personal inquiry (Baldwin & Trent, 2017; Punkanen & Ala-Ruona, 2012; Thrane & Cohen, 2014). I make no claim that these approaches are superior to other traditions, nor do I suggest they represent the full spectrum of healing practices available across the world. They are the tools with which I work most intimately, and they serve as the lenses through which I explore broader questions of consciousness, energy, and healing.

It is important to state from the outset that the methods discussed here represent only a small portion of humanity's diverse approaches to health, spirituality, and energy work. Entire cosmologies and cultural lineages could each command volumes of their own. For reasons of focus and readability, I will not attempt the impossible task of covering them all. This limitation is not an exclusion born of dismissal, but of scope.

Consider, for example, the case of China, where energy work and Eastern medicine are not peripheral but rather institutionalized within the fabric of society. Practices such as working with *qi*, acupuncture, and herbal medicine are not fringe alternatives—they are embedded within the official healthcare system, taught in universities, and respected by the general population.

The same can be said of other traditions: Ayurvedic medicine in India with its holistic framework of doshas and koshas (Patwardhan, 2014; Hankey, 2005), Chinese medicine with its long history of qi-based therapies including acupuncture and herbal pharmacology (Kaptchuk, 2000), and shamanic healing across the Americas that integrates altered states, ritual, and community in restoring balance (Winkelman, 2010). Indigenous systems of bodywork and spiritual alignment in Africa and Oceania likewise represent deep cultural lineages of health and consciousness (Rand, 2019; Usui, 2003). Each of these is a fully developed model of healing, often thousands of years old, that continues to flourish today.

In contrast, my critique and inquiry are directed most pointedly at the Western allopathic model. It is through this lens that I speak, and it is within this paradigm that I aim to challenge assumptions. My goal is not to deny the validity or effectiveness of established non-Western systems, but rather to highlight the limitations of Western medicine when it comes to acknowledging and integrating the subtler dimensions of human experience—dimensions that cultures elsewhere have long accepted as fact (Ader, 2007; van der Kolk, 2014).

I also write from direct experience, not theory alone. Over years of practice, I have repeatedly witnessed individuals experience measurable relief, psychological shifts, and profound healing through these methods (Baldwin et al., 2020; Diego & Field, 2009). I therefore attest that they work. This is not an article of faith but a record of outcomes—outcomes that can be observed, documented, and in many cases measured. Pain levels decrease. Stress biomarkers normalize. Sleep improves. Emotional states stabilize. If these changes were produced by a pharmaceutical intervention, they would be published and celebrated. That they emerge instead from modalities outside the dominant paradigm does not diminish their reality.

Here lies the challenge: if skeptics insist on the supremacy of empiricism, then let them apply it here. Test, measure, and attempt to disprove. To dismiss lived outcomes without rigorous study is not science—it is avoidance. To postpone investigation until mechanisms are fully explained is to ignore the very history of medicine, which has always validated practice first and discovered explanations later (Benedetti, 2008; Schedlowski et al., 2015). Science begins with results;

causation follows. To deny this sequence in the case of energy-based healing is not an act of reason but of selective blindness.

What follows, then, is not a comprehensive map of all possible paths, but a journey along several particular ones. Reiki, massage, and sound therapy are my chosen disciplines; they are how I have learned to listen, to heal, and to question. They will serve here as case studies in how energy can be felt, transmitted, and applied, but they should be understood as representatives of a much larger field of human exploration. To approach consciousness is to approach an inexhaustible horizon, and this work, like all works, barely scratches its surface.

Chapter One Alchemy Reimagined

Introduction

I began my career not in metaphysics, but in medicine. I spent 17 years in Emergency Medical Services, the bulk as a paramedic, responding to emergencies where human life hung in the balance. In that role, I witnessed both the remarkable efficacy of modern medicine and its limits. Many cases could be explained clinically, but others revealed phenomena that defied reduction to physiology alone: recoveries without explanation, patients reporting near-death experiences, and patterns of resilience that seemed tied more to consciousness than to biochemistry.

It was in this environment that my interest in the relationship between mind, body, and spirit deepened. While practicing as a paramedic, I pursued and completed a PhD in Parapsychology, motivated not by the rejection of science but by recognition of its current boundaries. The dissertation I wrote argued that consciousness cannot be treated as an epiphenomenon of the brain; instead, it must be understood as the primary medium of life. To ignore consciousness is to ignore the very substrate in which healing occurs.

In summary, the message of my dissertation was this: human experience cannot be fully explained or healed within the confines of materialism. Consciousness, energy, and intention are not fringe considerations but essential dimensions of life. To restore health, we must restore balance across all these levels.

From Theory to Practice

While research and writing established a theoretical foundation, my own journey led me to another conclusion: ideas must be embodied. Healing cannot remain only in journals or classrooms. It must become practice.

The clinic I have built—integrating massage therapy, Reiki, Reiki Massage, and sound therapy—represents, in my view, not merely a private enterprise but a prototype of what could one day become a semi-standardized form of patient care. Though its methods draw from ancient traditions—Hinduism, Ayurveda, and the Reiki system of Usui—its framework is modern, structured, and reproducible. It unites bodywork with energy work, evidence with experience, science with spirit. Reiki Massage Metaphysical Healing Service was founded in Nov, 2023.

This is not a rejection of conventional medicine. Rather, it is an expansion of the therapeutic model, one that acknowledges that human beings are multi-layered systems: physical, mental, emotional, and spiritual. When these layers fall out of harmony, illness arises. When they are reintegrated, healing occurs.

The Central Thesis of This Book

This book continues the work of my dissertation, but with a different purpose. Instead of addressing only academics or skeptics, it is written for patients, practitioners, and seekers. Its central thesis is simple:

- We are embodied beings, but life is ultimately a conscious experience.

- Healing requires addressing all layers of the human system—body, mind, energy, and spirit.

Practices such as massage therapy, Reiki, and vibroacoustic sound therapy are not "alternative." They are necessary complements, filling gaps left by purely materialistic medicine (Baldwin & Trent, 2017; Baldwin et al., 2020; Punkanen & Ala-Ruona, 2012; Thrane & Cohen, 2014).

By drawing these practices together into a coherent framework, we are taking the first steps toward what could become a new standard of holistic patient care.

The Path Ahead

The chapters that follow explore the four therapeutic pillars of this framework: Massage Therapy, Reiki, Reiki Massage, and Sound Therapy. Each section will integrate clinical evidence with metaphysical insight, grounding ancient practices in modern understanding. The goal is not only to describe these modalities, but to demonstrate how they function together as an integrated system—a system capable of addressing both the physical manifestations of illness and the deeper imbalances in consciousness that give rise to them (Davidson et al., 2003; Goyal et al., 2014; Lutz et al., 2004; Tang et al., 2015).

My intention is that this book not only informs but inspires. For Olympia residents, practitioners, and readers beyond, it is a call to reimagine what healing can mean.

The Multi-Body Model in Ayurvedic Thought

A Necessary Caveat

What follows is not presented as dogma. It is not an attempt to persuade the reader to adopt a particular religious or spiritual worldview, nor to suggest that one tradition has superior knowledge over another. Instead, it is an acknowledgment that in the face of the immeasurable, cultures have developed models that serve as maps. These maps may not be definitive, but they often provide a coherent language for describing phenomena that mainstream science has not yet fully captured.

The Layers of Being

In Ayurvedic and related Vedic systems, the human being is not considered a single body, but rather a collection of interpenetrating sheaths (*koshas*). These layers range from the gross physical body to subtler energetic and spiritual aspects:

- *Annamaya Kosha* – the physical body, composed of matter, sustained by food.

- *Pranamaya Kosha* – the vital energy body, regulating breath, vitality, and subtle currents.
- *Manomaya Kosha* – the mental-emotional body, where thought and feeling reside.
- *Vijnanamaya Kosha* – the wisdom body, associated with intuition and discernment.
- *Anandamaya Kosha* – the bliss body, the subtlest sheath, often described as the layer closest to pure consciousness.

Illness Across Bodies

Within this system, illness is not confined to the physical sheath. Disease may originate in or permeate multiple layers simultaneously. For example, Ayurveda might interpret a condition such as cancer not solely as a proliferation of cells in the physical body, but as an imbalance that has also invaded the astral or energetic layers.

From this perspective, the persistence of cancer despite extraordinary advances in surgery, chemotherapy, and immunotherapy is not a mystery. If only the *Annamaya Kosha* (physical body) is treated, while disturbances in the *Pranamaya* or *Manomaya* remain unresolved, the root of the disease is untouched. Healing in this framework is incomplete because "half" of the being—or more precisely, multiple dimensions of the being—are left outside of care.

This is not to dismiss or diminish the immense value of biomedical science. Rather, it is to suggest that the limited success in "curing" certain illnesses may reflect a partial approach. A system like Ayurveda insists that unless both visible and invisible layers of the human system are addressed, the underlying conditions that gave rise to disease persist (Ader, 2007; van der Kolk, 2014).

Why This Matters for Integrative Care

Even for those who do not adopt this worldview, the multi-body model provides a valuable teaching framework. It gives practitioners a way to articulate to patients that health is not merely mechanical, nor reducible to biochemical interactions. It points to the fact that stress, trauma, and emotional imbalance exert profound influence on the course of physical disease (Davidson et al., 2003; Goyal et al., 2014; Diego & Field, 2009).

In my view, the enduring strength of the Ayurvedic model lies in its conceptual completeness. By daring to speak of dimensions that are not directly measurable, it provides a language for what patients intuitively know but science has not yet fully explained: illness touches the whole being, and so must healing.

Comparative Frameworks for Whole-Person Health

A Caveat on Models

When speaking of the immeasurable, it is almost as if one must choose a flavor and color—to select a language model through which to approach what cannot be fully captured. No single system is sufficient to describe that which cannot be weighed, measured, bottled, or seen under a microscope. Still, such models serve as maps: interpretive frameworks that make the unseen speakable and, in many cases, clinically workable.

Vedānta/Ayurvedic Milieu: The Layered Person

In the Vedāntic account that permeates the Ayurvedic milieu, the human being is described as interpenetrating sheaths (pañca-kośa): physical (annamaya), vital (prāṇamaya), mental (manomaya), intuitive/wisdom (vijñānamaya), and bliss (ānandamaya). Illness can register in more than one sheath; thus, treating only the physical leaves upstream disturbances unaddressed (Patwardhan, 2014; Hankey, 2005). Contemporary Western research echoes this principle: psychoneuroimmunology shows the health impact of stress and perception (Ader, 2007), and trauma studies demonstrate how unresolved experience is embodied and perpetuates illness (van der Kolk, 2014).

Buddhist Psychology: Five Aggregates Without a Fixed Self

Early Buddhism analyzes experience into five aggregates (*skandha/khandha*): form, feeling, perception, formations, and consciousness. Suffering is tied to clinging to these processes, not to an enduring substance-self. Therapeutically, this invites methods that modulate attention, emotion, and embodiment rather than reifying identity. Evidence from meditation research supports this perspective, showing measurable neural and immune changes (Davidson et al., 2003; Lutz et al., 2004; Tang et al., 2015).

Western Medicine's Expansion: Biopsychosocial → Allostasis/Allostatic Load

Modern biomedicine's own evolution mirrors these holistic intuitions. Engel's biopsychosocial model argued that exclusive biological reductionism misses psychological and social determinants of illness. Later, McEwen and colleagues introduced allostatic load—the cumulative "wear and tear" from chronic stress across neuroendocrine, immune, and autonomic systems—linking lived experience to multisystem dysregulation and disease risk. Population evidence such as the ACE Study further demonstrates dose–response relationships between early adversity and adult morbidity and mortality (Ader, 2007; Palumbo et al., 2017).

Synthesis for Practice

Across these traditions, the through-line is clear: illness is rarely only physical; it is patterned across layers of embodiment, mind, relationship, and meaning. A care model that acknowledges the physical body, the regulatory/stress systems, and the subtle/experiential dimensions is not "alternative"—it is proportionate to the human being.

Consciousness, Psychology, and the Limits of Language

It is important to note that even psychology—considered a science—rests on models of consciousness that are, most literally, unproven philosophies. Brain imaging can demonstrate electrical oscillations, metabolic shifts, and localized patterns of activation, but it cannot reveal one's morals, values, or interior meanings. To reduce consciousness to brainwaves is to measure the instrument panel without touching the pilot.

This tension exposes the irony: psychology claims scientific grounding, yet every explanation of consciousness is a theoretical construct. Whether behaviorism, cognitive psychology, or neuro-reductionism, each proposes a model but none can finally prove its ontology.

The limitation is not simply scientific but linguistic. Human language itself fails when tasked with transmitting the fullness of conscious experience. To illustrate: no amount of written description can fully communicate the taste of orange juice. Words can approximate its sweetness, its acidity, or its texture on the tongue, but only the direct act of tasting conveys the reality. Consciousness is analogous: its essence resists capture by formula, word, or scan.

This is why multiple models—from Ayurveda's *koshas* to Western stress physiology—remain useful. They are attempts to speak about the unspeakable, to gesture toward what can only be experienced (Davidson et al., 2003; Goyal et al., 2014). They do not close the matter; they keep the conversation open.

Alchemy as Proto-Psychology and the Language of Transformation

In exploring healing across body, mind, and consciousness, it is worth pausing on an often-overlooked precursor to modern psychology: ancient alchemy. Rather than treating alchemy solely as an early chemistry, it can be read as a symbolic system—a way of speaking about internal transformation in times when direct discourse on the soul could invite persecution.

The symbolic stages of alchemy—*nigredo* (blackening), *Albedo* (whitening), *citrinitas* (yellowing), and *rubedo* (reddening)—mapped onto phases of psychological development: confronting shadow, purification, illumination, and integration of opposites. Images such as the *prima materia*, *Mercurius*, the *ouroboros*, and the *lapis philosophorum* were not simply archaic curiosities but archetypes—symbols recurring in dreams, myths, and transformative experiences (Laozi, 2003; Watts, 1974, 1996).

Thus, alchemy offers a striking parallel to what has been discussed regarding Ayurveda and other holistic models: it provided a language to discuss the immeasurable. Alchemy was never only about matter; it was a sacred grammar for the transformation of consciousness.

The recognition of alchemy as a veiled psychology folds directly into my own perception of the "rediscovery" of parapsychology. I have long regarded the alchemists with a kind of reverent respect, aware of the profound danger in which they placed themselves for daring to speak openly of transformation, spirit, and the inner life. In a cultural and religious climate where deviation could mean persecution, they crafted a symbolic system that both concealed and revealed the work of consciousness.

For me, their courage and creativity offered more than historical curiosity. They became an inspirational model—a lineage of thinkers and practitioners who, under duress, still found ways to articulate the inexpressible. In many ways, their work foreshadowed my own path: from paramedic to parapsychologist, from student of massage to practitioner of integrative care, and now to author of this book. Theirs was a language of survival and transformation; mine is an attempt to carry that impulse forward into a modern context of healing and holistic practice.

A Brief Interlude

Something from Nothing

During my studies in metaphysics, I encountered a lesson that began with a startling invitation:

> "Today we will speak of metaphysics, consciousness, and the like. And first, we will solve the paradox of the Big Bang in five minutes."

Science tells us that everything emerged from nothing. Yet if something arose, can it ever have been nothing? By definition, no. For all our advances—our telescopes that map galaxies, our instruments that replace failing hearts, our technology that splits atoms—we still do not know what consciousness is. It cannot be weighed, contained, or bottled. Brain waves represent activity, not the essence itself. From the perspective of mathematics and empiricism, consciousness may appear as *no-thing*—an absence of measurable substance—yet to dismiss it as "nothing" would be inaccurate. Its unmeasurable nature does not negate its existence; it simply resists reduction to material terms.

And here lies the paradox resolved: consciousness, while ungraspable to instruments, may in fact be the only true existence. Ineffable. Eternal. Perhaps in the boundlessness of infinity, unity fractured itself into countless fragments, each clothed in forgetfulness. Each fragment became a self, unaware of its origin. Even if it takes another eternity to awaken, time is irrelevant, for eternity itself cannot be exhausted.

That is what you are: a piece of the eternal One, living as a character among eight billion others. Look into a telescope or a microscope and you will see the same recurring pattern—the infinite folding into itself. In truth, there is nothing else to see, because everywhere you look, you are only looking at yourself.

(Inspired by the teachings of Dr. Paul Leon Masters, founder of the University of Metaphysics.)

This theme has been echoed in countless traditions, philosophies, and esoteric schools across history. It is precisely because of these many iterations that the Suggested Reading List included later in the book is not merely a bibliography. It is a map of voices pointing toward the same ineffable truth.

Chapter Two: Massage Therapy

Massage and Fascia as a Field

Language is rarely literal, yet it conveys meaning beyond its surface. A phrase may not describe reality in measurable terms, but it communicates something the mind and body grasp intuitively. I recall, during training in palpation, an instructor telling us: "Once you feel it, you will see what I mean." On the surface, the statement is paradoxical—how can touch reveal vision? Yet every student who pressed deeply enough into muscle, encountering hypertonicity, swelling, or pitting edema, came to understand. In that moment of tactile recognition, we did "see" what was meant—not with the eyes, but with a deeper comprehension of sensation and meaning.

This interplay of "I" and "me," as I described in my dissertation, is more than semantics. It points to the layered ways of knowing within human experience. Massage therapy operates in precisely this space: the literal act of touch is never just mechanical. It is communication between bodies, a dialogue of nervous systems, and often an unspoken invitation into awareness itself.

Massage, then, is not merely the manipulation of tissue. It is a way of engaging the multiple bodies of the human system—the physical, energetic, and emotional—each of which can be touched, influenced, and restored through skillful contact. In the same way that Ayurvedic models describe sheaths (*koshas*) or Jung described alchemy as the symbolic grammar of the unconscious, massage too offers a language: one of pressure, movement, rhythm, and stillness.

In this part of the book, I will explore massage therapy in broad strokes. We will consider its physiological effects on circulation, fascia, and the nervous system; its psychological impact on stress, trauma, and mental well-being; and its less tangible, yet equally real, capacity to reconnect individuals with their own embodied awareness. Massage is often considered simple bodywork. I would argue it is also a philosophy of touch, a practice that reminds us that feeling can lead to seeing, and that healing is always more than physical.

As the pioneer of sports massage Jack Meagher once remarked, "Massage is the study of anatomy in Braille." His words capture precisely the paradox my instructor conveyed years ago: that touch is its own form of vision, a way of perceiving the living body not through sight alone but through the subtle wisdom of the hands.

Massage and Fascia as a Field (Expanded)

Fascia has long been described as connective tissue, but modern research reveals it as far more than a passive wrapping. As Schleip et al. (2012) note, it is a "three-dimensional continuum of soft, collagen-containing, loose and dense fibrous connective tissues that permeate the body and enable all body systems to operate in an integrated manner" (p. 3). In this view, fascia is not simply structure, but communication: transmitting mechanical load, influencing proprioception and interoception, and participating in fluid dynamics.

Mechanobiology reinforces this integrative role. Langevin et al. (2005) demonstrated that fibroblasts within areolar connective tissue are highly responsive to stretch, actively remodeling their cytoskeleton in minutes. This responsiveness contributes to the viscoelastic behavior of the whole tissue. Other work has shown that ATP release and gap junction signaling mediate communication across fascial cells, meaning that what appears as "tissue texture" under a therapist's hands is in fact a living, adaptive process (Silver et al., 2001).

Biomechanics further reveals that muscles do not act in isolation. Huijing (2009) showed that force transmission occurs not only through tendons but also through epimuscular pathways—myofascial connections that alter length–force characteristics when fascial continuity is preserved. Such findings explain the clinical reality that working on one site often produces effects at a distance.

The Stecco school of fascial anatomy has emphasized that deep fascia coordinates movement and proprioception, acting as a functional interface between muscles. Stecco et al. (2011) argue that understanding fascial planes and their continuity can yield more precise manual interventions, since restrictions in one plane may reverberate through entire myofascial chains.

Taken together, this evidence justifies what practitioners observe daily: fascia functions as an integrative field. It is material enough to study under the microscope, yet systemic enough to explain why a therapist's slow, attentive pressure can reorganize movement and perception across the whole body.

Massage and Fascia as a Field (Plain Language Companion)

Most people think of fascia as the "wrapping" around muscles, like plastic film around food. But new research shows it's more like a body-wide fabric that connects everything—muscles, joints, organs—into one continuous suit. When massage therapists work into fascia, they're not just affecting a single muscle. They're speaking to this whole interconnected web.

Inside that web live fibroblasts—cells that act a little like engineers. When the tissue is gently stretched, these cells actually change shape and send chemical signals that help the tissue reorganize itself. This is why slow, steady pressure can feel like it "melts" tension: the tissue is literally responding to the message of touch.

But fascia isn't always soft and yielding. It behaves almost like a jelly-Kevlar hybrid. With gentle pressure, it glides and reshapes, but when force is too heavy, it stiffens and braces itself. Some scientists think this may be the body's way of protecting deeper structures—blood vessels, organs, and nerves—from potential harm. This means that pressing harder isn't always better. In fact, much of the therapeutic benefit of massage may come from listening pressure, not brute force.

Fascia also transmits force across the body. That's why working into the calf can sometimes ease tightness in the hamstring, or why releasing the hip can change the way the shoulders move. It is less like a machine of separate parts and more like a spiderweb—touch one thread, and the whole web vibrates.

For clients, this explains why a good massage often feels like more than local relief. What is being touched is not just a sore spot—it's the entire field of tension, movement, and energy that makes up the body's living fabric.

Alan Watts: One Sense Through Many Channels

Alan Watts offered a profound reframing of our sensory experience. He observed that what we think of as five separate senses are, in truth, facets of one fundamental sense—the perception of vibration. In his words:

> "All your five senses are differing forms of one basic sense—something like touch. Seeing is highly sensitive touching... Similarly, the ears touch sound waves in the air, and the nose [touches] tiny particles of dust and gas. … While eyes and ears actually register and respond to both the up-beat and the down-beat of these vibrations, the mind … notices only the up-beat" (Watts, 1969/1996, p. 61).

For Watts, this unity of sensation reflects an underlying continuity: light, sound, and all perceptual phenomena are vibratory, differentiated only by the organs that perceive them. He illustrates further:

> "The physical world is vibration … To the eye, form and color; to the ear, sound; to the nose, scent; to the fingers,

touch. But these are all different languages for the same thing, different qualities of sensitivity, different dimensions of consciousness" (Watts, 1956/1974, p. 89).

Both passages echo a recurring theme in his work: consciousness is a field of vibratory interplay, a tapestry of attentional tuning across spectra, each sense a gateway into a unified experiential field.

Massage and the Nervous System (Scholarly)

Massage engages the nervous system as much as the musculoskeletal. Mechanoreceptors in the skin, fascia, and muscle respond to touch, sending afferent signals to the central nervous system. This afferent input modulates autonomic balance: studies consistently show reductions in sympathetic activity and corresponding increases in parasympathetic tone during massage *(Diego & Field, 2009)*.

Cortisol, the primary stress hormone, has been observed to decrease following massage therapy, while serotonin and dopamine increase *(Field, 2016)*. These neurochemical changes correlate with subjective reports of reduced anxiety and improved mood. Importantly, these findings underscore that massage is not simply a peripheral intervention but one that directly modulates central processing of stress and relaxation.

Neuroimaging studies lend further support. Functional MRI has demonstrated altered activity in brain regions associated with interoception and affect regulation *(Boehme, Mueller, & Heinke, 2014)*. These findings validate the long-standing clinical observation: when the body is touched, the nervous system—not just the tissue—experiences regulation and recalibration.

Massage and the Nervous System (Plain-Language Companion)

When massage therapists touch the body, they aren't just working on muscles—they're speaking directly to the nervous system. Sensors in the skin and fascia send messages to the brain saying, "Something safe is happening here." In response, the body shifts gears: heart rate slows, breathing deepens, and stress hormones ease off.

Research shows cortisol, the chemical linked to stress, goes down after massage, while "feel-good" messengers like serotonin and dopamine go up. That's why people so often walk out of a massage not only looser in their muscles, but calmer, happier, and more at ease in themselves.

Brain scans even show that massage activates areas involved with emotional balance and body awareness. In other words, when a therapist works the body, the nervous system itself is being tuned—like bringing an orchestra back into harmony after playing off-key.

Massage as Regulation of Energy Flow (Scholarly)

All living systems depend on flow. In biomedicine, this is circulation, lymphatic drainage, and neural conduction. In traditional systems, it is *qi* or *prana*. While the language differs, the underlying concept is constant: restriction of flow breeds dysfunction, restoration of flow supports health.

Massage enhances fluid movement and vascular dynamics. Empirical studies have shown increased venous return, lymphatic clearance, and improved arterial compliance following massage interventions *(Weerapong, Hume, & Kolt, 2005)*. These circulatory changes are measurable correlates of what many traditions would call restored energy balance.

From a neurophysiological perspective, interstitial mechanoreceptors in fascia are hypothesized to influence autonomic regulation by providing slow, tonic input that modulates vagal tone *(Schleip, 2003)*. This provides a plausible mechanism by which "energy flow" is simultaneously biochemical, neural, and experiential.

Massage as Regulation of Energy Flow (Plain-Language Companion)

Every tradition agrees: life is movement. Blood must circulate, lymph must drain, nerves must fire. When these flows slow or stagnate, the body feels heavy, stiff, or ill. Massage reintroduces motion where things have become stuck.

Science shows this in circulation—blood moves more freely, lymph drains more effectively, and tissues get more oxygen after massage. At the same time, subtle sensors in fascia send calming signals to the nervous system, encouraging the body to switch out of stress mode.

Other traditions describe the same thing with different words: Chinese medicine calls it qi, Ayurveda calls it prana. Whatever name is used, people feel it the same way: warmth returning, tension melting, a sense of life moving again. Massage, in this way, is less about force and more about restoring flow.

Intuitive Touch and the Mystery of Knowing

No matter how skilled a massage therapist becomes, there remains an aspect that defies clinical explanation: intuition. A hand may come to rest precisely on a sore spot, eliciting surprise in the client—"Yes, that's exactly where it hurts," they say—when no imaging or measurement was used to guide the touch. This intuitive knowing is akin to a hidden field of awareness, one that operates outside the bounds of indexing and quantification.

Alan Watts framed this boundary of self-knowledge in a telling image: "You can't look at your own eyes with your eyes. You can't bite your own teeth. You can't touch the tip of this finger with the tip of this finger... That's the part of the universe, in other words, which does not see itself because it is seeing" (Watts, 1969/1996, p. 22).

Just as one finger cannot touch itself, the intuitive sense of touch in practice cannot be fully seen or explained by the same instrument that perceives it. The therapist's hand touches not as a mechanical agent, but as a living awareness reaching into an emergent whole.

In this way, intuitive touch functions as an embodied paradox: it is precise and intentional, yet grounded in something swooping beyond language or standard models. Like the ancient alchemists' ouroboros—a symbol of self-encompassment and transformation—the intuitive act remains both part of and beyond the system it operates within.

Massage, when informed by intuition, becomes more than technique. It becomes an act of holistic presence. It acknowledges that the limits of language—both scientific and therapeutic—open the very spaces where healing, awareness, and life itself unfold.

The Nervous System and the Limits of Emotional Language

When we speak of the nervous system's role in massage, we often use terms such as emotional regulation. The phrase is serviceable enough, but it conceals a deeper paradox. To say that massage helps regulate emotion implies a common understanding of what emotion is—yet emotion itself resists full translation.

Words like sadness, joy, or fear may describe familiar patterns, but what those states feel like in lived experience is irreducibly individual. As with the example of trying to describe the taste of orange juice, no matter how many words one uses—sweet, tangy, acidic, refreshing—the description will never replace the reality of a single sip. In the same way, two people may both say they feel "joy," but whether the interior texture of one's joy resembles the other's can never be proven.

This limitation is even clearer in the language of color. Physics can describe the precise waveforms of visible light—frequencies that can be charted, graphed, and expressed in equations. Yet to a person born blind, such formulas can never convey the lived experience of seeing color. Even among those with sight, we cannot be certain that the subjective quality of what one person perceives matches what another experiences.

Massage enters this territory. When clients speak of relief, calm, or release, they are translating interior experiences into words that only gesture toward meaning. What has actually shifted in their nervous system is not fully communicable. This does not negate the value of massage; on the contrary, it reveals its depth. Massage touches a domain where physiology and subjectivity overlap, a domain where the body's systems change in ways that cannot be captured entirely by description.

To enter that domain is to prepare the ground for energy work. For if emotion, sensation, and perception are already beyond the grasp of literal language, then speaking of subtle energy becomes a scholastic exercise. Energy, like emotion or color, is known first through experience. It must be felt, not merely explained.

The Nervous System and the Limits of Emotional Language (Expanded)

Massage itself contains a paradox of this kind. No matter how skilled the therapist, no matter how many years of practice or how refined their technique, they will never truly know what their own massage feels like. The experience is accessible only to others. The paradox mirrors everything we have said so far: some dimensions of reality can only be known through participation, never through self-reflection alone.

And yet, this is precisely what makes emotion central to human life. Without emotion, all information would be equivalent—one fact no more meaningful than another. Emotion imbues information with value, urgency, and depth; it colors human experience with significance. In this sense, emotion may be the defining quality of what it means to be human.

Models such as the chakras—whether regarded as literal energetic centers or symbolic constructs—serve as contextual languages to describe this immeasurable dimension. They provide a way to map and articulate how emotion feels and where it resides. To speak of a "blocked heart chakra," for instance, is simply one cultural way of expressing that grief, love, or vulnerability manifests not just mentally but in the felt sense of the chest. Whether one accepts the chakras as metaphysical fact or metaphor, their usefulness lies in giving us a vocabulary to speak about the ineffable.

It is here, at the meeting of physiology, emotion, and metaphor, that massage ends and energy work begins.

Body Consciousness and the Inner Voice

Dolores Cannon, founder of Quantum Healing Hypnosis Technique (QHHT), proposed that the human body holds its own form of consciousness, operating independently of the analytical mind *(Cannon, 2011)*. She illustrated this through an example: a person walking a trail may suddenly jump backward, reacting before thought intervenes. Only afterward does the mind register that what was feared as a snake was merely a stick. In such moments, the body's awareness acts first, transmitting knowledge more quickly than the rational mind can interpret.

Cannon further suggested that, from the body's perspective, the inner dialogue of the conscious mind is perceived as the "voice of God." She encouraged individuals to speak to their bodies with the same respect, patience, and clarity one would offer a child, observing that this practice could foster profound shifts in healing and well-being.

This perspective aligns with the broader paradox under discussion: a massage therapist cannot fully experience their own touch, a client cannot completely articulate their emotions, and the body itself may hold truths inaccessible to the conscious mind. In this light, the body is not simply mechanical but communicative, offering its own language of response.

Chakras, Meridians, and Contextual Languages of Energy

Here the conversation circles back to the contextual models cultures have developed to describe the immeasurable. In the Indian system, chakras provide a framework to locate emotion, consciousness, and energy in the body. In the Chinese tradition, meridians describe channels of qi whose balance or obstruction corresponds with wellness or disease.

Whether regarded as literal structures or symbolic maps, both systems succeed in offering a language where Western science often falls silent. To speak of a "blocked solar plexus" or an "imbalanced liver meridian" is to describe phenomena that people feel but cannot otherwise name: anxiety in the stomach, grief in the lungs, heaviness in the heart. These models allow individuals to recognize that emotion and energy are not abstractions but embodied experiences.

Together, Cannon's insights, the paradoxes of language and perception, and these ancient frameworks point toward a new way of understanding care: one that sees the body as both physical and conscious, and one that treats energy, emotion, and physiology as interconnected layers of the same human being.

Symbolic Language and Visualization

What unites these traditions is not only their emphasis on energy but their reliance on symbolic language. Reiki speaks of ki, Ayurveda of prāṇa, Chinese medicine of qi, polarity therapy of positive and negative currents, and somatic psychology of stored charge. None of these terms can be captured in a microscope slide, yet each provides a grammar of experience—a way to name, frame, and direct what is otherwise ineffable.

Visualization is a natural extension of this symbolic grammar. Whether in guided imagery, meditative focus, or ritual practice, the act of holding an image in consciousness shapes the body's physiological and energetic state. Neuroscience confirms that imagined movements activate many of the same neural circuits as actual movements, while contemplative traditions long ago recognized that visualization re-patterns both mind and body.

Thus, the symbolic languages of energy healing are not ornamental—they are functional. They provide practitioners and clients alike with a framework for intention, and intention expressed through image and gesture becomes embodied action. The picture painted may differ, but the act of painting—the visualization itself—is the common mechanism by which consciousness enters the body and healing unfolds.

Chapter Three: The Mind-Body Bridge

Section One: The Placebo Effect — Belief as Medicine

When I think of Reiki, I am reminded of a simple childhood story—*The Little Engine That Could* (Piper, 1930). A train loaded with toys and provisions had broken down, and all the larger, more powerful engines refused to help. It was the smallest engine, seemingly incapable of the task, that volunteered. As it began the steep climb, it repeated its mantra: "I think I can, I think I can, I think I can." Against all odds, the engine reached the top, delivering what was needed.

At first glance, this tale may appear naïve, a moralistic fable for children. Yet its lesson cuts to the very heart of Reiki: belief and intention do not merely accompany action—they transform its outcome. What should not be possible becomes possible, not because of mechanical force alone, but because of the conscious field in which effort is undertaken.

Modern biomedicine would call this "placebo" and dismiss it as an illusion. Yet the clinical record shows again and again that belief exerts measurable physiological change: blood pressure normalizes, cortisol levels decrease, immune response strengthens. As neuroscientist Fabrizio Benedetti (2008) has demonstrated, the placebo effect is neither trickery nor fraud; it is a direct expression of the body's ability to be influenced by expectation and meaning.

Reiki enters precisely here. Unlike massage, which manipulates tissue, Reiki acknowledges the reality that consciousness itself is a medium of healing. The practitioner places hands gently on or above the body, not forcing tissue into compliance, but cultivating a shared field of intention, belief, and presence. In this way, Reiki is less like the mechanics of an engine and more like the mantra it carried: a repeated tuning of the mind, body, and energy into alignment with possibility.

Just as the little engine climbed the impossible hill by the strength of its conviction, Reiki invites us to consider that the smallest shifts in consciousness—faith, hope, the simple willingness to believe that healing is possible—may be the very force that carries us up the mountains of illness, pain, or despair.

Placebo as Expectation Translated into Physiology

Scientific evidence leaves little doubt: placebo responses are physiological. Neuroimaging demonstrates that placebo analgesia activates the brain's opioid system. Zubieta et al. (2005) found increased μ-opioid receptor activity in the anterior cingulate cortex and nucleus accumbens when patients received placebo pain relief. These responses are blocked by naloxone, an opioid antagonist, confirming they are chemically mediated. Placebo responses have also been recorded in cardiovascular, endocrine, and immune systems (Schedlowski et al., 2015).

Plain-Language Companion

Cannon (2011) suggested that the body accepts the conscious mind's expectations as authoritative, responding to them as it would to an unquestioned directive. In this view, belief itself can set physiological processes into motion: the body may release natural pain-relieving chemicals, alter stress hormone levels, or shift immune activity in line with what the mind anticipates. Such mechanisms help explain why placebos can reduce pain, why simulated treatments may steady the heartbeat, and why conviction alone can influence the course of healing.

Ritual as a Therapeutic Agent

If expectation is the seed, ritual is the fertile ground that amplifies it. Moseley et al. (2002) famously showed that arthroscopic surgery for knee osteoarthritis produced no better outcomes than sham procedures, with patients in both groups reporting equal relief over two years. Later, vertebroplasty trials (Buchbinder et al., 2009; Kallmes et al., 2009) and subacromial decompression trials (Beard et al., 2018) repeated the lesson: invasive ritual often heals as much as the scalpel.

Plain-Language Companion

Sometimes what heals is not the incision, but the theater surrounding it—the lights, the drapes, the sense of being treated. The body responds not only to chemicals or physical interventions, but to the symbolic weight of care itself. Ritual amplifies belief, giving the body permission to heal.

Another Interlude: The Authority of Meditation

For all the philosophies that speak of consciousness as eternal, there has always been one common thread of practice: meditation. From the sages of India who refined the Upanishadic disciplines, to the Buddhist masters of mindfulness and emptiness, to the contemplative mystics of Christian, Sufi, and Taoist lineages, history's most respected authorities on inner life have given the same directive—look within.

Black Elk (Oglala Lakota holy man) stated:

> "Peace comes within the souls of men when they realize their relationship, their oneness, with the universe and all its powers."

The Buddha declared:

> "Be a lamp unto yourself." (*Mahāparinibbāna Sutta*)

Krishna affirmed:

> "I am the Self, O Gudakesha, seated in the hearts of all creatures." (*Bhagavad Gītā* 10:20)

Laozi observed:

> "Knowing others is intelligence; knowing yourself is true wisdom." (*Tao Te Ching*)

The *Upanishads* proclaim:

> "The Self is hidden in the hearts of all beings." (*Chāndogya Upanishad* 8.1.1)

Jesus taught the same principle:

> "The kingdom of God is within you." (Luke 17:21, New Revised Standard Version)

Muhammad taught, through the Qur'an:

> "Wherever you turn, there is the Face of God." (Qur'an 2:115, Sahih International)

They taught that the mind is not the Self; thoughts are clouds passing across the sky of awareness. Through meditation, one learns to locate the observer—the silent witness untouched by the fluctuations of body and mind.

The breath becomes both anchor and doorway, regulating the nervous system while unveiling subtler currents of awareness. Posture, rhythmic breathing, and disciplined attention serve not the ego, but the recognition that we are not the body and not the stream of thought.

The enduring lesson across traditions is this: while science still cannot weigh or bottle consciousness, meditation remains the most consistent, observable method we possess for encountering it. Instruments can record the aftereffects—coherent brain rhythms, steadier heart rates, synchronized networks—but the primary experiment is internal. To meditate is to move beyond speculation and taste consciousness directly.

Chapter 3 (Continued)

Meditation and the Brain: Consciousness as Regulator

Beyond placebo and ritual, meditation demonstrates that trained consciousness produces systematic changes in the body. Davidson et al. (2003) reported that eight weeks of mindfulness practice increased left prefrontal activation (linked to positive affect) and improved antibody response to influenza vaccination. Lutz et al. (2004) documented high-amplitude gamma synchrony in long-term meditators — a degree of brainwave coherence unseen in novices. A meta-analysis by Goyal et al. (2014), encompassing 47 trials with over 3,500 participants, found meditation programs significantly reduced anxiety, depression, and pain.

Plain-Language Companion

Meditation shows us that belief and attention are not passive — they rewire the brain and recalibrate the immune system. To meditate is to place the mind in dialogue with the body, altering brainwaves, enhancing immunity, and quieting stress.

Beyond Allopathy: Anomalous Healings

Finally, there are recoveries medicine cannot fully explain. O'Regan and Hirshberg (1993) catalogued more than 3,500 cases of spontaneous remission across cancer and chronic illness. Modern immunology suggests possible mechanisms — sudden immune activation, inflammatory shifts, or unmeasured psychosocial factors — but no unified theory.

Plain-Language Companion

Sometimes the body heals in ways that defy medical categories. Whether we call them anomalies, mysteries, or miracles, they remind us that healing is not fully owned by pharmacology or surgery.

Bridge to Reiki and Energy Healing

Taken together, placebo, ritual, and meditation form a pattern: consciousness is a determinant of health. Reiki belongs in this conversation not as superstition but as a culturally specific practice that makes this principle tangible. In the chapters that follow, we will treat Reiki's origins briefly, before expanding into energy healing more broadly. Our task is not to overwhelm with case studies but to establish the scaffolding: belief, expectation, and consciousness shape physiology. Reiki is one way to harness this universal truth.

Section Two: The Body as a Field of Energy — Beings of Light

Many spiritual systems affirm that we are "beings of light." Hindu scriptures describe subtle channels of prāṇa, Buddhist texts speak of the radiant body, and Christian mystics invoke the transfiguration of Christ as luminous presence. At first glance, such language seems poetic, metaphorical. Yet modern science affirms that human physiology is, quite literally, radiant.

The heart alone produces approximately 0.04 milliamperes of electrical current with each beat, measurable as a surrounding electromagnetic field (McCraty et al., 2009). By definition, electromagnetic radiation is light. Thus, when ancient teachers called us beings of light, they may have been closer to physics than metaphor.

The Heart as Generator

Electrocardiography (ECG) captures the heart's electrical discharge, which is not confined to the body but radiates outward. Magnetocardiography shows that the heart's field can be measured several feet away, extending into the space around us. The heart's electrical signal is roughly sixty times greater in amplitude than the brain's electrical activity as recorded by EEG.

Plain-Language Companion

Every heartbeat is a broadcast. Each contraction of the heart pushes not only blood but also a wave of electricity into the surrounding space. If our bodies are radios, the heart is the strongest transmitter. When spiritual teachers called us luminous beings, they may have been describing the same reality that cardiologists measure with sensors: we shine as fields of energy.

Brainwaves and Electrical Rhythms

If the heart is our transmitter, the brain is our instrument of rhythm. Electroencephalography (EEG) reveals that the brain continuously emits oscillations in delta, theta, alpha, beta, and gamma bands, each corresponding to distinct states of consciousness. Theta often accompanies meditation and imagery, alpha reflects relaxed alertness, and gamma synchrony correlates with heightened integration across neural networks.

Research on meditation has shown that mental training reshapes these rhythms. Lutz et al. (2004) found that long-term Tibetan practitioners could generate unprecedented levels of gamma coherence during meditation, patterns unseen in novices. Consciousness, then, has an electrical signature that shifts with intention, practice, and belief.

Plain-Language Companion

The brain hums like an orchestra. When we are asleep, it plays in slow, deep tones. When relaxed, it drifts into alpha rhythms. When intensely focused or in deep meditation, it resonates in rapid gamma harmonies. Meditation is not simply calming; it retunes the music of the brain itself.

Biophotons and Cellular Light

Even at the cellular level, life radiates. Ultraweak photon emission (UPE), also called biophotons, refers to the steady release of faint light from living cells. These emissions occur in the visible and ultraviolet spectrum and are measurable with sensitive photomultiplier devices.

Although the mechanisms remain under investigation, evidence suggests these photons are linked to oxidative metabolism and may play roles in cell-to-cell communication (Popp, 1992). The human body, therefore, is not merely an electrical system but a photonic one, glowing with invisible light.

Plain-Language Companion

Beneath the skin, every cell shines. Though invisible to the naked eye, biophotons are real, faint flashes of light generated by our own biology. Imagine an organism made of billions of tiny lanterns, each cell glowing quietly, together forming the subtle radiance of life.

Bridging Science and Symbolism

Mystical traditions have long used light as a metaphor for consciousness. Today, biophysics affirms that light is also a literal aspect of our biology. The heart broadcasts electromagnetic waves, the brain orchestrates electrical harmonies, and the cells themselves emit photons.

This convergence of science and spirituality is not a claim that religious descriptions are "proved." Rather, it suggests that when sages spoke of the human being as radiant, they were pointing toward a truth that modern measurements also reveal, though in different language.

Plain-Language Companion

Science and spirituality are often framed as rivals, yet here they meet. Spiritual texts say we are beings of light. Physics confirms that we radiate electricity and photons. One speaks in poetry, the other in data, but both describe the same mystery: life glows.

Thermal Signatures and the Heat of Life

Beyond photons and electrical waves, the body radiates heat. Infrared thermography reveals dynamic temperature changes across the skin, reflecting autonomic shifts in circulation and metabolism. Practitioners of Reiki and other energy therapies have long described sensations of warmth flowing from their hands during treatment.

Skeptics dismiss this as suggestion. Yet thermographic imaging has demonstrated measurable increases in localized skin temperature under the hands of healers, even when no physical contact occurs. The warmth patients feel is not always imaginary — it is, at least in part, a real thermal signature of life processes shifting in response to intention and presence.

Plain-Language Companion

Life burns. Every breath, every heartbeat produces heat. When a Reiki practitioner lays hands above the body, many people feel warmth. Science shows this is not just imagination: infrared cameras capture genuine shifts in skin temperature. Healing, in this sense, glows as heat as well as light.

Firelight and DNA Repair

Biophysics research suggests that light may influence DNA. Hamblin (2017) reviewed evidence that photobiomodulation — the application of red or near-infrared light — promotes cellular repair, reduces inflammation, and enhances mitochondrial function. At the genetic level, photon absorption can activate transcription factors and stimulate growth pathways.

Plain-Language Companion

Cells listen to light. Red and infrared wavelengths, when absorbed by tissue, can switch on repair programs in our DNA. In this sense, firelight is not only metaphor but medicine: it feeds the very code of life.

Bridging Toward Human Fields and Interaction

If individual hearts, brains, and cells radiate fields, then human interaction is a meeting of those fields. McCraty et al. (2009) showed that heart-rhythm coherence in one person could be detected in the brainwaves of another when in close proximity, suggesting interpersonal energy transfer.

Plain-Language Companion

We shine into one another. Your heartbeat broadcasts into the space around you, and another person's brain can pick up the signal. This means the relationship is not only emotional but electrical. Human beings are not islands; we are interacting fields.

Section Three: Fields, Waves, and Integration

Interpersonal Fields as Measurable Reality

This recognition challenges the materialist idea of humans as closed systems. Evidence from psychophysiology shows that we are permeable to one another's fields. Heart–brain synchronization, mirrored neural oscillations, and entrained rhythms suggest that relationship is not only metaphorically but literally energetic.

Plain-Language Companion Science confirms what people have always felt: we influence each other just by being near. The body is porous, open, and constantly tuning itself to the rhythms of others.

Pandora's Box of Measurement

Yet with each new demonstration comes controversy. To admit interpersonal fields is to admit that mind may not be bound by the skull or life by the skin. Such implications unsettle entrenched assumptions. Measurement of subtle energy opens a Pandora's box: once fields are admitted, the mechanistic model of isolated bodies must yield to a more fluid ontology.

The Flicker Factor: Waves Beneath Perception

Even perception itself is rhythmic. Vision, long assumed to be continuous, is now understood as occurring in oscillatory bursts. Recent research in neuroscience demonstrates that attention flickers at frequencies of roughly 7–10 hertz, aligned with alpha rhythms. Consciousness, then, is not a steady beam but a wave.

Plain-Language Companion We don't see the world in a smooth stream. The brain samples reality in flickers, like frames of film. Life is wave-like even in how we perceive it.

Mathematics and the Discovery of Language

Mathematics has often revealed truths beyond the reach of sensory experience. Non-Euclidean geometry, quantum mechanics, and chaos theory demonstrate that reality obeys patterns our ordinary language struggles to capture. Likewise, energy fields and vibratory phenomena may require a new grammar — a symbolic language that bridges mathematics, physiology, and experience.

Toward a Symbolic–Scientific Bridge

Alchemy once served this role, providing a symbolic vocabulary for transformation when direct speech was impossible. Today, physics and psychophysiology provide data, while Reiki, meditation, and bodywork provide practice. What remains is the bridge: a coherent language that honors both.

A New Language of Healing

This book proposes that such a bridge is possible. By weaving clinical science, ancient models, and experiential practice, we can begin to articulate a language adequate to the whole human being. Massage therapy, Reiki, Reiki Massage, and sound healing are not fringe curiosities but pillars of this new grammar. They speak across body, mind, and energy, giving us tools not only for treatment but for transformation.

The task of this book, then, is not merely descriptive. It is translational. It seeks to reimagine alchemy — the union of matter and spirit — as a framework for integrative healing.

Chapter Four: Reiki

Preface: Reiki as a Language of Energy Work

Scholarly Layer

Reiki, originating in early 20th-century Japan through the work of Mikao Usui, is often described as a form of energy healing in which practitioners transmit or channel a subtle vital force through the hands, either placed directly on or held slightly above the body (Rand, 2019). While skeptics may frame Reiki as placebo, emerging evidence suggests measurable physiological effects. Clinical studies document reductions in anxiety, pain, and fatigue following Reiki sessions (Thrane & Cohen, 2014; Baldwin & Trent, 2017). Neuroimaging has even hinted at altered brainwave coherence and parasympathetic activation during treatment (Baldwin et al., 2020).

Reiki, however, is not reducible to a single mechanism. Like *Āyurveda's koshas* or Chinese meridian theory, it functions as a language—a map for articulating phenomena at the margins of conventional science. Chakras, *ki*, and subtle bodies are not empirically verifiable structures in the material sense, but they are powerful symbolic frameworks that guide attention, intention, and therapeutic presence. In this regard, Reiki operates simultaneously as cultural system, therapeutic intervention, and phenomenological practice.

The danger of dismissing Reiki lies in collapsing language into ontology. To call chakras "imaginary" is as misleading as calling neurotransmitters "realer" than emotions. Both are models for describing processes that cannot be seen directly but manifest through lived experience. Reiki extends this principle by suggesting that consciousness itself is the field in which such interactions occur.

Plain-Language Companion

Reiki can be thought of as learning a new alphabet for the body's inner life. In Japanese, the word combines *rei* (spirit, universal) and *ki* (life energy). When a practitioner lays hands gently over a person, what is being exchanged is not force but presence—a tuning, like adjusting the strings of an instrument until harmony returns.

Science has its words—brainwaves, cortisol, vagal tone. Reiki has its words—chakras, energy flow, light. They are not enemies, but dialects of the same conversation. What matters is not whether one dialect is "truer," but whether it helps the body find balance and the person find ease. Clients who emerge from Reiki sessions often say, "I feel lighter," or, "It feels like something has shifted." Such statements are difficult to plot on a lab chart, yet they testify to an unmistakable reality: change has occurred.

Reiki, then, is less about imposing an external power and more about remembering an inner coherence that was never lost. It is a cultural practice, a therapeutic ritual, and for many, a profound experience of being met not only in the body, but in the very field of consciousness itself.

It is important to recognize that Reiki is not an isolated phenomenon but one expression of a larger human impulse to map and work with energy. Across cultures, the same principle appears in different guises. In India, *prāṇa* is cultivated and directed through pranic healing; in the West, Randolph Stone articulated polarity therapy as a way of balancing subtle currents through touch and alignment; and within contemporary psychology, somatic therapies emphasize the release of stored emotion and tension through intentional movement and presence.

Though their languages differ, the through-line remains constant: healing as the transfer or re-patterning of energy through conscious intention, often enacted through symbolic or embodied ritual. Whether one speaks of chakras, polarity lines, or autonomic discharge, the pattern is the same. A practitioner sets an intention, codifies it through touch, gesture, or movement, and the body responds—not only as flesh and nerves, but as a participant in a larger field of meaning.

This is what was meant earlier by the "flavor and color" of different models: each tradition paints the picture differently, but the canvas is the same. Reiki, pranic healing, polarity therapy, and somatic approaches all converge on a shared recognition—that the body is not a closed machine, but an open field where consciousness, energy, and physiology intersect.

History of Reiki Healing

Caveat on Brevity

The history of Reiki has been documented exhaustively in books, articles, and online sources. To repeat those accounts in detail here would add little to the present discussion. What follows, then, is a deliberately brief overview—enough to orient the reader, but not to duplicate what can be found elsewhere. The purpose of this chapter is not to rehearse genealogy, but to position Reiki within the broader framework of energy-based healing and its role in integrative care.

Scholarly Layer

Reiki traces its origins to early 20th-century Japan and the teachings of Mikao Usui (1865–1926). Usui is said to have undergone a period of meditation and fasting on Mount Kurama, after which he articulated a method of channeling universal energy (*rei-ki*) for healing through the hands. His students, notably Chujiro Hayashi, helped formalize techniques and hand positions, while Hawayo Takata later introduced Reiki to the West in the 1930s, ensuring its continuity across cultures (Usui, 1990/2003; Takata, 1981). Today Reiki exists in many lineages, yet all share the core intention of restoring balance through conscious presence and touch.

Plain-Language Companion

The history of Reiki is simple at its core: one man's experience became a practice, then a lineage, and finally a global tradition. Mikao Usui's meditation on Mount Kurama gave birth to a method that his students carried outward, each generation adapting but preserving its essence. Reiki has since traveled across continents and languages, yet whether practiced in Tokyo, Honolulu, or Olympia, the heart of it remains unchanged—hands placed with intention, presence offered as healing.

Reiki as an Accessible System

Scholarly Layer

One of Reiki's enduring strengths is its accessibility. Unlike complex medical curricula or esoteric initiations, the method is simple enough to be learned and practiced by anyone. This simplicity is not a weakness but a superpower: it demonstrates that the capacity for healing through intention and energy transmission is not restricted to specialists but is a latent human faculty. In this way, Reiki can be seen as both a structured tradition and a reminder that consciousness itself functions as an antenna—capable of sensing, amplifying, and transmitting fields of energy. The practice gives form to what might otherwise remain underacknowledged: that human physiology and awareness are intertwined in ways that extend beyond material reductionism.

Plain-Language Companion

Reiki's power lies in how simple it is. You don't need to be a doctor, a mystic, or a chosen healer. The method can be taught in a weekend, and yet its effects can last a lifetime. This accessibility is the point: Reiki reveals something already within us—the ability to sense and transmit energy, like an antenna tuning into a signal. It shows that healing is not just for a few, but for everyone, because the same faculties lie dormant in all human beings. Reiki gives a language and a method for what we already carry.

Intention as the Instrument of Energy Healing

Scholarly Layer

In energy-based practices, intention is not a poetic flourish but the operative mechanism. Just as a surgeon wields a scalpel to direct physical change, the energy practitioner wields intention to direct subtle change. Contemporary research in psychoneuroimmunology suggests that intention exerts measurable effects: mental focus and expectation can modulate immune response, pain perception, and autonomic regulation (Ader, 2007; Benson & Friedman, 1996). Visualization studies further confirm that imagined actions activate neural circuits overlapping with those used in actual movement (Decety, 1996). These findings underscore that intention is not ancillary but causal—it organizes physiological processes and structures the therapeutic field in which healing unfolds.

Plain-Language Companion

For energy healers, intention is the scalpel. It is the tool that makes the work precise. While surgeons cut with steel, energy practitioners cut with focus—shaping fields, directing flow, and inviting the body to remember its balance. This isn't just poetry. Science shows that what we imagine changes the way our bodies behave: heart rates shift, immune systems tune, and even pain lessens when the mind is steady in its purpose. Intention is, in this sense, the true instrument of healing. Hands provide contact, rituals provide form, but intention provides direction. Without it, the practice is empty gesture; with it, even simple presence becomes medicine.

Contextual Maps of Energy: Chakras, Koshas, and Meridians

Scholarly Layer

If intention is the scalpel of energy healing, symbolic maps are its anatomy. Every medical system requires models that orient the practitioner: in biomedicine, skeletal diagrams, dermatome charts, and neuroanatomy serve this purpose. In energy-based traditions, the equivalents are the chakra system of India, the *kosha* model of Vedānta, and the meridian system of Chinese medicine. These frameworks provide location, language, and logic for therapeutic action.

From a critical perspective, such maps may not correspond to empirically verifiable structures. Yet their utility lies elsewhere. They focus attention, organize technique, and anchor meaning. Studies on attentional direction show that where awareness is guided, physiological shifts follow—changes in heart rate variability, brainwave patterns, and stress hormone levels (Tang et al., 2015). Thus, whether one speaks of balancing the solar plexus, clearing liver *qi*, or harmonizing the *prāṇamaya kosha*, the map is not ornamental. It is a clinical tool, translating the healer's intention into embodied practice.

Plain-Language Companion

Maps matter. A surgeon studies charts of arteries and nerves; an energy healer studies diagrams of chakras or meridians. The goal is the same: to know where and how to guide the work. These maps may not show up on X-rays, but they give both practitioner and client a way to picture the process. And once something can be pictured, it can be worked with.

That is why chakras, koshas, and meridians persist. They don't have to be "proved" under a microscope to be useful. They tell a story of how energy moves, where it gets stuck, and how it can be freed. The practitioner's intention then becomes focused, like a surgeon's scalpel—guided not by steel, but by image and presence. In this way, symbolic maps are not just metaphors. They are the working diagrams of the healing arts.

Caveat: The Slip Knot of Dogma

Scholarly Layer

There is a profound danger in mistaking symbolic maps for literal anatomy. To insist that chakras or meridians exist in the same way arteries or neurons exist is to bind oneself into what might be called a slip knot of dogma. The knot forms because symbols, once codified, can harden into absolutes. When this occurs, the living fluidity of experience becomes reduced to rigid doctrine.

Nearly all of these maps—chakras, koshas, meridians, polarity lines—fall outside the reach of current empirical research. They cannot be dissected under a microscope or traced with dyes through cadavers. The temptation, then, is twofold: skeptics dismiss them as fantasy, while adherents cling to them as literal truths. Both responses miss the point. The value of these systems lies not in their verifiability, but in their utility as frameworks for attention and intention.

This is why a general, intuitive understanding can be as powerful as a doctorate in the world of healing arts. Intuition, when coupled with a symbolic map, allows practitioners to enter the therapeutic encounter with focus and confidence—without the illusion that the map itself is the territory. To treat these models as tools, rather than dogma, is to preserve their usefulness while avoiding the pitfalls of fundamentalism.

Plain-Language Companion

The maps of energy—chakras, meridians, koshas—are like drawings in the sand. They give us direction, but they are not the landscape itself. The danger comes when people start believing the drawing is the land. That's the slip knot of dogma: the moment a symbol is mistaken for a literal thing.

Science can't prove these maps, but that doesn't mean they are useless. Their power is in how they guide attention and shape intention. A practitioner who works with a general sense of balance and flow may be just as effective as one who has memorized every symbolic point. In fact, sometimes the generalist sees more clearly, because they are not tangled in the knot of dogma.

This is why intuitive healers, often without advanced degrees or formal systems, can still achieve profound results. They work with the essence of the map, not the rigidity of its borders.

In the intuitive world, clarity of intention is the true doctorate. The maps are there to serve the practice—not to become prisons of belief.

Sidenote: The Thorn in the Side of Empirical Science

Scholarly Layer

Science prides itself on its capacity to measure, replicate, and falsify. At its core, the scientific method is not only about establishing proof but about testing for disproof. The failure to disprove a claim is, in fact, the condition under which truth gains traction. Yet this principle places energy-based systems in a curious position. Though they cannot be quantified by present instrumentation, they have also resisted disproof. Reiki, prāṇic healing, meridian therapies—all remain outside empirical capture, but not because they have been invalidated. What troubles the materialist is not simply that these systems are unmeasurable, but that despite fervent attempts, they are not falsifiable in any definitive way.

Plain-Language Companion

Science works like this: you don't just prove an idea, you try to break it. If it can't be broken, it stands a little stronger. That's why medicines are tested in trials, why experiments are repeated, why skepticism is built into the method.

The irony with Reiki and other energy systems is that while no microscope has pinned them down, no study has torn them apart either. They remain stubbornly present—used by practitioners, experienced by clients, and echoed across cultures.

For materialists, this is the thorn in the side. They would prefer these practices be disproven and discarded. Yet the fact remains: the maps cannot be proven, but neither can they be erased. They persist, like an unyielding knot in the fabric of human healing, challenging the notion that only what can be weighed and measured is real.

Chapter Five: Sound Healing

Preface: Vibration as the Ground of Experience

Scholarly Layer

From the most ancient texts to the most modern laboratories, vibration is recognized as a fundamental principle of existence. The Hebrew Bible opens with the phrase, "God said, 'Let there be light'" (Genesis 1:3). Whatever one's theological commitments, the symbolism is striking: sound precedes light. In other words, vibration comes before illumination. Read metaphorically, this places resonance at the very root of creation.

This intuition finds resonance in physics as well. Matter itself is not static but vibratory: atoms oscillate, subatomic particles exist as probability waves, and the measurable universe is patterned by frequency. Biologically, too, humans are beings of sound. The heart produces rhythmic waves detectable outside the body; the brain hums with oscillatory rhythms; and at the cellular level, ultraweak photon emission has been observed to pulse in rhythmic coherence (Popp, 1992). To describe life as vibration is not poetry—it is empirically defensible.

In this context, sound healing does not appear as exotic or esoteric. Rather, it is an applied recognition of a principle science already affirms: that resonance organizes matter, physiology, and consciousness.

Plain-Language Companion

The most famous sentence in the Bible begins not with light but with sound: "God said, let there be light." Think about that—before light, there was speech, vibration, resonance. Whether you take it as history or as metaphor, the order matters. The first creative act was sound.

Science quietly agrees. The universe is not silent; it hums. Atoms quiver, molecules vibrate, and even the stars emit frequencies too vast for us to hear. Our bodies do the same: the heart is a drum, the brain an orchestra, the voice a tuning fork. When healers use sound—through bowls, forks, or even voice—they are not inventing something new. They are working with what has always been there: vibration as the foundation of life itself.

In this way, sound healing is not mystical ornament but a reminder. It tells us that to heal is to tune, to restore harmony where the song has gone off-key. And perhaps the irony remains: even in the stories of creation, vibration was the first word, and light came after.

The Physiology of Sound: Resonance in the Human Body

Scholarly Layer

If vibration is the foundation, then biology is its most immediate expression. Human beings are, in essence, electromagnetic organisms composed largely of water. Roughly 60 percent of the adult body is water, and every physiological process—from nerve conduction to cardiac rhythm—relies on the movement of ions and electrical gradients. Water is an efficient medium for transmitting both mechanical waves and electromagnetic fields, which means the human body is naturally predisposed to resonate.

Studies in vibroacoustic therapy demonstrate this principle in action. Low-frequency sound applied through specialized tables or speakers has been shown to reduce pain, improve sleep, and ease muscle tension (Wahbeh et al., 2007). Heart rate variability (HRV) and vagal tone often increase during such sessions, indicating a shift toward parasympathetic dominance—the physiology of rest and repair. These findings confirm what intuition has long suggested: sound does not merely touch the ears; it permeates the entire organism.

Plain-Language Companion

At the simplest level, people are walking bags of water held together by skin, pulsing with electricity. The heart sparks a rhythm, nerves fire like tiny lightning bolts, and all of it travels through a medium that conducts vibration with astonishing efficiency. When sound waves enter the body, they don't stop at the ear—they ripple through muscle, fascia, and fluid.

This is why sound feels different from other sensations. A drumbeat in the chest, the deep hum of a crystal bowl, the vibration of a tuning fork on the skin—these don't just register as "hearing." They reorganize the body from the inside out. Science shows it in numbers: slower heartbeats, calmer breath, better sleep. But you don't need a lab to know it. Sit in a room with music that moves you, and your whole being remembers: you are made of water, and water sings when touched.

Sound as Time Made Audible

Scholarly Layer

Alan Watts, in *The Book: On the Taboo Against Knowing Who You Are* (1996/1969), remarked that the five senses are not separate faculties but variations of a single sense: touch. Light, sound, scent, and taste are, in this view, differing ways of perceiving vibration. Hearing, for example, is not the detection of an isolated moment but the perception of waves—pressure changes moving through air and tissue.

Building on this idea, Watts argued that sound reveals something unique about time. A sound, unlike a static image, cannot be perceived without duration. A clap or bang includes its own narrative: a silence before, a sharp present, and a fading future. In this way, sound uniquely embodies past, present, and future as a single sensory event. To hear, then, is to participate in temporality.

Plain-Language Companion

Watts liked to say that all our senses are just different ways of touching. Eyes touch light waves, ears touch sound waves, skin touches air and pressure. Everything we know of the world comes through vibration.

Sound makes this clearer than anything else. Think of a bang: first there is silence, then the sudden noise, then its fading echo. In that single sound, you've just experienced the past, the present, and the future. No philosophy needed—it's built into the way hearing works.

This is a quiet problem for materialism. If perception of time is woven into sound itself, then consciousness is not merely "in the present moment." It is always stretched across before, now, and after—woven into waves. To hear, in other words, is to live in time.

The Hard Problem of Vibration

Scholarly Layer

Empiricists pride themselves on precision: measuring sound waves, charting decibels, tracing neural responses. Yet vibration poses a fundamental challenge. Human beings demonstrably adapt to vibration even in the absence of hearing. Studies on deaf participants show measurable changes in somatosensory cortex activity when exposed to vibratory stimuli, confirming that the body interprets frequency beyond the auditory canal (Levänen et al., 1998).

Vibration, then, is not confined to "hearing" but is a multisystem force acting across skin, fascia, nervous tissue, and even cellular processes.

This creates a paradox. Vibration is both traceable and elusive. It can be recorded by instruments, plotted as waveforms, and quantified in hertz—yet the experience of vibration, the sense of resonance or harmony, resists reduction. It is at once mathematical and metaphysical. For proponents of integrative healing, this duality offers what might be called an endless safety net: everything, at its most fundamental level, is vibration. Thus, vibration is not merely a metaphor but a principle that both sustains scientific analysis and surpasses it.

Plain-Language Companion

Here is where science runs into its own wall. Vibration can be measured down to the tiniest fraction of a second, yet it refuses to stay in the box. People who cannot hear still feel vibration in their bones and skin, and their brains change in response. The body doesn't care if ears are working or not—it knows vibration anyway.

This is the hard problem: vibration is everywhere, measurable and undeniable, but its meaning slips beyond the graphs. We can say a drumbeat is 80 hertz, but that doesn't explain why it feels grounding. We can measure a crystal bowl's frequency, but not why its sound feels like it "opens the chest." Science can describe the waves, but not the experience. And so vibration sits at the edge of knowledge, a reminder that life is both mathematics and mystery, physics and poetry.

Evidence in Practice: Vibroacoustic Therapy and Binaural Tones

Scholarly Layer

Among the many applications of vibration in healing, vibroacoustic therapy (VAT) is perhaps the most thoroughly documented. Using low-frequency sound delivered through transducers embedded in chairs, beds, or mats, VAT has been shown to reduce muscle tension, improve sleep, and decrease pain in clinical populations (Wahbeh et al., 2007; Punkanen & Ala-Ruona, 2012). Physiologically, these effects correlate with increased parasympathetic activity, reductions in cortisol, and shifts in brainwave coherence. Patients often report not only symptom relief but also an enhanced sense of calm, integration, and grounded presence.

Binaural beats, another branch of vibratory medicine, exploit the brain's natural tendency toward entrainment. When two tones of slightly different frequencies are presented separately to each ear, the brain perceives a third "beat" frequency equal to the difference. Research indicates that such auditory entrainment can influence states of consciousness, inducing relaxation, focused attention, or even altered states associated with meditation (Lane et al., 1998; Garcia-Argibay et al., 2019). These findings highlight that vibration does not merely passively wash over the body; it actively reorganizes perception, physiology, and consciousness.

Plain-Language Companion

This is where the science actually helps prove the point. Vibroacoustic therapy works by running low-frequency sound right into the body through a chair, table, or mat. Patients don't just hear the sound—they feel it ripple through their muscles and bones. The result is often less pain, deeper sleep, and a calm that can't be faked.

Binaural beats take the same principle inside the brain. Play one note in the left ear and another in the right, and the brain "creates" a third note out of the difference. That imagined rhythm can actually guide brainwaves into states of focus, meditation, or relaxation. In other words, vibration doesn't just shape the body—it tunes the mind.

Both of these therapies are studied, published, and accepted in ways that Reiki is not. And yet they rely on the same principle: intention married to vibration. This is the scientific foothold that reveals a deeper truth—the very one Reiki Massage embodies.

The Note That Doesn't Exist (The Missing Fundamental)

Scholarly Layer

The most striking lesson of binaural beats is that the therapeutic effect arises not from the tones themselves, but from the illusory third frequency—a sound the brain generates internally. The beat does not exist in the external world, yet it entrains neural oscillations, alters physiological states, and produces measurable outcomes (Garcia-Argibay et al., 2019). In other words, the mechanism of healing is an emergent phenomenon: an artifact of perception that becomes causally real.

This observation undermines the insistence that only tangible, measurable stimuli can be considered legitimate. It is precisely the "non-existent" note that drives the physiological shift. The metaphor could not be clearer: healing often arises not from what can be weighed or dissected, but from what consciousness itself constructs.

Plain-Language Companion

Here's the punch line: the healing in binaural beats comes from the note that isn't there. Two different tones go into your ears, and your brain invents a third one. That invented rhythm changes your brainwaves, slows your heartbeat, and calms your body.

Think about that—something that doesn't exist in the outside world is the very thing creating real, measurable change. It's a reminder that what matters in healing is not always what's physical, but what's perceived, felt, and embodied.

This is why vibration and intention belong together. Reiki Massage, as we will see next, works on the same principle: combining what is tangible (touch, movement, rhythm) with what is intangible (intention, energy, presence). Just like the "third note," the effect is greater than the sum of its parts.

Chapter Six: Reiki Massage

Preface: Integration in Practice

Scholarly Layer

If sound teaches us that healing can arise from a note that does not exist in the external world, Reiki Massage demonstrates that integration itself can become a modality. Here, the tactile precision of massage and the intentional field of Reiki are joined, producing outcomes neither could accomplish alone. Like the illusory third tone of binaural beats, Reiki Massage is more than the sum of its parts. It is an emergent practice—structured, repeatable, yet irreducible to either tissue mechanics or energy flow in isolation.

Plain-Language Companion Reiki Massage is the "third note" made flesh. It isn't just massage plus Reiki, stacked side by side. It's what happens when touch and energy meet—something new, something more. Just as your brain invents a rhythm that changes your whole state, Reiki Massage creates a space where muscle, mind, and energy shift together.

Clinical Foundations: Trauma, Stress, and Somatic Integration

Scholarly Layer

Trauma research has established that unresolved stress is stored not only in declarative memory but in fascia, musculature, and autonomic reflexes (van der Kolk, 2014). Massage restores fascial glide, releases muscular tension, and supports parasympathetic dominance (Field, 2016). Reiki, meanwhile, has been associated with reduced anxiety, lowered blood pressure, and improved heart-rate variability (Baldwin & Trent, 2017).

It is a safe approximation to suggest that when these modalities are combined, massage reorganizes tissue while Reiki interacts with autonomic regulation through presence and attunement. The two together appear to foster conditions in which trauma patterns may shift more readily.

Plain-Language Companion

Trauma doesn't just live in memory—it hides in the body. Muscles tense, nerves stay on alert, breathing shortens. Massage unwinds the knots. Reiki calms the invisible alarm system underneath. Together, they create a setting where the body finally believes: "You are safe, you can let go."

Deep Relaxation and Vagal Tone

Scholarly Layer

Studies confirm that massage stimulates vagal afferents, reducing cortisol and increasing oxytocin (Diego & Field, 2009). Reiki sessions correlate with heart-rate variability improvements and parasympathetic "reset" (Baldwin et al., 2020).

It is logical to suppose that Reiki Massage combines these mechanisms: the tactile rhythm of massage activates mechanoreceptors, while Reiki's intentional stillness sustains vagal dominance. These shifts may represent the physiological correlates of what practitioners describe as "deep sinking" or "centered calm."

Plain-Language Companion

Relaxation isn't just a nice feeling; it's the body's repair mode. Massage starts the switch, slowing the heart and calming the breath. Reiki helps keep it switched on long enough for the body to truly reset. That's why clients often describe sinking into themselves—it's the body remembering how to heal once safety returns.

What Reiki Does: Proximity as Mechanism

Scholarly Layer

When hands hover near the body, studies confirm measurable changes: surface temperature increases (Peper & Ancoli, 1979), subtle electrical potentials fluctuate (Seto et al., 1992), and heart–brain rhythms can synchronize between practitioner and client (Palumbo et al., 2017). Magnetocardiography has established that the heart's electromagnetic field extends several feet outward (McCraty et al., 2009).

It is a safe approximation to suggest that such responses may represent part of what Reiki practitioners intuitively engage with. The act does not depend on conscious analysis of these dynamics. Reiki operates through felt attunement, in ways that remain ineffable even when science can measure correlates.

Plain-Language Companion

Science shows what happens when hands come close: skin warms, tiny electrical shifts occur, rhythms sometimes fall into sync. These are facts. Reiki may be working with those same forces, though not in a way that requires naming them. Practitioners feel their way into the moment. It's less about knowing and more about listening with presence.

Proximity and Non-Locality: Complement, Not Contradiction

Scholarly Layer

Reiki traditions emphasize that energy transmission is not bound by proximity. Practitioners describe sending energy across distance, into the past or future, and even through dimensions of consciousness. These claims extend beyond current scientific measurement. Proximity, however, does create conditions where correlates—heat, field shifts, entrainment—can be recorded.

It is a reasonable deduction that Reiki may operate both locally and non-locally: proximity provides a measurable subset, while distance practice represents a broader, less accessible dimension of the same phenomenon.

Plain-Language Companion

Reiki healers often say distance doesn't matter. Energy can be sent across miles—or even across time. Science isn't ready to measure that yet. What it can see is what happens up close: warmth under the hands, rhythms syncing, fields shifting. Both belong to the picture—Reiki may reach far, while in person it offers data points science can follow.

Beyond Proximity: Distance, Time, and Dimensions

Scholarly Layer

Some Reiki lineages hold that energy transmission can extend into the past, future, or alternate dimensions. These assertions cannot be confirmed with present methods, yet they are not incoherent. Alan Watts observed that vibration inherently contains temporality: a bang embodies silence before, sound present, and echo after—past, present, and future within one oscillatory event (Watts, 1974). Physics also acknowledges non-local correlation through quantum entanglement.

It is a safe approximation to suppose that Reiki's claims of non-local action may represent intuitive engagement with such vibratory structures, even if science has not yet learned to measure them.

Plain-Language Companion

Some Reiki practitioners say energy can reach not just across the world but into the past or future—even into other layers of reality. Science doesn't have tools for that yet. But sound already shows how time overlaps: one bang holds before, during, and after. Physics also admits particles can shift together across vast distances. Reiki may be sensing what science hasn't named yet.

Vibration as a Common Foundation

Scholarly Layer

Physics affirms that all matter is oscillatory: atoms, cells, organs, and galaxies vibrate. Biophysics shows that cells emit ultraweak photons, the heart radiates electrical fields, and the brain hums in rhythmic bands.

It is reasonable to suggest that Reiki's symbolic language of flow, timelessness, and resonance may be intuitive descriptions of this vibratory substrate. The difficulty for materialism is that vibration can be measured in hertz, yet its experiential qualities—harmony, dissonance, resonance—resist reduction. Reiki inhabits this paradox: grounded in the vibratory fabric of life, yet insisting consciousness can shape those vibrations in ways science has not yet framed.

Plain-Language Companion

Everything vibrates—atoms, hearts, brains, even galaxies. Science measures the waves. Reiki may be another way of describing how those waves are felt and shaped by consciousness. Both speak to the same ground, just in different languages.

Intention as Scalpel

Scholarly Layer

Psychoneuroimmunology has shown that focused mental imagery alters cortisol, immune markers, and cardiovascular activity (Ader, 2007; Benson & Friedman, 1996). Visualization studies demonstrate that imagined actions activate overlapping neural circuits with real movement (Decety, 1996). These findings confirm that intention has physiological effects.

It is a safe approximation to suggest that Reiki codifies this principle: hands may create measurable proximity effects, while intention organizes them; consciousness may extend across distance, while intention directs the current. In this sense, intention is the scalpel of energy work—the alchemical fire that transforms diffuse presence into coherent healing.

Plain-Language Companion

Science shows focus changes the body—slowing the heart, shifting hormones, even boosting immunity. Reiki takes this truth and turns it into practice. Whether near or far, intention focuses the current, shaping vibration into healing. Reiki isn't just presence—it is presence guided, like raw material transmuted into gold.

Chapter Seven: Consciousness as Contextual Medium

Universality of Healing Traditions

Scholarly Layer

Energy healing is not confined to one culture or lineage. Nearly every civilization has preserved its own form of faith or energy healing. Ancient Egypt invoked *Sekhmet* through temple sleep and laying-on-of-hands. Indigenous shamans across Africa, the Americas, and Oceania transmitted power through smoke, song, and touch. Christianity enshrined healing by touch as sacrament, while Sufi Islam described *baraka*—divine blessing conveyed through presence. Jewish ritual invoked *ruach*, the breath of spirit.

Across Asia, *prāṇa*, *qi*, and *ki* were codified into elaborate maps of body and cosmos. The recurrence of these practices suggests not coincidence but universality. Whether named as spirit, *pneuma*, energy, or vibration, the gesture of channeling life-force through presence and intention appears across cultures as old as humanity itself.

Plain-Language Companion

Reiki isn't alone. Egyptians healed through touch and prayer. Shamans used drumming, smoke, and song. Christians laid on hands. Sufis spoke of *baraka*. Jews called on *ruach*, the spirit-breath. Africans invoked ancestors, Indigenous healers cleansed with plants and fire. The languages differ, but the act is the same: presence, intention, and life-force moving between people. Almost every culture has done it. That's not an oddity—that's a pattern.

Contextual Languages of Healing

Scholarly Layer

These traditions, diverse as they are, share a deeper implication: each is a contextual language. Ayurveda speaks of *prāṇa* and *koshas*; Chinese medicine of *qi* and meridians; Buddhism of skandhas and emptiness; Reiki of *ki* and symbols; Christianity of Spirit; neuroscience of neurotransmitters, oscillations, and vagal tone. Each brings certain truths into focus while leaving others unseen.

It is humility, not condescension, to recognize that some of these systems are religious at their root. Their vocabularies are not merely medical but devotional. Science, too, has its creed: only what is measured is real.

This, too, is a kind of faith. In this sense, all systems—sacred and secular—are languages through which human beings describe and work with consciousness as medium.

Plain-Language Companion

Healing systems are like languages. Ayurveda speaks of *prāṇa*. Chinese medicine speaks of *qi*. Reiki speaks of *ki*. Christians speak of Spirit. Scientists speak of data and brainwaves. None of them are wrong—they just choose different words.

Some of these languages are openly religious. Some pretend they're not. Science doesn't call itself faith, but it has its creed too: only what can be measured is real. Each system highlights one part of truth and hides another. That's why this book keeps saying: it's not either/or. It's all of them. Healing is bigger than any one language.

Consciousness as the Medium

Scholarly Layer

If all of these traditions are taken seriously on their own terms, a startling convergence emerges: consciousness itself functions as the medium of healing. This is not metaphor alone. Placebo research demonstrates that belief alters physiology. Quantum physics acknowledges that observation shapes outcome. Neuroscience finds that intention modulates immune and cardiovascular markers. Religion names the same principle in terms of spirit, grace, or blessing. It is a safe approximation to propose that what Reiki practitioners, shamans, priests, and physicians alike engage with is this same medium—consciousness structured by language and practice.

Plain-Language Companion

Look closely and you'll see the common thread. Belief heals in the placebo effect. Attention changes what physics observes. Focus shifts the body's rhythms. Religion calls it spirit. Science calls it mind. Reiki calls it energy. They're all naming the same thing: consciousness is the medium through which healing happens.

Limits of Language

Scholarly Layer

Each tradition is both true and partial. Language defines what is observable: *qi* makes meridians visible; neurotransmitters make brain scans visible; Spirit makes sacrament visible. Yet none of these terms exhaust the phenomenon they point toward. The difficulty—and the opportunity—is that language not only describes but also shapes reality. What cannot be spoken in a given framework often cannot be seen within it. This is as true for science as for religion. In this sense, the humility required is universal: no single system owns truth. All of them are contextual grammars for perceiving and participating in consciousness.

Plain-Language Companion

Every language shows part of the picture and hides part of it. *Qi* makes you notice energy flow. Science makes you notice chemicals. Religion makes you notice spirit. None of them capture the whole. That's why this book keeps saying: it's not either/or. It's all of them. Healing is bigger than any one language.

Closing Movement of Chapter Seven

Scholarly Layer

If energy healing traditions are universal, and if science itself is a language among languages, then we must entertain the possibility that all of them are correct—each pointing toward consciousness as the shared medium. This does not diminish their differences. It honors their integrity while situating them within a larger alchemy: measured and unmeasured, empirical and symbolic, all participating in the same reality.

Plain-Language Companion

If almost every culture has done energy healing, and if science is just one more way of speaking, then maybe the point is this: they're all right. Each tradition points to consciousness in its own way. Together, they show us that healing is not the property of one system, but the language of life itself.

Chapter Eight: Attunement and the Clinical Field

Attunement Defined

Scholarly Layer

If consciousness is the medium of healing, attunement is the process by which practitioner and client enter resonance within that medium. The term itself is instructive. To attune is to bring into harmony, as instruments are adjusted until they vibrate on the same frequency. The word carries its own etymology: *attention*—the focus of awareness—and *tune*—the act of aligning vibration. Attunement, then, is both cognitive and vibratory: it is the focused presence that allows two beings to fall into coherence.

Empirical research supports this dual meaning. Studies of heart-rate variability have documented synchronization between patient and clinician during empathic encounters (McCraty et al., 2009). EEG studies show brainwave entrainment between therapist and client during moments of deep rapport (Konvalinka et al., 2011). Psychotherapy research consistently finds that "therapeutic alliance"—often described as being "in sync" with the patient—predicts outcomes more reliably than specific techniques (Horvath & Symonds, 1991). These findings suggest that attention itself is a tuning fork, shaping not only the subjective experience of connection but also measurable physiological states.

Plain-Language Companion

Attunement means "to tune with." The word hides its truth in plain sight: attention plus tune. To be attuned is to give attention in such a way that two people fall into rhythm together. Musicians know this—two instruments adjust until they sound right. Healers know it too—two people adjust until they feel right.

Science has caught glimpses of this. Heartbeats can sync. Brainwaves can fall into rhythm. Even without touch, presence itself can line people up. Practitioners call it being "in tune." Patients call it "feeling seen." Both are pointing to the same event: attunement.

Attunement as Observed in Science

Scholarly Layer

Evidence for attunement extends across multiple fields of study. Research in psychophysiology shows that when two individuals engage deeply, their autonomic systems can synchronize, producing measurable heart-rate and breath coherence (Palumbo et al., 2017). Neuroscience adds further support: mirror neuron activity provides a neural basis for empathy, while hyperscanning EEG studies reveal synchronized brain activity across individuals in cooperative or therapeutic interactions (Dumas et al., 2010).

It is a safe approximation to propose that such findings provide physiological correlates of what practitioners describe as "energetic resonance." While science names the oscillations and neural firings, the healer feels them directly as rapport, flow, or presence. Both accounts—empirical and experiential—may be understood as languages describing the same reality.

Plain-Language Companion

Science has shown what healers have always felt: when two people connect deeply, their bodies sync up. Heart rates line up. Breathing slows together. Even brainwaves can fall into rhythm.

A healer may not call it "mirror neurons" or "hyperscanning." They just feel it as being in sync, as energy moving between them. Two languages, one event.

Remote Attunement: The Metaphor of Tools

Scholarly Layer

The question arises: if attunement is real in local settings, how might it extend across distance? Here, science itself offers countless precedents. Astronomers engage galaxies through telescopes, mediated by light-years of space. Oceanographers work on the deep sea via remotely operated vehicles, extending reach to depths no human body can survive. Surgeons perform delicate procedures with robotic instruments, sometimes from across the globe. Microscopists examine living cells through layers of optics and computation, "seeing" realities otherwise invisible.

Across these examples, human attention and intention are extended through tools—visual, mechanical, digital—without losing fidelity. The work remains real even when direct contact is impossible.

Remote Reiki practice may be understood as a symbolic analogue of this same principle. Consciousness provides its own instruments: focused attention, visualization, and symbolic acts. Neuroscience shows that visualization activates many of the same neural circuits as physical actions

Integration Into Care: Revelation

Hypothesis Delivered – The Final Push

Attunement, in the language of intuitive healing, is not a vague metaphor but a volitional act: the deliberate practice of aligning one's consciousness with another. This thesis advances the audacious suggestion that what has been called attunement may in fact be the lived expression of the very synchrony and coherence that medicine has already observed as anomalies yet failed to integrate.

Research has documented that the brain waves of two individuals can fall into rhythm during shared states, and that heartbeats can entrain when people interact deeply. These findings have been noted in passing, but left unexplored. This book insists they are not curiosities. They may be the first evidence that attunement, as consciously practiced by healers, operates within the very same domain.

Closing Argument: Subtle Forces in Medicine

Modern medicine has accumulated a vast record of signals: electrocardiograms, electroencephalograms, magnetic traces, thermal shifts, heart-rate variability, stress markers, and more. Within this record lies a detail too often treated as incidental: the tendency of these signals to synchronize. Heart with heart, brain with brain, rhythms of one life aligning with another. These events have been noted, sometimes reported, yet rarely pursued. They have been treated as curiosities rather than clues.

The argument of this book is that such synchrony is not an accident to be filed away. It is the doorway. These so-called anomalies may be the first indicators of a field science has not yet known to look for, the bridge toward a measure medicine has not conceived because it has not imagined such a thing could exist. To ignore them is to miss the very evidence that could redefine the nature of healing. To focus on them with deliberate rigor is to admit that the unknown has already brushed against the known.

The anomalies medicine has recorded in heart rhythms, brain waves, and other physiological signals should not be treated as curiosities awaiting cleaner instruments. They may be the first hints of an entirely new measure—evidence of dynamics for which no present category or tool exists. Synchrony, coherence, entrainment: these are not errors in data, nor metaphors for connection. They may be the fingerprints of a dimension science has not yet conceived, a variable hidden in plain sight that demands new models, new instruments, and new questions.

This is the heart of integration. Not a polite addition to existing practice, but a radical expansion of its foundation. Healing has never arisen from chemistry and steel alone. It has always drawn strength from alignment —between patient and practitioner, intention and act, field and body. The synchrony hidden in our instruments is the residue of that alignment. To treat it as noise is to throw away the very signal we most need.

Volition vs. Wishful Thinking

The critical sign is volition. When intuitives and energy workers engage in their practice, they do not stumble into results—they act consciously, intentionally. This volition marks the difference between imagination and interaction, between wishful thought and measurable influence. It is the green flag that signals we are not dealing with fantasy, but with the first stirrings of a science that has yet to name its subject.

If consciousness can act upon these fields deliberately, then integration is not a matter of faith but of method. Document the outcomes, correlate them with the anomalies already known, and expand the frame of medicine to include what patients and practitioners have experienced all along. The real measure may remain hidden, but the path toward it is visible. It runs through synchrony, through coherence, through the relational fingerprints scattered across the physiological record.

This is why the argument belongs to parapsychology rather than merely to the clinic. Not because healing is too small a frame, but because healing is the first proof of a principle that may extend far beyond health. To take these anomalies seriously is to admit that science has been circling the edge of a truth it has not yet had the courage to face.

This is Alchemy Reimagined: to give voice to what has been glimpsed but left unspoken, to turn the private burden of intuition into a language the collective can test, repeat, and build upon. For what is at stake is not healing alone. If these anomalies truly point to a field in which consciousness interacts with matter, then the implications stretch to the very boundaries of human possibility. Gnostics would have called it release from the prison of flesh. Magicians, invisibility. Science fiction, teleportation. Intuitives and mediums may have been brushing against it all along without naming it. The sages of all ages have iterated every metaphor imaginable expressing the same idea.

Outlandish? Only in the way every revolution in knowledge first appears. Germs were invisible until microscopes, electricity until conductors, relativity until clocks could measure the difference. Synchrony is our next instrument. Through it we may discover that the impossible was always here, waiting to be seen.

Epilogue: The Long Arc of Gravity

Part I: The Obvious Step — Look Up

Scholarly Layer

Humanity's first science was the sky. Long before mathematics, people watched stones fall, rain pour, and stars sweep their patterns overhead. To look up was the most obvious experiment, and to mark what was seen became the earliest form of data. The bulk of collective consciousness agreed, implicitly, that these motions were real. The falling body was not an illusion; the rising moon was not a trick.

Science is not built on proving what is already assumed but on testing what can be disproved. By this standard, gravity has never failed. Every attempt to deny it—whether through philosophical conjecture, mystical re-description, or later, fringe denial—has collapsed under measurement. These counter-claims stand outside the scientific tradition not because they are unpopular but because they have failed the true measure of science: disproof by repeatable observation. This chapter is not about them. It is about the long history of how the impossible was slowly brought into the range of measurement.

Plain-Language Companion

The first science was simple: look up. Stones fall, rivers flow, stars cross the sky. People knew this long before anyone had equations for it. The agreement was almost universal: these things are real. Science didn't need to prove them—it needed to see if they could ever be disproved. Gravity has never failed that test. Those who argue otherwise don't stand in science's tradition. They've already lost the measure. This story is about something else: how people learned to measure the impossible.

The Rebel Step: Measure

Scholarly Layer

Aristotle described falling bodies as seeking their "natural place." He argued that heavier objects fall faster because they contain more of the element earth. For centuries this explanation held, but anomalies accumulated. Comets refused the rules. Planetary retrograde motion mocked "natural place."

The first true break came with Galileo. Refusing to lean only on philosophy, he rolled spheres down inclined planes and timed their descent with water clocks and his own pulse *(Galilei, 1914/1638)*. His observations were radical: bodies fall with equal acceleration regardless of weight. The prevailing wisdom was disproved. Galileo had not explained why things fall, but he had shown how. In so doing, he established the scientific principle that would echo through centuries: outcomes measured honestly outrank theories, no matter how venerable.

Plain-Language Companion

Aristotle thought things fall because they want to reach their "natural place." Heavy things, he said, fall faster. But when Galileo rolled balls down ramps and timed them, he saw they all fell the same way *(Galilei, 1914/1638)*. That single act of measuring overthrew centuries of "common sense." Galileo still didn't know why things fall—but he proved how they fall. And that was enough to change everything.

The Elegant Step: Describe

Scholarly Layer

Newton took Galileo's observations and crafted them into universal law. An apple's fall and a planet's orbit, he showed, could be described by the same mathematics. For the first time, Earth and cosmos were bound by a single principle. Yet Newton admitted his ignorance of mechanism. He refused to hypothesize the cause of gravity, writing *hypotheses non fingo*—"I feign no hypothesis" *(Newton, 1687/1999)*.

This is the critical lesson: for two centuries, the world ran on Newton's laws without any mechanism at all. Ships navigated seas, engineers built machines, astronomers charted orbits—outcomes were sufficient. Science advanced because measurement and description were enough. The "why" could wait.

Plain-Language Companion

Newton made gravity into math. He showed apples and planets obey the same rules. For the first time, the Earth and stars followed one law. But Newton admitted: I don't know why. He wouldn't guess. For 200 years, people lived and worked on Newton's math without explanation. Ships sailed, clocks ticked, planets were charted. The "why" could wait. The "what" was enough.

Part II: Einstein and the Impossible

The Radical Step: Rethink the Medium

Scholarly Layer

By Newton's time, gravity was law but remained mysterious. The equations worked, yet no one knew why distant bodies could exert force across the void. Newton himself called the idea of "action at a distance" absurd. Still, ships sailed, planets circled, and the math held.

Then came Einstein. In 1915, with the general theory of relativity, he reframed the question. Gravity, he proposed, is not a force but a property of spacetime itself. Matter tells spacetime how to curve; curved spacetime tells matter how to move *(Einstein, 1915; 1916/2005)*. The falling apple is not "pulled" by Earth but follows the curve of the Earth's geometry.

This radical idea produced predictions no prior theory had made: light should bend around massive objects, time itself should dilate in gravitational fields, and ripples of spacetime—gravitational waves—should propagate through the universe. At the time, these outcomes were judged impossible to measure.

Plain-Language Companion

Newton's gravity worked but made no sense. How could Earth "pull" the moon across empty space? Newton admitted he didn't know.

Einstein looked again and said: maybe gravity isn't a force at all. Maybe space itself bends, and matter just follows the curve. An apple falls not because Earth tugs it but because Earth bends the ground of space under it *(Einstein, 1915; 1916/2005)*.

This idea was shocking—but it made bold predictions. Light would bend around stars. Time would slow in strong gravity. Space itself would ripple with invisible waves. At first, no one believed these effects could ever be measured.

The First Impossible: Bend the Light

Scholarly Layer

Einstein's first prediction to be tested was the bending of starlight by the Sun. During a total solar eclipse in 1919, Arthur Eddington led expeditions to measure the apparent shift of stars near the Sun's edge.

The results confirmed Einstein's theory: light bent exactly as predicted *(Dyson, Eddington, & Davidson, 1920)*.

This was more than confirmation. It was proof that science could test even what seemed untestable. A phenomenon invisible in ordinary conditions became measurable with creativity, patience, and the willingness to look when the universe itself dimmed the lights.

Plain-Language Companion

Einstein said: light bends around the Sun. Astronomers said: impossible. But in 1919, during a solar eclipse, Arthur Eddington tested it. When the Sun's glare was blocked, stars near its edge appeared shifted—just as Einstein predicted *(Dyson et al., 1920)*.

Einstein was right. The impossible had been measured.

The Next Impossible: Catch the Ripples

Scholarly Layer

Gravitational waves, predicted in 1916, were another matter. These ripples in spacetime were expected to be so faint that Einstein himself doubted they could ever be detected. For decades, the idea remained a theoretical curiosity.

Yet in the late 20th century, scientists began to build instruments that could test the untestable. LIGO (Laser Interferometer Gravitational-Wave Observatory) was conceived: twin detectors, each with arms four kilometers long, designed to measure distortions smaller than a proton. Critics called it folly. But in September 2015, LIGO recorded the merger of two black holes, sending ripples across the cosmos that reached Earth 1.3 billion years later—confirming them as gravitational waves *(Abbott et al., 2016)*.

This was not a metaphor. It was spacetime itself ringing like a drum—and humanity hearing it for the first time.

Plain-Language Companion

Einstein also predicted that space could ripple, like water when a stone is thrown. He doubted we'd ever hear it. The waves would be too small.

But scientists built giant detectors called LIGO, stretching four kilometers in each direction. In 2015, they caught it: two black holes colliding billions of years ago made space itself ring, and the ripple reached Earth *(Abbott et al., 2016)*.

The impossible had been caught, measured, proven.

Part III: The Tools of the Impossible

Building the Eyes to See

Scholarly Layer

To detect gravitational waves was to attempt the absurd. Einstein's equations said the ripples would distort space by less than one part in 10^{21} *(Einstein, 1916/2005)*. For comparison, this is like measuring a change in distance smaller than the width of a proton across a four-kilometer span. Many physicists argued the task was hopeless.

Yet the pursuit continued. In the 1970s, Rainer Weiss at MIT outlined a design using laser interferometry *(Weiss, 1972)*. Two perpendicular arms, each kilometers long, would bounce lasers back and forth, measuring interference patterns caused by infinitesimal distortions of spacetime. Kip Thorne and Ronald Drever joined the effort, securing U.S. National Science Foundation backing *(Thorne, 1994)*. Decades of skepticism, funding battles, and engineering obstacles followed.

The solution was not a single experiment but a system. The Laser Interferometer Gravitational-Wave Observatory (LIGO) was built in two sites: Livingston, Louisiana, and Hanford, Washington *(Abbott et al., 2016)*. Both detectors had to operate in synchrony, eliminating local noise—from seismic tremors, trucks passing, even quantum fluctuations in the lasers themselves. Vacuum chambers ran the length of the arms, maintained at pressures lower than outer space. Mirrors were polished to atomic precision, suspended by silica fibers to dampen vibration.

The scale was staggering: billions of dollars, thousands of collaborators, decades of labor. Yet the rationale was simple: if reality hides its truths at this scale, then instruments must be built at this scale.

Plain-Language Companion

Catching a gravitational wave meant measuring something smaller than a proton—a billionth of a billionth of a meter. Most scientists thought it was impossible. But a few refused to stop. They designed giant "L" shaped machines with lasers bouncing back and forth along four-kilometer arms. If a ripple in space passed through, the lasers would shift ever so slightly.

It took decades, billions of dollars, and two huge detectors working together in Louisiana and Washington. Everything had to be perfect: mirrors polished smooth at the atomic level, vacuum tunnels cleaner than outer space, even the hum of nearby trucks filtered out. Thousands of people worked for years just to give reality a chance to reveal itself.

The Breakthrough

Scholarly Layer

On September 14, 2015, at 5:51 a.m. Eastern Time, both LIGO detectors registered the same signal: a brief "chirp" lasting less than half a second *(Abbott et al., 2016)*. The data matched the predicted waveform of two black holes spiraling together and merging 1.3 billion years ago. Independent teams verified the signal.

On February 11, 2016, the collaboration announced the discovery to the world *(Abbott et al., 2016)*. The "impossible" had become data. Gravitational waves were not an abstract prediction but a measurable reality. The Nobel Prize in Physics was awarded in 2017 to Weiss, Thorne, and Barish for their roles in the discovery *(Nobel Prize, 2017)*.

Plain-Language Companion

In 2015, both LIGO detectors picked up the same sound—a tiny "chirp" from space. It was exactly what Einstein's math predicted: two black holes colliding more than a billion years ago.

What was once "impossible" was now measured. Einstein's waves had been caught. The scientists who built the machines won the Nobel Prize.

The Lesson

Scholarly Layer

The path from Aristotle to LIGO was not a straight line but a long arc of method: observe, measure, describe, rethink, build. Each stage required abandoning the demand for immediate mechanism and accepting outcomes as sufficient proof that inquiry must continue.

Gravity was not understood before it was accepted. Its effects were measured long before its nature was explained. And when explanation seemed to outstrip measurement, humanity built new tools until the "impossible" was revealed.

This is not a story of faith, nor of metaphor. It is science at its most honest: the courage to measure before knowing, and the persistence to build instruments equal to the mysteries they pursue.

This arc—Galileo to Newton to Einstein to LIGO—says the quiet part out loud: science advances by measuring outcomes before it understands mechanisms. We sailed ships on Newton's math for two centuries without knowing "why." The obligation is identical in healing: when outcomes exist, we measure them—then we argue about mechanisms. To delay integration until explanation arrives is not scientific caution; it is cultural hesitation.

Plain-Language Companion

The story of gravity is the story of science itself: first watch, then measure, then describe, then rethink, then build. Each step came long before the "why" was understood.

People trusted the outcomes—stones fall, planets orbit—long before they knew the reason. And when Einstein predicted things too small to measure, people built tools until the impossible became real.

That's how science works when it's at its best: measure first, explain later.

Part IV: The Lesson for Healing

Outcomes Before Mechanisms

Scholarly Layer

The story of gravity is a cautionary tale for healing. For centuries, the world ran on Newton's laws without any mechanism. Ships navigated, astronomers charted, outcomes were sufficient. Science advanced because measurement and description were enough. The "why" could wait.

Plain-Language Companion

Newton's gravity made no sense. But the world used his math for 200 years without knowing why. Ships sailed, planets were predicted, clocks ticked. The "what" was enough.

The Responsibility of Science

Scholarly Layer

By Newton's time, gravity was law but remained mysterious. The equations worked, yet no one knew why distant bodies could exert force across the void. Newton himself called the idea of "action at a distance" absurd. Still, ships sailed, planets circled, and the math held.

Einstein looked again and said: maybe gravity isn't a force at all. Maybe space itself bends, and matter just follows the curve. An apple falls not because Earth tugs it but because Earth bends the ground of space under it *(Einstein, 1915; 1916/2005)*.

This idea was shocking—but it made bold predictions. Light would bend around stars. Time would slow in strong gravity. Space itself would ripple with invisible waves. At first, no one believed these effects could ever be measured.

Plain-Language Companion

Newton's idea of action at a distance made no sense. Einstein said: maybe space itself bends. Matter just follows the curve.

It sounded shocking, but it predicted things no one thought could be measured: bent light, slowed time, rippling space. At first, no one believed it.

Turning the Mirror

Scholarly Layer

The refusal to integrate rests on a contradiction. The justification is "lack of data," yet data exists in the most meaningful form—outcomes. What is missing is not observation but willingness: the courage to subject these outcomes to the same rigor applied to any other intervention. To wait for mechanisms before measuring is to confess that the barrier is not science but culture.

Plain-Language Companion

The excuse is "not enough data." But the data that matters—outcomes—already exists. That's how science always starts: see the results first, explain them later.

The truth is, it's not a science problem. It's a culture problem.

The Closing Challenge

Scholarly Layer

Humanity's first science was the sky. Long before mathematics, people watched stones fall, rain pour, and stars sweep their patterns overhead.

To look up was the most obvious experiment, and to mark what was seen became the earliest form of data. The bulk of collective consciousness agreed, implicitly, that these motions were real. The falling body was not an illusion; the rising moon was not a trick.

This intuition finds resonance in physics as well. Matter itself is not static but vibratory: atoms oscillate, subatomic particles exist as probability waves, and the measurable universe is patterned by frequency. Biologically, too, humans are beings of sound. The heart produces rhythmic waves detectable outside the body; the brain hums with oscillatory rhythms; and at the cellular level, ultraweak photon emission has been observed to pulse in rhythmic coherence *(Popp, 1992)*. To describe life as vibration is not poetry—it is empirically defensible.

Plain-Language Companion

The first science was the sky. Look up—stones fall, stars sweep, rain pours. These things are real.

Science today still finds the same truth: life itself vibrates. Atoms, waves, rhythms in the heart and brain, even tiny pulses of light inside our cells *(Popp, 1992)*. To call life vibration isn't poetry. It's fact.

The Latent Human Ability

Scholarly Layer

The argument is not that energy healing deserves a trial. It is that its systematic integration is already overdue. The outcomes are measurable now, just as falling bodies and planetary orbits were measurable long before their causes were known. Science has always begun here: with results in hand, explanation trailing after.

The cost is profound. Humanity may be delaying abilities that could reshape medicine, psychology, and perhaps even our understanding of reality itself.

Plain-Language Companion

We aren't asking for permission to be studied. We're asking why healing practices haven't already been built into the system. The excuse is "not enough data." But the data that matters—outcomes—already exists. That's how science always starts: see the results first, explain them later.

The truth is, it's not a science problem. It's a culture problem. While we wait, human abilities that could change medicine and even change life itself are left sitting in the dark. The real question isn't whether energy healing works—it's why we still haven't built it in.

Conclusion: Toward One Possible System

As this book closes, I must clarify what it is not. It is not a declaration of dogma, nor a final word on energy healing, consciousness, or integrative medicine. To assert certainty in matters as vast as consciousness would be to betray the very subject itself.

What I have outlined here is not the system, but a system—one possible framework of application. It is provisional, porous, and deliberately unfinished. It arises from my own practice—Reiki, massage therapy, sound healing, decades of observation—but it does not claim jurisdiction over other lineages, traditions, or ways of knowing.

The framework, at its simplest, rests on a few working principles: consciousness as baseline, resonance as mechanism, intention as scalpel, presence as medicine. In practice, this manifests as an integrative method where touch, vibration, and attunement converge in the clinical space. The aim is coherence, not conquest; harmony, not hierarchy.

This proposal is less a conclusion than an invitation. It asks to be tested, challenged, refined, even overturned. In truth, what we do not know dwarfs what we claim to understand. Any honest framework must be built on humility and the expectation of being surpassed.

If this book has value, it is not in proving Reiki, or explaining sound therapy, or dismantling materialism. Its value, if any, is in provoking further inquiry—by scholars, by practitioners, by skeptics, by patients. My contribution is only one voice in a larger chorus. The hope is that others will expand it, contradict it, or replace it entirely.

Consciousness is not a closed system; neither should healing be. The work remains unfinished, and must remain unfinished. If there is a philosopher's stone, it is not a hidden formula but the willingness to keep searching, testing, and remaining open.

So the circle closes: from zero, polarity, oscillation, return. From silence, vibration, and resonance. From nothing, everything—and always, back to nothing again.

The Women Who Captured Starlight

The Spectrum of the Night Sky

When we look into the night sky, we are not simply gazing into a void scattered with points of light. We are looking into a living spectrum. Each star emits not only brightness but also color — a vibration of energy written in bands, hidden to the naked eye yet traceable through the prism's patient work. What we call "light" is not uniform. It is layered, differentiated, and encoded with information. The universe, it turns out, is speaking in wavelengths (Ogilvie, 2000).

Decoding the Mystery of Stars

The mystery, for centuries, was whether that language could be read. To early astronomers, the stars were distant fires, divine lanterns, or, at most, glowing spheres like our own Sun. It would take the painstaking labor of women — marginalized, underpaid, and largely forgotten in their time — to reveal that stars were not merely points of beauty, but messages. It was they who decoded the hidden grammar of starlight (Ogilvie, 2000).

The Harvard Computers

At the Harvard Observatory in the late 19th and early 20th centuries, women were employed as "computers." Their task was to study glass photographic plates of the heavens, captured each night by telescopes, and to classify, measure, and describe what they saw. To most of the scientific establishment, these women were anonymous clerks, nameless assistants in a masculine pursuit. But their quiet work became nothing less than the foundation of modern astrophysics (Ogilvie, 2000).

Annie Jump Cannon: Creating Order from Chaos

Annie Jump Cannon created order out of stellar chaos. Looking at the faint bands of color etched into the plates, she discerned patterns no one else could see. She gave us the sequence still taught to students today: O, B, A, F, G, K, M (Cannon, 1901–1907). Each letter, each category, was not arbitrary but encoded with meaning. A star's color told its temperature, its stage of life, its nature. What seemed to the eye as a uniform scatter of white points became, under her vision, a cathedral of classification (Ogilvie, 2000). Just as a healer senses subtle gradations of energy between one body and another, Cannon sensed the subtle differences in the voices of stars.

Cecilia Payne-Gaposchkin: Revealing Stellar Composition

Then came Cecilia Payne-Gaposchkin, whose courage was equal to her genius. In her 1925 doctoral thesis at Radcliffe College, she advanced what was then unthinkable: "that stars are composed almost entirely of hydrogen and helium" (Payne, 1925, p. 53). The great bodies of the heavens, long assumed to share the same stuff as Earth, were revealed to be fundamentally other. She had heard the deeper resonance of the spectrum and declared that starlight itself carried the record of a star's chemistry. Senior astronomers, including Henry Norris Russell, dismissed her claim and urged restraint, but Russell himself later confirmed her conclusions (Russell, 1929). Her conclusion, now considered axiomatic, redefined our place in the cosmos (Smithsonian Magazine, 2025).

Henrietta Swan Leavitt: Measuring Cosmic Distances

Henrietta Swan Leavitt added yet another dimension. Studying variable stars whose brightness waxed and waned in rhythmic pulses, she discovered that their period of fluctuation corresponded directly to their intrinsic brightness (Leavitt, 1912). This meant that a single star's pulse could serve as a cosmic ruler, measuring distances across the universe. Without Leavitt, Edwin Hubble could not have shown that the cosmos is expanding. Without her, the scale of creation would have remained immeasurable. It was Leavitt who translated rhythm into distance — vibration into architecture.

Translators of Energy

These women, known to history as the "Harvard Computers," did more than classify or calculate. They listened. They perceived what others ignored. They trusted the evidence of vibration. In this sense, they were translators of energy, just as much as healers who map meridians, mystics who trace the flow of breath, or therapists who attune to the rhythm of trauma in the body (Ogilvie, 2000).

Metaphoric Gifts and Hidden Order

Their gift was not only scientific but metaphoric. They showed that vibration is never empty. Whether in starlight, sound, or the human nervous system, there is always a hidden order waiting to be revealed by attention and trust. Just as Cannon discerned patterns (Cannon, 1901–1907), Payne heard chemistry in light (Payne, 1925), and Leavitt measured the universe in pulsations (Leavitt, 1912), so too can we learn to read the languages of energy in our own practice.

Honoring the Legacy

To honor them is to affirm the central premise of this work: that mystery, when studied with patience, yields not less but more wonder. The stars did not shrink under analysis. They expanded. The universe, once assumed static and finite, was revealed as vast, living, and still becoming (Russell, 1929).

A Model of Inquiry

The women who captured starlight gave us more than astronomy. They offered a model of inquiry: to listen for what is hidden, to trust vibration as carrier of truth, and to let humility before mystery guide us toward understanding. Their work, like ours, stands as a bridge between silence and speech, symbol and signal, ineffable experience and empirical form (Ogilvie, 2000).

The Women Who Computed the Stars

The Hidden Figures of NASA

If Annie Jump Cannon and Cecilia Payne-Gaposchkin gave us the language of starlight, it was the women of the mid-20th century who built the algorithms that allowed us to journey into that starlight. They were not celebrated, not immortalized in bronze, but they carried the equations that lifted rockets into orbit, mapped galaxies, and gave humanity the tools to see the universe as it is. Their gift was translation once more: to take the intangible language of vibration and transform it into the trajectories of spacecraft and the catalogues of stars.

At NASA, before computers meant machines, the word referred to people — and most of them were women. Katherine Johnson, Dorothy Vaughan, and Mary Jackson became known much later as the "Hidden Figures" (Shetterly, 2016). In their time, they were simply "computers." It was Johnson who verified John Glenn's orbital trajectory in 1962. Glenn, when told to trust a room-sized IBM, responded: "Get the girl to check the numbers. If she says they're good, then I'm ready to go" (NASA, 2017). In that act, a woman's hand-calculated figures became the final arbiter of whether humanity was ready to leave Earth. The trajectory was right, and Glenn orbited safely.

From Chalkboards to Code

This was not an isolated miracle. Dorothy Vaughan taught herself and her team FORTRAN programming when NASA transitioned to electronic computers (Shetterly, 2016). Mary Jackson, an aeronautical engineer, mastered fluid dynamics in wind tunnels and then rewrote equations for re-entry vehicles (NASA, 2020). These women transformed raw mathematics into survival. They turned abstraction into flight.

While their work enabled astronauts to reach orbit, another wave of women was preparing humanity to see further still.

Nancy Roman and the Vision of Hubble

Nancy Roman, later called the "Mother of Hubble," was NASA's first Chief of Astronomy (Roman, 1991). She pressed for a space-based telescope when many in the agency considered it science fiction. Roman's vision became the Hubble Space Telescope, and through it humanity learned to see galaxies receding, dark matter bending light, and the deep time of the universe unfolding in color (NASA, 2019).

From Harvard to Hipparcos and Gaia

Parallel efforts unfolded in Europe. The European Space Agency launched the Hipparcos satellite in 1989 — the first space-based astrometry mission. Its task was audacious: to measure the positions and motions of more than 100,000 stars with unprecedented accuracy (Perryman et al., 1997). Hipparcos would be followed decades later by Gaia, which now charts over a billion stars (Gaia Collaboration et al., 2016).

Behind these missions were teams of astronomers, coders, and mathematicians — many of them women — who translated stellar spectra into data streams, algorithms, and ultimately into maps of the cosmos. Where Annie Jump Cannon had once sorted stars by eye, now vast catalogues were computed with the labor of many unseen hands, extending her legacy into the computer age.

Translation as Continuum

The lineage is clear: Leavitt measured stellar rhythms; Cannon classified spectra; Payne revealed composition. Johnson, Vaughan, and Jackson then took those vibrations and turned them into orbital pathways. Roman and her colleagues wrote the future of telescopes into being. The unnamed analysts of Hipparcos and Gaia then wove light into digital cartographies of the Milky Way. Each generation of women extended the work of the last, holding the thread of translation: vibration into pattern, pattern into number, number into map.

This chapter is an owed debt, for without these women, we would not have the means to explore at all. They transformed what was once invisible into navigable form. They showed that starlight was not only beauty but trajectory. That vibration was not only symbol but coordinate. That energy was not only mystery but pathway.

Energy Work and Celestial Work

There is a parallel here that must be drawn. In energy work, we often speak of resonance, of vibration carrying meaning, of patterns in the invisible shaping outcomes in the visible. The women who computed the stars were engaged in precisely the same translation, though theirs was cast in the language of mathematics. They read the ineffable and made it empirical. They built bridges between symbol and signal, just as healers attempt in the therapeutic setting.

Katherine Johnson's equations are not so different in spirit from the pulse of a Reiki practitioner's hand sensing an energetic block. Both are readings of hidden flows. Dorothy Vaughan's translation of code echoes the healer's translation of sensation into meaning. Nancy Roman's insistence that telescopes must leave Earth to truly see parallels the healer's insistence that perception must leave the body's surface to touch the subtle.

Mapping the Cosmos

When Hipparcos delivered its star catalogue in the 1990s, humanity's map of the heavens leapt forward (Perryman et al., 1997). Gaia has since given us a living atlas of over a billion stars, their positions, motions, and even their chemical identities (Gaia Collaboration et al., 2016). The irony is striking: the instruments may be satellites, but the algorithms — the ability to interpret — stand upon the shoulders of those who were once called merely "computers."

To speak of them is to acknowledge a hidden continuity. Women who were denied recognition nonetheless gave us the keys to the cosmos. They were translators of energy, mediators of mystery, and, like the healers whose work fills these pages, they transformed what was once ineffable into something that could guide others.

Conclusion — Translators of Light

So let us remember them not as background figures in a masculine epic of rockets and telescopes, but as the true architects of the path. They showed us that starlight is not only wonder to be gazed at, but information to be lived with. They revealed that trajectories through space are as much acts of listening as they are of thrust and fire.

If we owe Cannon, Payne, and Leavitt for giving us the grammar of starlight, we owe Johnson, Vaughan, Jackson, and Roman — and the anonymous women of Hipparcos and Gaia — for writing the algorithms that carried us into it. The universe is not silent. It is filled with messages. These women taught us how to listen, how to compute, and how to turn vibration into journey.

This, then, is the true continuum: from prism to plate, from chalkboard to telescope, from healing hand to satellite array. Mystery, always, translated by those willing to sit with it, to compute it, and to transform it into a language we can travel by.

Nothing to It — How Zero Explains Everything

Zero as Potential

Zero is often described as "nothing." Yet in mathematics, zero is not a void — it is the most powerful placeholder in history. Without it, positional numbering collapses, algebra fails, and calculus disappears. Zero is not the absence of value but the field of potential, the silent axis upon which all values swing (Kaplan, 2000; Seife, 2000).

Emission and Polarity

From zero, positive and negative values emerge. The moment you graph them, oscillation appears. Zero does not just sit there; it generates polarity, and polarity becomes a wave. This is the simplest act of creation: from nothing, something — or rather, from zero, everything (Feynman et al., 1963).

The Waveform as Common Language

Waves are the one thing skeptics and mystics both respect. Physics describes light, sound, electromagnetism, and even the probability fields of quantum mechanics as waves (Hecht, 2016). Metaphysics speaks of vibration, resonance, and frequency. Healing traditions invoke attunement and coherence. All describe the same form: oscillation from baseline, resolution back to equilibrium (Capra, 1975).

The Big Bang, Simplified

Cosmology's great paradox is how "something" came from "nothing." Zero answers it in under five minutes. Zero is not empty; it is the substrate of polarity. Positive and negative emerge, oscillate, and create waves. Sound, then light, then matter. "God said," vibration appeared, and "there was light." The Vedic Brahman hummed as Om. Physics calls it the birth of photons. The formulas match the scriptures (Hawking, 1988; Guth, 1997).

Zero as Consciousness

What zero is to mathematics, consciousness is to ontology. Both are invisible, unmeasurable directly, yet absolutely indispensable. Zero emits values, then integrates them back. Consciousness emits experiences, then receives them back. Both are baseline and return. Both are paradoxically nothing and everything (Chalmers, 1996; Penrose, 1994).

Fun but Serious Conclusion

Skeptics may scoff, but they can't delete zero from their equations. And once you accept zero as potential, the rest follows: polarity, oscillation, waveform, creation. Consciousness as zero is not mysticism — it is ontological math. Nothing to it, really.

Sidebar: Zero in a Nutshell

You don't need a PhD to see it. Start with zero. Add a positive, add a negative, and you get a wave. Plot it and the universe appears. Light, sound, gravity, heartbeats, brainwaves — all are oscillations from baseline, resolving back to zero. Call it math, call it physics, call it Brahman or "Let there be light." Either way, the formula doesn't lie: nothing is the mother of everything.

The Nothing Formula

At its simplest, oscillation is expressed by the sine function:

$$f(x) = \sin(x)$$

Zero is the equilibrium axis — the centerline about which all values rise and fall (Boyce & DiPrima, 2017).

- Positive and negative values alternate symmetrically around zero.
- The result is a waveform: oscillation from baseline, through polarity, returning to baseline.

In its generalized form, the sine wave becomes:

$$f(x) = A \cdot \sin(\omega x + \phi)$$

Where:

- **A = amplitude** (the intensity of expression: energy, force, vibration).
- **ω = frequency** (the rate of cycles per unit: sound, light, neural rhythms).
- **φ = phase** (the unique starting point or offset, like a fingerprint).

This simple formula is astonishingly versatile. It describes:

- acoustic vibrations (sound waves),

- electromagnetic radiation (light, radio, X-rays),
- electrical signals (AC current, EKG, EEG),
- and even quantum probability fields (wavefunctions).

Mathematically, sine does not "create" polarity, but it models polarity in perfect balance. Zero itself is not generative, but it provides the axis of symmetry that makes oscillation possible. Without zero, there is no midpoint, no balance point, no return.

Philosophical Bridge

Here, mathematics and metaphysics converge. Physicists describe the universe through oscillations (Feynman et al., 1963). Mystics describe creation through vibration, resonance, or sound (Capra, 1975). Both point to the same structure: fluctuation around a baseline.

- To the physicist, zero is equilibrium.
- To the mystic, zero is potential.
- To both, oscillation is the language of creation.

Consciousness, by this analogy, resembles the sine wave: it arises from a baseline of stillness, expands into polarity, and resolves back again.

As Above, So Below: The Microcosm and Macrocosm

Corpus Hermeticum

"What is above is like what is below; and what is below is like what is above, to accomplish the miracle of the One." (*Corpus Hermeticum I: Poimandres*, 2nd century CE; Copenhaver, 1992, p. 1)

Emerald Tablet of Hermes Trismegistus

"That which is below is like that which is above, and that which is above is like that which is below, to accomplish the miracles of the One Thing." (*Emerald Tablet*, trans. Newton, 17th century; in Dobbs, 1988, p. 183)

Plato, *Timaeus*

"This world is indeed a living creature endowed with a soul and intelligence… a visible god." (*Timaeus* 30b–c; Plato, trans. Cornford, 1937, p. 33)

Plotinus, *Enneads*

"The All is everywhere present… Each thing is in sympathy with the Whole, and the Whole with each thing." (*Enneads* IV.4.32; Plotinus, trans. Armstrong, 1984, p. 223)

Gospel of Thomas

"When you make the two one, and when you make the inner as the outer and the outer as the inner, and the above as the below… then you will enter the Kingdom." (*Gospel of Thomas*, logion 22; Meyer, 2007, p. 129)

Paracelsus

"Man is a microcosm, or little world, because he is an extract from all the stars and planets of the heavens, from the earth and the elements; and so he is their quintessence." (*Paragranum*, 1530; Paracelsus, trans. Gutman, 1996, p. 47)

Robert Fludd

"The whole world is man, and man is the whole world." (*Utriusque Cosmi Historia*, 1617; Debus, 1979, p. 114)

Eastern Esoteric & Persian-Medieval Parallels

Upanishads (Hinduism)

"As is the human body, so is the cosmic body. As is the human mind, so is the cosmic mind. As is the microcosm, so is the macrocosm." (*Yajur Veda, Shukla Upanishad*, c. 800 BCE; Radhakrishnan, 1953, p. 121)

Chāndogya Upaniṣad

"Now, the Self that is free from evil, free from old age, free from death, free from sorrow, free from hunger and thirst, whose desire is the real, whose thought is the real — that is what should be sought, that is what one should desire to understand." (*Chāndogya Upaniṣad* 8.7.1–3; Olivelle, 1998, p. 152)

Tao Te Ching (Daoism)

"The Tao gives birth to One. One gives birth to Two. Two gives birth to Three. Three gives birth to all things." (*Tao Te Ching* ch. 42; Laozi, trans. Lau, 2003, p. 58) "The nameless is the origin of Heaven and Earth; the named is the mother of ten thousand things." (*Tao Te Ching* ch. 1; Laozi, trans. Lau, 2003, p. 3)

Avicenna (Ibn Sīnā)

"The human being is a microcosm; all that exists in the world exists within man." (*Kitāb al-Shifāʾ*, c. 1020 CE; Gutas, 2001, p. 144)

Suhrawardī

"Man is a world in little, and the world is a man in great." (*Ḥikmat al-Ishrāq* / *The Philosophy of Illumination*, 12th century CE; Walbridge & Ziai, 1999, p. 98)

Rumi

"You are not a drop in the ocean. You are the entire ocean in a drop." (*Masnavi*, 13th century CE; Nicholson, 1926/1990, Book I, p. 36)

Al-Bīrūnī

"The relations of the stars in the heavens are mirrored in the nature of man on earth; as above, so below." (*Kitab al-Tafhim*, c. 1030 CE; Wright, 1934, p. 75)

Ikhwān al-Ṣafā' (Brethren of Purity)

"Man is a microcosm containing in himself all the elements and all the powers of the universe." (*Epistles of the Brethren of Purity*, 10th century CE; Netton, 1982, p. 201)

Suggested Reading

A Modern Alchemical Table of Correspondence

Preface

This Suggested Reading List is more than a bibliography. It is both a scholarly guide and an alchemical chart — a modern table of correspondences, much like the symbolic tables of the alchemists of old. In the pages of this book, we have embarked on a provocative journey into the non-locality of consciousness — a realm where the boundaries of self dissolve into the vast interconnectedness of existence. We challenge the rigid confines of Western allopathic medicine, exposing its blindness to what cannot be reduced, and argue for energy work as the necessary complement to materialist models of healing.

What follows is not an exhaustive catalog — no such catalog could exist — but a curated concordance of texts that together form a mosaic of inquiry. These works span philosophy, psychology, neuroscience, physics, geology, and astrophysics; they travel through politics, anthropology, and social upheaval; they speak to non-human sentience in the animal kingdom and plant intelligence, as well as to the planetary consciousness hinted at in ecology and earth sciences. They enter the skies of aeronautics and space exploration, dive into the mathematics of linear and non-linear equations, probe quantum entanglement and the paradoxes of time, and confront the mysteries of shamanism, alchemy, and esoteric traditions. Collectively, they demonstrate that the evidence for non-local consciousness has always been present, if only ignored.

Like the alchemical tables of old, this list is meant not merely for reference but for transformation — to guide, provoke, and ultimately dismantle the illusion that only the measurable is real. Its breadth reflects the truth that consciousness is not a compartmentalized puzzle of biology, but a phenomenon written into the very structures of matter, time, and society. To ignore one domain is to weaken the whole. To trace their intersections is to glimpse the totality.

How to Use This Suggested Reading List

This Suggested Reading List is designed to support your exploration of consciousness, subjectivity, and the immeasurable, as presented in the accompanying book. It is organized across a wide range of disciplines — from foundational philosophy to advanced physics, from bodywork modalities to studies of non-human intelligence, from ecological systems to the frontiers of aeronautics and space.

To use this list effectively, consider the following approach:
Identify Your Focus

Begin by choosing the domain that most resonates with you — whether philosophy, physics, neuroscience, ecology, or esoteric traditions. Each provides a starting point for deep dives into specific facets of the topic.

Trace the Overlap

Many themes recur across disciplines. Shamanism speaks not only to anthropology but also to psychology and spirituality. Quantum entanglement has implications for physics, cosmology, and even theories of time. Social upheaval appears in political philosophy, history, and psychology alike. These overlaps are intentional, offering diverse angles of consideration and reminding us that no inquiry stands alone.

Cross-Reference for Depth

Follow threads between domains. Exploring non-human intelligence may lead you from animal cognition to plant communication to planetary consciousness. Investigating time may take you from relativity to non-linear mathematics to esoteric traditions of cyclical return. The connections matter as much as the sources themselves.

Engage Actively

Treat each entry as an invitation to question and integrate. Start with broad, foundational works and then progress to more specialized explorations. Use annotations and primary sources to deepen your context.

Search for Points of Inquiry

This list highlights varied perspectives — empirical, esoteric, and experiential. Use it to uncover data and insight that mainstream frameworks overlook, from parapsychology to psychedelic research, from geology to cosmology. Cross-pollinate ideas across disciplines to build a robust challenge to reductionism.

This list is a living tool. Return to it as your inquiry evolves, using its overlaps and breadth to uncover the immeasurable within the measurable. It is a map of humanity's search for itself — one that demands you look both beyond and within, or risk never seeing at all.

Suggested Reading List - Table of Correspondence

Foundations of Consciousness and Philosophy

1.1 Consciousness, Psychology, and Philosophy

- Chalmers, D. J. (1995). Facing up to the problem of consciousness. *Journal of Consciousness Studies, 2*(3), 200–219. → Introduces the "hard problem" of consciousness, foundational for your metaphysical ↔ empirical translation.
- James, W. (1890). *The principles of psychology* (Vols. 1–2). Henry Holt. → Early psychological framework emphasizing lived experience.
- James, W. (1902). *The varieties of religious experience: A study in human nature*. Longmans, Green, and Co. → Links mystical states with psychology.
- Jung, C. G. (1968). *Psychology and alchemy* (R. F. C. Hull, Trans.; 2nd ed., Vol. 12). Princeton University Press. (Original work published 1944).
- Jung, C. G. (1980). *Alchemical studies* (R. F. C. Hull, Trans.; Vol. 13). Princeton University Press. (Original work published 1967).
- Jung, C. G. (1973). *Synchronicity: An acausal connecting principle* (R. F. C. Hull, Trans.). Princeton University Press. (Original work published 1952). → Jung's trilogy here anchors alchemy, symbolism, and non-causal explanation.
- Heidegger, M. (1962). *Being and time* (J. Macquarrie & E. Robinson, Trans.). Harper & Row. (Original work published 1927). → Landmark text on ontology, temporality, and authenticity, influential in existentialism and spiritual phenomenology.
- Sartre, J.-P. (1993). *Being and nothingness* (H. Barnes, Trans.). Washington Square Press. (Original work published 1943). → Existential philosophy engaging freedom, responsibility, and human consciousness.
- Whitehead, A. N. (1978). *Process and reality* (Corrected ed., D. Griffin & D. Sherburne, Eds.). Free Press. (Original work published 1929). → A metaphysical system integrating science, philosophy, and spirituality; influential in theology and ecology.
- Foucault, M. (1995). *Discipline and punish: The birth of the prison* (A. Sheridan, Trans.). Vintage Books. (Original work published 1975). → Exposes power structures shaping body and spirit, relevant to critical metaphysical inquiry.

- Derrida, J. (1997). *Of grammatology* (G. C. Spivak, Trans.). Johns Hopkins University Press. (Original work published 1967). → Foundational text of deconstruction, reframing metaphysics and language.
- Deleuze, G., & Guattari, F. (1987). *A thousand plateaus: Capitalism and schizophrenia* (B. Massumi, Trans.). University of Minnesota Press. (Original work published 1980). → Post-structuralist metaphysics, exploring multiplicity, flows, and non-linear systems of meaning.
- Wilber, K. (2000). *A theory of everything: An integral vision for business, politics, science, and spirituality*. Shambhala. → Contemporary synthesis of psychology, spirituality, and systems theory; influential in modern integrative practice.
- Planck, M. (1932). *Where is science going?* W. W. Norton & Company. → Nobel physicist's reflections on matter, energy, and consciousness.
- Watts, A. (1951). *The wisdom of insecurity: A message for an age of anxiety*. Pantheon.
- Watts, A. (1974). *Still the mind: An introduction to meditation*. New World Library. (Original work published 1956).
- Watts, A. (1996). *The book: On the taboo against knowing who you are*. Vintage Books. (Original work published 1969). → Alan Watts' works provide the philosophical bridge between East/West.
- Westen, D. (1998). The scientific legacy of Sigmund Freud: Toward a psychodynamically informed psychological science. *Psychological Bulletin, 124*(3), 333–371.

1.2 Ontology, New Age Spiritualism, and Self-Transformation

1.2.1 Ontology & Being

- Heidegger, M. (1962). *Being and time* (J. Macquarrie & E. Robinson, Trans.). Harper & Row. (Original work published 1927).
- Sartre, J.-P. (1993). *Being and nothingness* (H. Barnes, Trans.). Washington Square Press. (Original work published 1943).
- Tillich, P. (2001). *The courage to be*. Yale University Press. (Original work published 1951).
- Merleau-Ponty, M. (2012). *Phenomenology of perception*. Routledge. (Original work published 1945).

1.2.2 New Age Spiritualism & Popular Metaphysics

- Byrne, R. (2006). *The secret*. Atria Books.
- Gawain, S. (2010). *Creative visualization*. New World Library. (Original work published 1978).
- Chopra, D. (1994). *Quantum healing*. Bantam. (Original work published 1989).
- Tolle, E. (2004). *The power of now*. New World Library. (Original work published 1997).
- Tolle, E. (2005). *A new earth*. Penguin.
- Redfield, J. (1993). *The Celestine prophecy*. Warner Books.

1.2.3 Esoteric Psychology & Transformation

- Assagioli, R. (2000). *Psychosynthesis*. Penguin Books. (Original work published 1965).
- Wilber, K. (1997). *The eye of spirit*. Shambhala.
- Ferrer, J. N. (2002). *Revisioning transpersonal theory*. SUNY Press.
- Almaas, A. H. (1996). *Essence*. Shambhala.

1.3 Nihilism, Atheism, and Radical Skepticism

1.3.1 Nihilism & Existentialism

- Nietzsche, F. (2006). *Thus spoke Zarathustra* (G. Parkes, Trans.). Oxford University Press. (Original work published 1883–1885). → Philosophical-poetic work anticipating depth psychology, myth, and modern existentialism.
- Kierkegaard, S. (1989). *The sickness unto death*. Princeton University Press. (Original work published 1849). → Existential theology and the problem of despair, highly influential in religious philosophy.
- Camus, A. (1991). *The myth of Sisyphus*. Vintage International. (Original work published 1942).
- Camus, A. (1991). *The stranger*. Vintage International. (Original work published 1942).
- Cioran, E. M. (1992). *A short history of decay*. Arcade Publishing. (Original work published 1949).
- Cioran, E. M. (2012). *The trouble with being born*. Arcade Publishing. (Original work published 1973).
- Zapffe, P. W. (1993). The last Messiah. *Philosophy Now*, (45). (Original work published 1933).
- Ligotti, T. (2010). *The conspiracy against the human race*. Hippocampus Press.

1.3.2 Atheism & Critiques of Religion

- Dawkins, R. (2006). *The God delusion*. Houghton Mifflin.
- Dennett, D. (2006). *Breaking the spell*. Viking.
- Harris, S. (2004). *The end of faith*. W. W. Norton.
- Hitchens, C. (2007). *God is not great*. Twelve Books.
- Russell, B. (2004). *Why I am not a Christian*. Routledge. (Original work published 1927).
- Hume, D. (1999). *An enquiry concerning human understanding*. Oxford University Press. (Original work published 1748).
- Feuerbach, L. (1989). *The essence of Christianity*. Prometheus Books. (Original work published 1841).
- Nagel, T. (1971). The absurd. *Journal of Philosophy, 68*(20), 716–727.

1.3.3 Philosophical Skepticism

- Hume, D. (1999). *An enquiry concerning human understanding*. Oxford University Press. (Original work published 1748).
- Kant, I. (1998). *Critique of pure reason*. Cambridge University Press. (Original work published 1781).
- Wittgenstein, L. (1999). *Tractatus logico-philosophicus*. Dover. (Original work published 1921).
- Wittgenstein, L. (2009). *Philosophical investigations*. Wiley-Blackwell. (Original work published 1953).

1.3.4 Modern Nihilism & Pessimism

- Nietzsche, F. (1994). *On the genealogy of morals*. Vintage. (Original work published 1887).
- Nietzsche, F. (2006). *Thus spoke Zarathustra*. Oxford University Press. (Original work published 1883–1885).
- Camus, A. (1991). *The myth of Sisyphus*. Vintage International. (Original work published 1942).
- Camus, A. (1991). *The stranger*. Vintage International. (Original work published 1942).
- Kierkegaard, S. (1989). *The sickness unto death*. Princeton University Press. (Original work published 1849).

1.4 Hard Problems, Paradoxes, and the Limits of Thought

1.4.1 The Hard Problem of Consciousness

- Chalmers, D. J. (1995). Facing up to the problem of consciousness. *Journal of Consciousness Studies, 2*(3), 200–219.
- Nagel, T. (1974). What is it like to be a bat? *The Philosophical Review, 83*(4), 435–450.
- Chalmers, D. J. (1996). *The conscious mind*. Oxford University Press.
- Nagel, T. (1974). What is it like to be a bat? *The Philosophical Review, 83*(4).
- Jackson, F. (1982). Epiphenomenal qualia. *The Philosophical Quarterly, 32*(127).
- Levine, J. (1983). Materialism and qualia. *Pacific Philosophical Quarterly, 64*(4).

1.4.2 Classic Paradoxes

- Zeno of Elea. (2001). Fragments and paradoxes. Oxford. (Original work published c. 450 BCE).
- Russell, B. (1996). *The principles of mathematics*. W. W. Norton. (Original work published 1903).
- Carroll, L. (1995). What the tortoise said to Achilles. Macmillan. (Original work published 1895).

1.4.3 Modern Logical and Semantic Paradoxes

- Gödel, K. (1986). On formally undecidable propositions. Princeton. (Original work published 1931).
- Tarski, A. (1944). The semantic conception of truth. *Philosophy and Phenomenological Research, 4*(3).
- Kripke, S. (1980). *Naming and necessity*. Harvard University Press.
- Putnam, H. (1981). *Reason, truth, and history*. Cambridge University Press.

1.4.4 Epistemic & Metaphysical Limits

- Kant, I. (1998). *Critique of pure reason*. Cambridge University Press. (Original work published 1781).
- Wittgenstein, L. (1999). *Tractatus logico-philosophicus*. Dover. (Original work published 1921).
- Wittgenstein, L. (2009). *Philosophical investigations*. Wiley-Blackwell. (Original work published 1953).
- Heidegger, M. (1962). *Being and time*. Harper & Row. (Original work published 1927).

1.4.5 "Busted" or Reframed Paradoxes

- Dennett, D. C. (1991). *Consciousness explained*. Little, Brown.
- Hofstadter, D. R. (1979). *Gödel, Escher, Bach*. Basic Books.
- Searle, J. R. (1980). Minds, brains, and programs. *Behavioral and Brain Sciences, 3*(3).
- Sorensen, R. (2003). *A brief history of the paradox*. Oxford University Press.

1.5 Linguistic Models and Unsolvable Equations

1.5.1 Limits of Formal Systems

- Gödel, K. (1986). On formally undecidable propositions of Principia Mathematica and related systems I. In S. Feferman (Ed.), *Kurt Gödel: Collected works* (Vol. I). Oxford University Press. (Original work published 1931).
- Turing, A. M. (2004). On computable numbers, with an application to the Entscheidungsproblem. In B. Jack Copeland (Ed.), *The essential Turing*. Oxford University Press. (Original work published 1936).
- Chaitin, G. J. (1994). *Algorithmic information theory*. Cambridge University Press.

1.5.2 Language as Model and Constraint

- Wittgenstein, L. (2001). *Tractatus logico-philosophicus*. Routledge. (Original work published 1921).
- Wittgenstein, L. (2009). *Philosophical investigations*. Wiley-Blackwell. (Original work published 1953).
- Lakoff, G., & Johnson, M. (1980). *Metaphors we live by*. University of Chicago Press.
- Chomsky, N. (1965). *Aspects of the theory of syntax*. MIT Press.

1.5.3 Where Language Meets the Unsolvable

- Hofstadter, D. R. (1979). *Gödel, Escher, Bach: An eternal golden braid*. Basic Books.
- Nagel, E., & Newman, J. R. (2001). *Gödel's proof*. NYU Press. (Original work published 1958).
- Barrow, J. D. (1992). *Pi in the sky: Counting, thinking, and being*. Clarendon Press.

1.5.4 Speculative and Integrative Perspectives

- Penrose, R. (1989). *The emperor's new mind*. Oxford University Press.
- Deacon, T. W. (1997). *The symbolic species: The co-evolution of language and the brain*. Norton.
- Dennett, D. C. (2017). *From bacteria to Bach and back: The evolution of minds*. W. W. Norton.

1.6 Philosophical Debates on Free Will

1.6.1 Classical Foundations

- Augustine. (1998). *On free choice of the will*. Hackett. (Original work published 397).
- Spinoza, B. (1996). *Ethics*. Penguin. (Original work published 1677).
- Kant, I. (1997). *Critique of practical reason*. Cambridge University Press. (Original work published 1788).

1.6.2 Determinism and Mechanistic Models

- Hobbes, T. (1996). *Leviathan*. Oxford University Press. (Original work published 1651).
- Hume, D. (2007). *An enquiry concerning human understanding*. Oxford University Press. (Original work published 1748).
- Laplace, P. S. (1951). *A philosophical essay on probabilities*. Dover. (Original work published 1814).

1.6.3 Modern Compatibilism and Its Critics

- Frankfurt, H. G. (1969). Alternate possibilities and moral responsibility. *Journal of Philosophy, 66*(23), 829–839.
- Dennett, D. C. (1984). *Elbow room: The varieties of free will worth wanting*. MIT Press.
- Strawson, P. F. (1962). Freedom and resentment. *Proceedings of the British Academy, 48*, 1–25.

1.6.4 Neuroscience and the Challenge to Free Will

- Libet, B. (1985). Unconscious cerebral initiative and the role of conscious will in voluntary action. *Behavioral and Brain Sciences, 8*(4), 529–566.
- Wegner, D. M. (2002). *The illusion of conscious will*. MIT Press.

- Soon, C. S., Brass, M., Heinze, H. J., & Haynes, J. D. (2008). Unconscious determinants of free decisions in the human brain. *Nature Neuroscience, 11*(5), 543–545.

1.6.5 Contemporary Reframings

- Kane, R. (1996). *The significance of free will*. Oxford University Press.
- Pereboom, D. (2001). *Living without free will*. Cambridge University Press.
- Harris, S. (2012). *Free will*. Free Press.
- Smilansky, S. (2000). *Free will and illusion*. Oxford University Press.

1.7 Imagination

- Casey, E. S. (1976). *Imagining: A phenomenological study*. Indiana University Press.
- Finke, R. A. (1996). *Imagery, creativity, and emergent structure*. Erlbaum.
- Johnson, M. (1987). *The body in the mind: The bodily basis of meaning, imagination, and reason*. University of Chicago Press.
- Jung, C. G. (1969). *The structure and dynamics of the psyche* (Collected Works Vol. 8). Princeton University Press.
- Kosslyn, S. M. (1994). *Image and brain: The resolution of the imagery debate*. MIT Press.
- Piaget, J. (1962). *Play, dreams and imitation in childhood*. Norton.
- Ricoeur, P. (1994). *Imagination in discourse and action*. Northwestern University Press.
- Sartre, J. P. (1940). *The psychology of imagination*. Philosophical Library.
- Vygotsky, L. S. (2004). Imagination and creativity in childhood. *Journal of Russian & East European Psychology, 42*(1), 7–97.

1.8 Freud vs. Jung: Comparative Studies & Neuroscience Reinterpretations

- Ellenberger, H. F. (1970). *The discovery of the unconscious: The history and evolution of dynamic psychiatry*. Basic Books.
- Fordham, M. (1957). Jungian psychology: A review. *Journal of Analytical Psychology, 2*(1), 5–15.
- Homans, P. (1989). *Jung in context: Modernity and the making of a psychology*. University of Chicago Press.

- Kerr, J. (1993). *A most dangerous method: The story of Jung, Freud, and Sabina Spielrein.* Knopf
- McGuire, W., & Hull, R. F. C. (Eds.). (1974). *The Freud/Jung letters.* Princeton University Press.
- Noll, R. (1994). *The Jung cult: Origins of a charismatic movement.* Princeton University Press.
- Shamdasani, S. (2005). *Jung and the making of modern psychology: The dream of a science.* Cambridge University Press.
- Kandel, E. R. (1999). Biology and the future of psychoanalysis: A new intellectual framework for psychiatry revisited. *American Journal of Psychiatry, 156*(4), 505–524.
- Solms, M. (2018). The neurobiological underpinnings of psychoanalysis: Freud's theories revisited in light of modern neuroscience. *Frontiers in Psychology, 9,* 2200.
- Hogenson, G. B. (2009). Archetypes as action patterns: Complexity theory, neurobiology, and the archetypal image. *Journal of Analytical Psychology, 54*(3), 355–371.
- Panksepp, J., & Solms, M. (2012). *What is neuropsychoanalysis?* Karnac.
- Westen, D. (1998). The scientific legacy of Sigmund Freud: Toward a psychodynamically informed psychological science. *Psychological Bulletin, 124*(3), 333–371.

1.9 Myth, Archetypes & Comparative Symbolism

- Campbell, J. (2008). *The hero with a thousand faces.* New World Library. (Original work published 1949).
- Eliade, M. (1964). *Shamanism: Archaic techniques of ecstasy.* Princeton University Press.
- Lévi-Strauss, C. (1978). *Myth and meaning.* Schocken Books.
- Neumann, E. (1954). *The origins and history of consciousness.* Princeton University Press.
- Segal, R. A. (1999). *Theorizing about myth.* University of Massachusetts Press.

1.10 Time & Temporality Beyond Physics

- Bergson, H. (1910). *Time and free will: An essay on the immediate data of consciousness.* Macmillan.
- Husserl, E. (1991). *On the phenomenology of the consciousness of internal time (1893–1917)* (J. B. Brough, Trans.). Springer.

- Kubler, G. (1962). *The shape of time: Remarks on the history of things.* Yale University Press.
- Ricoeur, P. (1984). *Time and narrative* (Vol. 1). University of Chicago Press.

1.11 Ethics of Consciousness Expansion

- Bostrom, N. (2014). *Superintelligence: Paths, dangers, strategies.* Oxford University Press.
- Jonas, H. (1984). *The imperative of responsibility: In search of an ethics for the technological age.*

Psychology, Trauma, and Human Behavior

2.1 Clinical, Somatic, and Trauma Studies

- Engel, G. L. (1977). The need for a new medical model: A challenge for biomedicine. *Science, 196*(4286), 129–136.
- Goodrich-Dunn, B., & Greene, M. (2004). *The psychology of the body.* Lippincott Williams & Wilkins.
- van der Kolk, B. A. (2014). *The body keeps the score: Brain, mind, and body in the healing of trauma.* Viking.

2.2 Criminal Minds, Psychopathy, and Self-Confessed Crimes

2.2.1 Psychopathy & Forensic Psychology

- Cleckley, H. (1988). *The mask of sanity.* Mosby. (Original work published 1941).
- Hare, R. D. (2003). *Without conscience.* Guilford Press. (Original work published 1993).
- Babiak, P., & Hare, R. D. (2006). *Snakes in suits.* HarperCollins.
- Fallon, J. (2013). *The psychopath inside.* Current.

2.2.2 Self-Professed Criminal Accounts

- Capote, T. (2005). *In cold blood.* Vintage International. (Original work published 1966).
- Abbott, J. H. (1981). *In the belly of the beast.* Random House.
- Kuklinski, R., & Carlo, P. (2003). *The ice man: Confessions of a mafia contract killer.* HarperCollins.
- Bundy, T., & Michaud, S. G. (2012). *Ted Bundy: Conversations with a killer.* Authorlink. (Original work published 1989).

- Manson, C., & Emmons, N. (1986). *Manson in his own words*. Grove Press.

2.2.3 Criminology & Case Studies

- Douglas, J. E., & Olshaker, M. (1995). *Mindhunter*. Scribner.
- Ressler, R. K., & Shachtman, T. (1992). *Whoever fights monsters*. St. Martin's Press.
- Hickey, E. W. (2015). *Serial murderers and their victims*. Cengage Learning.
- Holmes, R. M., & Holmes, S. T. (2009). *Profiling violent crimes*. Sage.

2.3 Psychological Trends, Personality, and Cultural Expressions

2.3.1 Narcissism & Psychopathy

- Lasch, C. (1979). *The culture of narcissism*. W. W. Norton.
- Twenge, J. M., & Campbell, W. K. (2009). *The narcissism epidemic*. Free Press.
- Hare, R. D. (2003). *Without conscience: The disturbing world of the psychopaths among us*. Guilford Press. (Original work published 1993).
- Babiak, P., & Hare, R. D. (2006). *Snakes in suits*. HarperCollins.

2.3.2 Contemporary Psychological Trends

- Beck, A. T. (1967). *Depression: Clinical, experimental, and theoretical aspects*. University of Pennsylvania Press.
- Seligman, M. E. P. (1990). *Learned optimism*. Knopf.
- Haidt, J. (2012). *The righteous mind: Why good people are divided by politics and religion*. Vintage.
- Kahneman, D. (2011). *Thinking, fast and slow*. Farrar, Straus and Giroux.

2.3.3 Clothing, Fashion, and Identity

- Entwistle, J. (2000). *The fashioned body: Fashion, dress, and modern social theory*. Polity.
- Wilson, E. (2003). *Adorned in dreams: Fashion and modernity*. I.B. Tauris. (Original work published 1985).
- Hollander, A. (1993). *Sex and suits*. Knopf.
- Steele, V. (2005). *Fashion, Italian style*. Yale University Press.

2.3.4 Diet & Food Culture

- Pollan, M. (2006). *The omnivore's dilemma*. Penguin.
- Nestle, M. (2002). *Food politics: How the food industry influences nutrition and health*. University of California Press.
- Harris, M. (1985). *Good to eat: Riddles of food and culture*. Waveland Press.
- Fischler, C. (1988). Food, self, and identity. *Social Science Information, 27*(2), 275–292.

2.4 Sex, Beauty, and Reproductive Rights

2.4.1 Sexuality & Culture

- Foucault, M. (1990). *The history of sexuality* (Vol. 1). Vintage Books. (Original work published 1976).
- Rubin, G. (2011). Thinking sex: Notes for a radical theory of the politics of sexuality. Duke University Press. (Original work published 1984).
- Kinsey, A. C., Pomeroy, W. B., & Martin, C. E. (1948). *Sexual behavior in the human male*. W. B. Saunders.
- Kinsey, A. C., et al. (1953). *Sexual behavior in the human female*. W. B. Saunders.

2.4.2 Beauty, Gender, and Power

- Wolf, N. (1990). *The beauty myth: How images of beauty are used against women*. William Morrow.
- Bordo, S. (2003). *Unbearable weight: Feminism, Western culture, and the body*. University of California Press. (Original work published 1993).
- Gill, R. (2007). *Gender and the media*. Polity Press.
- Mulvey, L. (1975). Visual pleasure and narrative cinema. *Screen, 16*(3), 6–18.

2.4.3 Reproductive Rights & Bodily Autonomy

- Sanger, M. (1997). *Woman and the new race*. Charles Kerr. (Original work published 1920).
- Solinger, R. (2005). *Pregnancy and power: A short history of reproductive politics in America*. NYU Press.
- Petchesky, R. P. (1990). *Abortion and woman's choice*. Northeastern University Press. (Original work published 1984).
- Ginsburg, F. D. (1989). *Contested lives: The abortion debate in an American community*. University of California Press.

2.5 Autism, Telepathy, and the Edges of Communication

2.5.1 Autism and Altered Communication Frameworks

- Grandin, T. (1995). *Thinking in pictures: And other reports from my life with autism.* Vintage.
- Baron-Cohen, S. (1995). *Mindblindness: An essay on autism and theory of mind.* MIT Press.
- Happé, F. (1994). *Autism: An introduction to psychological theory.* Routledge.

2.5.2 Telepathy and Anomalous Communication Research

- Rhine, J. B. (1948). *The reach of the mind.* William Sloane Associates.
- Sheldrake, R. (2003). *The sense of being stared at: And other aspects of the extended mind.* Crown.
- Radin, D. (2006). *Entangled minds: Extrasensory experiences in a quantum reality.* Paraview Pocket Books.

2.5.3 Bridging the Two: From Nonverbal Cognition to Shared Fields

- Dawson, G., & Mottron, L. (2004). *Autism: Brain and behavior.* Oxford University Press.
- Trevarthen, C. (1998). The concept and foundations of infant intersubjectivity. In S. Bråten (Ed.), *Intersubjective communication and emotion in early ontogeny* (pp. 15–46). Cambridge University Press.
- Savant, K. (2010). Autism and the telepathic mind [Independent essays].

2.5.4 Cautionary and Integrative Perspectives

- Frith, U. (2003). *Autism: Explaining the enigma* (2nd ed.). Wiley-Blackwell.
- Cardeña, E., Palmer, J., & Marcusson-Clavertz, D. (Eds.). (2015). *Parapsychology: A handbook for the 21st century.* McFarland.

2.6 The Problem of Allopathy in Psychiatry

2.6.1 Historical Foundations of Allopathic Psychiatry

- Kraepelin, E. (2002). *Dementia praecox and paraphrenia.* Thoemmes Press. (Original work published 1919).

- Bleuler, E. (1950). *Dementia praecox, or the group of schizophrenias*. International Universities Press. (Original work published 1911).
- Shorter, E. (1997). *A history of psychiatry: From the era of the asylum to the age of Prozac*. Wiley.

2.6.2 The Pharmaceutical Era and Its Discontents

- Healy, D. (2002). *The creation of psychopharmacology*. Harvard University Press.
- Moncrieff, J. (2009). *The myth of the chemical cure: A critique of psychiatric drug treatment*. Palgrave Macmillan.
- Whitaker, R. (2010). *Anatomy of an epidemic*. Crown.

2.6.3 Consciousness, Meaning, and the Limits of Allopathy

- Laing, R. D. (1960). *The divided self*. Tavistock.
- Szasz, T. (1961). *The myth of mental illness*. Harper & Row.
- Foucault, M. (1988). *Madness and civilization*. Vintage. (Original work published 1965).

2.6.4 Integrative & Phenomenological Alternatives

- Grof, S. (1985). *Beyond the brain: Birth, death, and transcendence in psychotherapy*. SUNY Press.
- van der Kolk, B. (2014). *The body keeps the score*. Viking.
- Corlett, P. R., Fletcher, P. C., & Frith, C. D. (2009). From drugs to deprivation: A Bayesian framework for understanding models of psychosis. *Biological Psychiatry, 65*(7), 572–578.

2.6.5 Toward a Reframing of Psychiatric Care

- Parnas, J., & Zahavi, D. (2002). The role of phenomenology in psychiatric diagnosis and classification. *International Review of Psychiatry, 14*(2), 97–108.
- Lewis-Fernández, R., & Kirmayer, L. J. (2019). Cultural concepts of distress and psychiatric disorders: Understanding symptom experience and expression across cultures. *Transcultural Psychiatry, 56*(6), 1119–1133.

2.7 Social Psychology, Obedience & Collective Behavior

- Asch, S. E. (1951). Effects of group pressure upon the modification and distortion of judgments. In H. Guetzkow (Ed.), *Groups, leadership, and men* (pp. 177–190). Carnegie Press.
- Darley, J. M., & Latané, B. (1968). Bystander intervention in emergencies: Diffusion of responsibility. *Journal of Personality and Social Psychology, 8*(4), 377–383.
- Janis, I. L. (1972). *Victims of groupthink: A psychological study of foreign-policy decisions and fiascoes*. Houghton Mifflin.
- Milgram, S. (1963). Behavioral study of obedience. *Journal of Abnormal and Social Psychology, 67*(4), 371–378.
- Milgram, S. (1974). *Obedience to authority*. Harper & Row.
- Zimbardo, P. G. (2007). *The Lucifer effect: Understanding how good people turn evil*. Random House.
- Christensen, J., & Stuart-Fox, D. (2021). The myth of lemming mass suicide: Evidence from behavior and biology. *Frontiers in Ecology and Evolution, 9*, 682123.

2.8 Mass Psychology, Propaganda & Collective Movements

- Canetti, E. (1960). *Crowds and power*. Viking Press.
- Freud, S. (1922). *Group psychology and the analysis of the ego* (J. Strachey, Trans.). International Psycho-Analytical Press.
- Le Bon, G. (1896). *The crowd: A study of the popular mind*. Macmillan.
- Lippmann, W. (1922). *Public opinion*. Harcourt, Brace & Company.
- Orwell, G. (1949). *Nineteen eighty-four*. Secker & Warburg.
- Reicher, S. D., Spears, R., & Postmes, T. (1995). A social identity model of deindividuation phenomena. *European Review of Social Psychology, 6*(1), 161–198.
- Tufekci, Z. (2017). *Twitter and tear gas: The power and fragility of networked protest*. Yale University Press.

2.9 Visualization, Dreams & Transference

- Decety, J. (1996). The neurophysiological basis of motor imagery. *Behavioural Brain Research, 77*(1–2), 45–52.

- Freud, S. (1958). The dynamics of transference. In J. Strachey (Ed.), *The standard edition of the complete psychological works of Sigmund Freud* (Vol. 12, pp. 97–108). Hogarth Press. (Original work published 1912).
- Hobson, J. A. (2002). *Dreaming: An introduction to the science of sleep.* Oxford University Press.
- Horowitz, M. J. (1970). *Image formation and cognition.* Appleton-Century-Crofts.
- Jung, C. G. (1954). *The practice of psychotherapy.* Princeton University Press.
- Krippner, S. (1993). *The psychology of the future.* Prometheus Books.
- LaBerge, S. (1985). *Lucid dreaming.* Ballantine Books.
- Ogilvie, R. D., & Hunt, H. T. (1989). Lucid dreaming and the EEG: Induction and measurement. *Journal of Mental Imagery, 13*(1), 25–40.
- Ullman, M., Krippner, S., & Vaughan, A. (1973). *Dream telepathy.* Macmillan.
- Watkins, J. G. (1978). *The therapeutic self.* Human Science Press.

2.10 Human Feats, Peak Performance, and Sports Psychology

2.10.1 Endurance & Extreme Achievement

- Noakes, T. (2012). *Lore of running* (4th ed.). Human Kinetics.
- Hutchinson, A. (2018). *Endure.* William Morrow.
- Strayed, C. (2012). *Wild.* Knopf.
- Reinhold, M. (2011). *High altitude.* Cicerone Press.

2.10.2 Sports Psychology & Flow States

- Csikszentmihalyi, M. (2008). *Flow.* Harper Perennial. (Original work published 1990).
- Loehr, J. (1994). *The mental game.* Plume.
- Moran, A. (2012). *Sport and exercise psychology.* Routledge.
- Hardy, L., Jones, G., & Gould, D. (1996). *Understanding psychological preparation for sport.* Wiley.

2.10.3 Neuroscience of Performance

- Eccles, D. W., & Arsal, G. (2017). Deliberate practice in sport. *Current Opinion in Psychology, 16,* 1–5.
- Erickson, K. A., et al. (2009). The role of deliberate practice. *High Ability Studies, 20*(1), 9–18.

- Seifert, L., et al. (2013). Skill acquisition and expertise development. *Frontiers In Psychology, 4*, 1–9.

2.10.4 Cultural Narratives of Feats & Resilience

- McDougall, C. (2009). *Born to run*. Knopf.
- Murakami, H. (2008). *What I talk about when I talk about running*. Knopf.
- Messner, R. (2009). *The crystal horizon: Everest—the first solo ascent*. Mountaineers Books.
- Attia, P. (2023). *Outlive*. Harmony.

Metaphysical and Esoteric Traditions

3.1 Metaphysical and Esoteric Explorations

- Anonymous. (2002). *Meditations on the tarot: A journey into Christian hermeticism* (R. Powell, Trans.). Tarcher/Putnam. (Original work published 1980). → Anonymously authored classic of modern Christian Hermeticism, deeply Jungian in tone, using the Major Arcana as a path of inner transformation.
- Blavatsky, H. P. (1877). *Isis unveiled: A master-key to the mysteries of ancient and modern science and theology* (Vols. 1–2). J. W. Bouton.
- Blavatsky, H. P. (1888). *The secret doctrine: The synthesis of science, religion, and philosophy* (Vols. 1–2). Theosophical Publishing Company. → Foundational Theosophical text merging Eastern and Western metaphysics.
- Cannon, D. (1993). *Between death and life: Conversations with a spirit*. Ozark Mountain Publishing.
- Cannon, D. (2011). *The convoluted universe: Book four*. Ozark Mountain Publishing. → Case studies exploring reincarnation, consciousness, and healing metaphors.
- Crowley, A. (1909). *The equinox* (Vol. 1, No. 1). Simpkin, Marshall, Hamilton, Kent & Co.
- Crowley, A. (1929). *Magick in theory and practice*. Lecram Press.
- Crowley, A. (1997). *Liber ABA (Book 4)*. Weiser Books. (Original work published 1938). → Crowley's masterwork synthesizing yoga, mysticism, and ceremonial magick.
- DuQuette, L. M. (1995). *The chicken qabalist*. Weiser Books. → Accessible introduction to Qabalah and ceremonial practice.

- DuQuette, L. M. (2003). *The magick of Aleister Crowley: A handbook of the rituals of Thelema*. Weiser Books.
- Frost, G., & Frost, Y. (1972). *The witch's bible*. New World Library.
- Frost, G., & Frost, Y. (1975). *The magic power of witchcraft*. New American Library.
- Frost, G., & Frost, Y. (1999). *The prophet's bible*. University of Minnesota Press. → The Frosts integrate Wiccan energy practices, with Gavin's physics background informing attempts at empirical validation of energy work.
- Godwin, D. (1999). *Godwin's cabalistic encyclopedia: A complete guide to cabalistic magic* (4th rev. ed.). Llewellyn Publications. → Definitive reference for Qabalistic correspondences, bridging Hermetic, magical, and mystical traditions.
- Hall, M. P. (1928). *The secret teachings of all ages: An encyclopedic outline of Masonic, Hermetic, Qabbalistic and Rosicrucian symbolical philosophy*. H. S. Crocker Company. → A sweeping compendium of Western esotericism and symbolism.
- Ichazo, O. (1982). *The human process for enlightenment and freedom*. Arica Institute Press. → Foundational Arica School text integrating psychology, philosophy, and esoteric development.
- Ichazo, O. (1991). *Enneagram of personality types*. Arica Institute Press. → Ichazo's original presentation of the enneagram system as a map of human consciousness.
- Kiev, A. (1974). *Magic and schizophrenia*. International Universities Press. → Groundbreaking exploration of overlaps between magical thinking and psychiatric states.
- Lévi, É. (1896). *Transcendental magic: Its doctrine and ritual* (A. E. Waite, Trans.). Rider. (Original work published 1856). → Classic synthesis of Hermeticism, Kabbalah, and occult philosophy.
- Regardie, I. (2004). *The tree of life: An illustrated study in magic*. Weiser Books. (Original work published 1932). → A systematic presentation of ceremonial magic in the Western esoteric tradition.
- Regardie, I. (1989). *The golden dawn: The original account of the teachings, rites, and ceremonies of the Hermetic Order*. Llewellyn Publications. (Original work published 1937). → The most complete documentation of Golden Dawn ritual and philosophy.

- Skinner, S. (2006). *The complete magicians' tables.* Golden Hoard Press. → Authoritative reference aligning Qabalah, astrology, alchemy, and grimoires.
- Skinner, S. (2009). *Geomancy in theory and practice.* Golden Hoard Press. → Definitive modern text on the ancient art of geomancy.
- Skinner, S. (2010). *The keys to the gateway of magic: Summoning spirits in the Solomonic tradition.* Golden Hoard Press. → Scholarly edition of Solomonic magical texts with commentary.
- Sri Aurobindo. (2005). *The life divine.* Lotus Press. (Original work published 1939–1940). → A modern Vedantic vision integrating consciousness, evolution, and divinity.
- Trajkovic, N. R. (2019–2023). *The anatomy of the abyss* (Vols. 1–3). Aeon Sophia Press. → A contemporary exploration of the Abyss in Qabalah, Thelema, and mystical philosophy, synthesizing modern scholarship with classical occult sources.
- Vatsyayan, K. (1997). *The square and the circle of the Indian arts.* Abhinav Publications. → Contemporary Vedic and aesthetic theory, linking cosmology to form and practice.
- Waite, A. E. (1888). *The real history of the Rosicrucians: Founded on their own manifestoes and on facts and documents collected from the writings of initiated brethren.* George Redway. → Scholarly historical survey of Rosicrucian texts and traditions.
- Waite, A. E. (1910). *The secret doctrine in Israel: A study of the Zohar and its connections.* William Rider & Son. → A critical exploration of Kabbalah, mysticism, and Rosicrucian influences.
- Waite, A. E. (1911). *The hidden church of the Holy Graal.* Rebman. → Rosicrucian and mystical interpretation of the Grail legend.
- Winkler, G. (2003). *Magic of the ordinary: Recovering the shamanic in Judaism.* North Atlantic Books. → Explores Jewish shamanic traditions and the intersection of magic and daily life.
- Yronwode, C. (2002). *Hoodoo herb and root magic: A materia magica of African-American conjure.* Lucky Mojo Curio Company. → Definitive modern text on rootwork and folk-magic practice.
- Yronwode, C. (2006). *The art of hoodoo candle magic in rootwork, conjure, and spiritual church services.* Lucky Mojo Curio Company.

- Yronwode, C. (2006). *The art of hoodoo candle magic in rootwork, conjure, and spiritual church services*. Lucky Mojo Curio Company.
- Crowley, A. (1976). *The book of the law (Liber AL vel Legis)*. Weiser Books. (Original work published 1904).
- Crowley, A. (1998). *The vision and the voice (Liber 418)*. Weiser Books. (Original work published 1911).
- Fortune, D. (2001). *Psychic self-defense*. Weiser Books. (Original work published 1930).
- DuQuette, L. M. (2001). *Psychic self-defense and the mysteries of magic*. Weiser Books.
- Roberts, J. (1972). *Seth speaks*. Prentice-Hall.
- Roberts, J. (1974). *The nature of personal reality*. Prentice-Hall.

3.2 Shamanism & Indigenous Mysticism

- Eliade, M. (1964). *Shamanism: Archaic techniques of ecstasy*. Princeton University Press. → Foundational cross-cultural study, documenting universal shamanic techniques of initiation, trance, and healing. Still the most cited academic reference on shamanism.
- Harner, M. (1980). *The way of the shaman*. Harper & Row. → Introduced "core shamanism" to Western readers, emphasizing journeying and drumming. Practical and widely used in training, though debated in anthropology.
- Walsh, R. (1990). *The spirit of shamanism*. Jeremy P. Tarcher. → Integrates anthropology, psychology, and practice. Scholarly yet accessible, bridging research with lived instruction.
- Harner, M. (1990). *The way of the shaman*. HarperOne. (Original work published 1980).
- Narby, J. (1998). *The cosmic serpent*. Tarcher/Putnam.
- Luna, L. E., & Amaringo, P. (1991). *Ayahuasca visions*. North Atlantic Books.
- Viveiros de Castro, E. (2014). *Cannibal metaphysics*. Univocal. (Original work published 1998).
- Taussig, M. (1987). *Shamanism, colonialism, and the wild man*. University of Chicago Press.
- Deloria, V., Jr. (1992). *God is red*. Fulcrum.
- Deloria, V., Jr. (2006). *The world we used to live in*. Fulcrum.
- Brown, J. E. (1989). *The sacred pipe*. University of Oklahoma Press. (Original work published 1953).
- Lame Deer, J. F., & Erdoes, R. (1994). *Lame Deer, seeker of visions*. Washington Square Press. (Original work published 1972).

- Irwin, L. (1994). *The dream seekers*. University of Oklahoma Press.
- Mooney, J. (1991). *The ghost-dance religion*. University of Chicago Press. (Original work published 1896).
- Estes, N. (2019). *Our history is the future*. Verso.

3.3 Sacred Texts & Commentaries Referenced in Esoteric Traditions

- Rig Veda (Doniger, Trans., 1981).
- Upaniṣads (Olivelle, 1998; Radhakrishnan, 1994).
- Bhagavad Gita (Mascaró, 1962).
- Tao Te Ching (Mitchell, 1988).
- Analects (Confucius, Waley, 1997).
- I Ching (Legge, 1963).
- Zhuangzi (Watson, 1968).
- Dhammapada (Müller, 1881).
- Lotus Sutra (Watson, 1993).
- Holy Bible — King James Version (1611/2017), New American Bible Revised Edition (2011), New Revised Standard Version (1989).
- Holy Qur'an (Ali, 2001; Nasr, 2015).
- Zohar (Pritzker, 2003).
- Nag Hammadi Library (Robinson, 1990).
- Buddhist I Ching (Cleary, 1993).

3.4 Theosophy, Numerology, and Astrology

3.4.1 Theosophical Traditions

- Blavatsky, H. P. (1970). *The secret doctrine*. Theosophical Publishing House. (Original work published 1888).
- Besant, A. (1897). *Ancient wisdom*. Theosophical Publishing Society.
- Steiner, R. (1997). *Theosophy*. Anthroposophic Press. (Original work published 1904).

3.4.2 Numerology and Sacred Number

- Pythagoras. (1987). The golden verses of Pythagoras. Phanes Press. (Original work published c. 500 BCE).
- Balliett, L. D. (1913). *The philosophy of numbers*. The Sacred Science Society.
- Jung, C. G. (1973). *Synchronicity*. Princeton University Press. (Original work published 1952).

3.4.3 Astrology as Archetypal Science

- Ptolemy. (1940). *Tetrabiblos*. Harvard University Press. (Original work published 2nd century).
- Greene, L., & Arroyo, S. (1976). *Astrology and the modern psyche*. CRCS Publications.
- Tarnas, R. (2006). *Cosmos and psyche*. Viking.

3.5 Alchemy, Symbol, and the Language of the Unconscious

3.5.1 Classical Alchemy

- Paracelsus. (2008). *Selected writings*. Princeton University Press. (Original work published 1567).
- Flamel, N. (1994). *Exposition of the hieroglyphical figures*. Kessinger. (Original work published c. 1400).
- Jung, C. G. (1968). *Psychology and alchemy*. Princeton University Press. (Original work published 1944).

3.5.2 Renaissance and Esoteric Revivals

- Dee, J. (2003). *The hieroglyphic monad*. Weiser Books. (Original work published 1564).
- Khunrath, H. (1999). *Amphitheatrum sapientiae aeternae*. University of Minnesota Press. (Original work published 1595).
- Evola, J. (1995). *The hermetic tradition*. Inner Traditions.

3.5.3 Alchemy as Inner Transformation

- Eliade, M. (1978). *The forge and the crucible*. University of Chicago Press. (Original work published 1956).
- Dobbs, B. J. T. (1975). *The foundations of Newton's alchemy*. Cambridge University Press.
- Principe, L. M. (2013). *The secrets of alchemy*. University of Chicago Press.

3.5.4 Jung and the Symbolic Imagination

- Jung, C. G., von Franz, M.-L., Henderson, J. L., Jacobi, J., & Jaffé, A. (1964). *Man and his symbols*. Dell.
- Jung, C. G. (1969). *The archetypes and the collective unconscious*. Princeton University Press. (Original work published 1959).
- Jung, C. G. (1973). *Synchronicity*. Princeton University Press. (Original work published 1952).

3.5.5 Symbol, Myth, and Art as Universal Language

- Campbell, J. (2008). *The hero with a thousand faces*. New World Library. (Original work published 1949).
- Eliade, M. (1963). *Myth and reality*. Harper & Row. (Original work published 1957).
- Cirlot, J. E. (2001). *A dictionary of symbols*. Routledge. (Original work published 1962).

3.5.6 Depth Psychology and Symbol Systems

- Hillman, J. (1975). *Re-visioning psychology*. Harper & Row.
- Neumann, E. (2015). *The origins and history of consciousness*. Princeton University Press. (Original work published 1954).
- Edinger, E. F. (1994). *Ego and archetype*. Shambhala.

3.5.7 Toward an Integrative Symbolic Science

- Corbin, H. (1998). *Alone with the alone*. Princeton University Press. (Original work published 1964).
- Ricoeur, P. (1967). *The symbolism of evil*. Beacon Press.
- Kearney, R. (1984). *The wake of imagination*. Routledge.

3.6 Freemasonry and Secret Societies

3.6.1 Origins and Symbolic Framework

- Anderson, J. (2005). *The constitutions of the free-masons*. Kessinger. (Original work published 1723).
- Mackey, A. G. (2005). *The symbolisms of Freemasonry*. Kessinger. (Original work published 1873).
- Pike, A. (2011). *Morals and dogma of the ancient and accepted Scottish Rite of Freemasonry*. Forgotten Books. (Original work published 1871).

3.6.2 Esoteric Continuities and Influences

- Hall, M. P. (2003). *The secret teachings of all ages*. Tarcher. (Original work published 1928).
- Waite, A. E. (2003). *The secret tradition in Freemasonry*. Cosimo Classics. (Original work published 1921).
- Yates, F. A. (2001). *Giordano Bruno and the hermetic tradition*. University of Chicago Press. (Original work published 1964).

3.6.3 Secret Societies and Cultural Power

- Roberts, J. M. (2008). *The mythology of the secret societies*. Routledge. (Original work published 1972).
- Stevenson, D. (1988). *The origins of Freemasonry: Scotland's century, 1590–1710*. Cambridge University Press.
- Ridley, J. (2011). *The Freemasons: A history of the world's most powerful secret society*. Arcade.

3.6.4 Contemporary Symbolic Resonance

- Baigent, M., Leigh, R., & Lincoln, H. (1982). *The holy blood and the holy grail*. Delacorte.
- Knight, C., & Lomas, R. (1996). *The Hiram key: Pharaohs, Freemasons and the discovery of the secret scrolls of Jesus*. Century.
- Brown, D. (2003). *The Da Vinci code*. Doubleday.

3.7 Monsters, Entities, and the Edges of Perception

3.7.1 Archetypes of the Shadow

- Jung, C. G. (1969). *Aion: Researches into the phenomenology of the self*. Princeton University Press. (Original work published 1951).
- Campbell, J. (2008). *The hero with a thousand faces*. New World Library. (Original work published 1949).
- Cohen, J. J. (1996). *Monster theory: Reading culture*. University of Minnesota Press.

3.7.2 Vampires, Ghouls, and Cultural Archetypes

- Stoker, B. (1997). *Dracula*. Oxford University Press. (Original work published 1897).
- Summers, M. (2000). *The vampire: His kith and kin*. Senate. (Original work published 1928).
- Barber, P. (1988). *Vampires, burial, and death: Folklore and reality*. Yale University Press.

3.7.3 Demons, Daimons, and Intermediary Beings

- Pagels, E. (1995). *The origin of Satan*. Vintage.
- Kelsey, M. T. (1973). *Encounter with the demonic*. Fortress Press.
- Hillman, J. (1975). *Re-visioning psychology*. Harper & Row.

3.7.4 Fourth-Dimensional Entities and Anomalous Beings

- Abbott, E. A. (1991). *Flatland: A romance of many dimensions*. Princeton University Press. (Original work published 1884).
- Vallee, J. (2014). *Passport to Magonia*. Daily Grail Press. (Original work published 1969).
- Keel, J. A. (1991). *Operation Trojan Horse*. Illuminet Press. (Original work published 1970).

3.7.5 The Function of the Monstrous

- Kristeva, J. (1982). *Powers of horror: An essay on abjection*. Columbia University Press.
- Warner, M. (1998). *No go the bogeyman: Scaring, lulling, and making mock*. Chatto & Windus.
- Douglas, M. (2002). *Purity and danger*. Routledge. (Original work published 1966).

3.8 The Pyramids and Ancient Egypt: Architecture of Mystery

3.8.1 The Pyramid as Sacred Science

- Lehner, M. (1997). *The complete pyramids*. Thames & Hudson.
- Bauval, R., & Gilbert, A. (1994). *The Orion mystery: Unlocking the secrets of the pyramids*. Crown.
- West, J. A. (1993). *Serpent in the sky: The high wisdom of ancient Egypt*. Quest Books.

3.8.2 Egypt as the Root of Western Esotericism

- Hornung, E. (1992). *Idea into image: Essays on ancient Egyptian thought*. Princeton University Press.
- Assmann, J. (2001). *The search for God in ancient Egypt*. Cornell University Press.
- Budge, E. A. W. (2009). *The Egyptian book of the dead*. Dover. (Original work published 1904).

3.8.3 The Pyramid as Symbol of Transformation

- Schwaller de Lubicz, R. A. (1998). *The temple of man*. Inner Traditions. (Original work published 1949).
- Hancock, G. (1995). *Fingerprints of the gods*. Crown.
- Naydler, J. (1996). *Temple of the cosmos: The ancient Egyptian experience of the sacred*. Inner Traditions.

3.8.4 From Egypt to Alchemy, Masonry, and Psychology

- Yates, F. A. (2001). *Giordano Bruno and the hermetic tradition*. University of Chicago Press. (Original work published 1964).
- Pike, A. (2011). *Morals and dogma of the ancient and accepted Scottish Rite of Freemasonry*. Forgotten Books. (Original work published 1871).
- Jung, C. G. (1970). *Mysterium coniunctionis*. Princeton University Press. (Original work published 1954).

3.9 Niche Energy Healing

- Brennan, B. A. (1987). *Hands of light: A guide to healing through the human energy field*. Bantam.
- Brennan, B. A. (1993). *Light emerging: The journey of personal healing*. Bantam.
- Brennan, B. A. (2017). *Core light healing*. Hay House.
- Hover-Kramer, D. (2002). *Healing touch: A guidebook for practitioners*. Delmar Cengage.
- Krieger, D. (1979). *The therapeutic touch: How to use your hands to help or to heal*. Prentice Hall.
- Krieger, D. (2002). *Therapeutic touch inner workbook: Ventures in transpersonal healing*. Bear & Company.
- Randolph, S. (1997). *Polarity therapy: The complete collected works of Randolph Stone*. CRCS Publications.
- Stone, R. (1986). *Polarity therapy: The power that heals*. CRCS Publications.
- Sui, C. K. (2004). *Miracles through pranic healing* (3rd ed.). Institute for Inner Studies.
- Wardell, D. W., & Weymouth, K. F. (2004). Review of studies of healing touch. *Journal of Nursing Scholarship, 36*(2), 147–154.

3.10 Embodied Mastery & Extreme Practices

- Iyengar, B. K. S. (1966). *Light on yoga*. Schocken Books.
- Patanjali. (1990). *The Yoga Sutras of Patanjali* (S. Vivekananda, Trans.). Dover. (Original work published ca. 400 CE).
- Shahar, M. (2008). *The Shaolin monastery: History, religion, and the Chinese martial arts*. University of Hawaii Press.
- van der Kolk, B. A. (2014). *The body keeps the score*. Viking.
- Wong, K. (1996). *The art of Shaolin Kung Fu*. Tuttle Publishing.

3.11 Ritual, Transgression & Alternative Systems of Awareness

- Aquino, M. (2015). *The temple of Set*. CreateSpace Independent Publishing.
- Crowley, A. (1973). *Magick in theory and practice*. Weiser Books. (Original work published 1929–1930).
- Dyrendal, A., Lewis, J. R., & Petersen, J. A. (2015). *The invention of Satanism*. Oxford University Press.
- Flowers, S. E. (1997). *Lords of the left-hand path: Forbidden practices and spiritual heresies*. Rûna-Raven Press.
- LaVey, A. S. (1969). *The Satanic Bible*. Avon.
- LaVey, A. S. (1972). *The Satanic rituals*. Avon.
- Regardie, I. (1984). *The Golden Dawn*. Llewellyn Publications. (Original work published 1937).
- Urban, H. B. (2006). *Magia sexualis: Sex, magic, and liberation in modern Western esotericism*. University of California Press.

3.12 Ceremonial Magic: Scholarly Analyses

- Asprem, E. (2012). *Arguing with angels: Enochian magic and modern occultism*. SUNY Press.
- Asprem, E., & Granholm, K. (Eds.). (2014). *Contemporary esotericism*. Routledge.
- Hanegraaff, W. J. (2012). *Esotericism and the academy: Rejected knowledge in Western culture*. Cambridge University Press.
- Hanegraaff, W. J., Faivre, A., van den Broek, R., & Brach, J.-P. (Eds.). (2005). *Dictionary of gnosis and Western esotericism*. Brill.
- Hutton, R. (1999). *The triumph of the moon: A history of modern pagan witchcraft*. Oxford University Press.
- Pasi, M. (2012). Aleister Crowley and the temptations of politics. *Aries, 12*(1), 83–113.
- Stuckrad, K. von. (2005). *Western esotericism: A brief history of secret knowledge*. Equinox.
- Versluis, A. (2007). *Magic and mysticism: An introduction to Western esotericism*. Rowman & Littlefield.

Anomalies, Parapsychology, and Unexplained Phenomena

4.1 Anomalies & Human Extremes

- Abrahams, P. H. (1995). Spontaneous human combustion: A medical assessment. *Journal of the Royal Society of Medicine, 88*(1), 13–16.

- Arnold, L. (1995). *Spontaneous human combustion*. Little, Brown
- Green, E. E., & Green, A. M. (1977). *Beyond biofeedback*. Delacorte Press.
- Playfair, G. L. (1980). *This house is haunted: The true story of the Enfield poltergeist*. St. Martin's Press.
- Radin, D. (1997). *The conscious universe: The scientific truth of psychic phenomena*. HarperOne.
- Ricard, M., Lutz, A., & Davidson, R. J. (2014). *Altered traits*. Avery.
- Rhine, J. B. (1934). *Extra-sensory perception*. Boston Society for Psychic Research.
- Zöllner, J. C. F. (1878). *Transcendental physics*. Kegan Paul.

4.2 Psychic Research & Parapsychology

4.2.1 Foundational Works

- Rhine, J. B. (1934). *Extrasensory perception*. Boston Society for Psychic Research.
- Rhine, J. B., & Pratt, J. G. (1957). *Parapsychology: Frontier science of the mind*. Charles C. Thomas.
- Ullman, M., Krippner, S., & Vaughan, A. (1973). *Dream telepathy*. Macmillan.
- Rhine, J. B. (2003). *Extra-sensory perception*. Boston Society for Psychic Research. (Original work published 1934).
- Ullman, M., Krippner, S., & Vaughan, A. (1973). *Dream telepathy*. Macmillan.

4.2.2 Government & Institutional Research

- Targ, R., & Puthoff, H. E. (1977). *Mind-reach*. Delacorte Press.
- McMoneagle, J. (1993). *Mind trek*. Hampton Roads.
- May, E. C., & Marwaha, S. B. (2018). *ESP wars: East and West*. Anomalist Books.
- CIA. (1995). Stargate remote viewing documents (declassified).
- McMoneagle, J. (1993). *Mind trek*. Hampton Roads.
- Smith, P. H. (2005). *Reading the enemy's mind*. Forge Books.

4.2.3 Academic & Statistical Analyses

- Radin, D. (1997). *The conscious universe*. HarperOne.
- Radin, D. (2006). *Entangled minds*. Simon & Schuster.

- Jahn, R. G., & Dunne, B. J. (1987). *Margins of reality*. Harcourt Brace Jovanovich.
- Radin, D. (2006). *The conscious universe*. HarperOne. (Original work published 1997).
- Radin, D. (2009). *Entangled minds*. Simon & Schuster.

4.2.4 Recent and Contemporary Research

- Cardeña, E., Lynn, S. J., & Krippner, S. (Eds.). (2014). *Varieties of anomalous experience* (2nd ed.). American Psychological Association.
- Mossbridge, J., & Radin, D. (2018). *The precognition code*. Watkins.
- Cardeña, E., Palmer, J., & Marcusson-Clavertz, D. (Eds.). (2015). *Parapsychology: A handbook for the 21st century*. McFarland.

4.3 Psychic Prediction & Consensus Reality

- Chalmers, D. J. (1996). *The conscious mind: In search of a fundamental theory*. Oxford University Press.
- Honorton, C., & Ferrari, D. C. (1989). "Future telling": A meta-analysis of forced-choice precognition experiments, 1935–1987. *Journal of Parapsychology, 53*(4), 281–308.
- Mossbridge, J., & Radin, D. (2018). *The precognition code*. Watkins.
- Radin, D. (2006). *Entangled minds*. Paraview Pocket Books.
- Tart, C. T. (2009). *The end of materialism*. New Harbinger.
- Targ, R., & Harary, K. (1984). *The mind race*. Villard.
- William James. (1986). Essays in psychical research. Harvard University Press. (Original work published 1896).

4.4 Psychic Phenomena, Out-of-Body Experiences, and Telepathy

4.4.1 Foundational Parapsychology

- Rhine, J. B. (2003). *Extra-sensory perception*. Boston Society for Psychic Research. (Original work published 1934).
- Ullman, M., Krippner, S., & Vaughan, A. (1973). *Dream telepathy*. Macmillan.
- Radin, D. (2006). *The conscious universe*. HarperOne. (Original work published 1997).
- Radin, D. (2009). *Entangled minds*. Simon & Schuster.

4.4.2 Out-of-Body & Near-Death Experiences

- Monroe, R. A. (1971). *Journeys out of the body*. Anchor Books.
- Monroe, R. A. (1985). *Far journeys*. Doubleday.
- Moody, R. A. (2001). *Life after life*. HarperOne. (Original work published 1975).
- Ring, K. (1980). *Life at death*. Coward, McCann & Geoghegan.
- Greyson, B. (2021). *After*. St. Martin's Essentials.

4.4.3 Telepathy, Clairvoyance, and Precognition

- Targ, R., & Puthoff, H. (1977). *Mind-reach*. Delacorte.
- Targ, R. (2012). *The reality of ESP*. Quest Books.
- Bem, D. J. (2011). Feeling the future. *Journal of Personality and Social Psychology, 100*(3), 407–425.
- Dunne, J. W. (2001). *An experiment with time*. Hampton Roads. (Original work published 1927).

4.4.4 Cross-Cultural & Esoteric Perspectives

- Leadbeater, C. W. (1993). *Clairvoyance*. Quest Books. (Original work published 1899).
- Steiner, R. (1994). *Knowledge of the higher worlds*. Anthroposophic Press. (Original work published 1923).
- Blavatsky, H. P. (1977). *The secret doctrine*. Theosophical University Press. (Original work published 1888).

4.4.5 Government & Military Programs

- CIA. (1995). Stargate remote viewing documents (declassified).
- McMoneagle, J. (1993). *Mind trek*. Hampton Roads.
- Smith, P. H. (2005). *Reading the enemy's mind*. Forge Books.

4.5 Ancient Aliens, Forbidden Archaeology, and Lost Histories

4.5.1 Foundational "Ancient Astronaut" Theories

- von Däniken, E. (1999). *Chariots of the gods?* Berkley Books. (Original work published 1968).
- von Däniken, E. (1972). *Gods from outer space*. Bantam Books.
- Sitchin, Z. (2002). *The 12th planet*. Harper. (Original work published 1976).

4.5.2 Babylonian, Sumerian & Ancient Texts

- Kramer, S. N. (1999). *The Sumerians: Their history, culture, and character*. University of Chicago Press. (Original work published 1963).
- Dalley, S. (2009). *Myths from Mesopotamia: Creation, the flood, Gilgamesh, and others*. Oxford University Press. (Original work published 1989).
- Bottéro, J. (2001). *Religion in ancient Mesopotamia*. University of Chicago Press.
- George, A. (2003). *The epic of Gilgamesh*. Penguin Classics.

4.5.3 Alternative Archaeology & Historical Anomalies

- Hancock, G. (1995). *Fingerprints of the gods*. Crown.
- Hancock, G. (2015). *Magicians of the gods*. St. Martin's Press.
- Schoch, R. M. (1992). Redating the Great Sphinx of Giza. *Geological Society of America abstracts with programs, 24*(7), 231.
- Bauval, R., & Gilbert, A. (1994). *The Orion mystery*. Crown.
- Childress, D. H. (1993). *Lost cities of Atlantis, ancient Europe & the Mediterranean*. Adventures Unlimited Press.

4.5.4 Modern Theorists Expanding the Ancient Alien Hypothesis

- Tellinger, M. (2005). *Slave species of god: The story of mankind's genetic origins*. Zulu Planet.
- Tellinger, M. (2012). *African temples of the Anunnaki*. Bear & Company.
- Martell, J. (2001). *Knowledge apocalypse: Ancient astronauts and the search for planet X*. Adventures Unlimited Press.
- Martell, J. (2010). *Ancient alien question*. New Page Books.
- Tsoukalos, G. A. (2011–present). *Ancient Aliens* [Television series]. History Channel.

4.5.5 Modern Discoveries that Challenge History

- Schoch, R. M., & McNally, R. A. (2002). *Voices of the rocks*. Harmony.
- Collins, A. (2002). *Gateway to Atlantis*. Arrow.
- West, J. A. (1993). *Serpent in the sky*. Quest Books.

4.5.6 Critical Engagements

- Feder, K. L. (2010). *Frauds, myths, and mysteries*. McGraw-Hill.
- Fagan, B. (2006). *Archaeological fantasies*. Routledge.
- Card, J. J. (Ed.). (2018). *Spooky archaeology*. University of New Mexico Press.

Science, Technology, and Systems

5.1 Technology, AI, Systems, Space, and Mathematics

5.1.1 Technology & AI

- Wiener, N. (1948). *Cybernetics*. MIT Press.
- Turing, A. M. (1950). Computing machinery and intelligence. *Mind, 59*(236), 433–460.
- Russell, S., & Norvig, P. (2021). *Artificial intelligence: A modern approach* (4th ed.). Pearson.
- Shannon, C. E. (1948). A mathematical theory of communication. *Bell System Technical Journal, 27*(3), 379–423.
- von Neumann, J. (1958). *The computer and the brain*. Yale University Press.
- Kurzweil, R. (2005). *The singularity is near*. Viking.
- Floridi, L. (2014). *The fourth revolution*. Oxford University Press.
- Turing, A. M. (1950). Computing machinery and intelligence. *Mind, 59*(236), 433–460.
- Turing, A. M. (2004). On computable numbers. In *The essential Turing*. Oxford. (Original work published 1936).
- Wiener, N. (1961). *Cybernetics: Or control and communication in the animal and the machine*. MIT Press. (Original work published 1948).
- McCarthy, J., Minsky, M., Rochester, N., & Shannon, C. E. (1955). A proposal for the Dartmouth Summer Research Project on Artificial Intelligence.
- Searle, J. R. (1980). Minds, brains, and programs. *Behavioral and Brain Sciences, 3*(3), 417–457.
- Dennett, D. C. (1991). *Consciousness explained*. Little, Brown.
- Kurzweil, R. (2005). *The singularity is near: When humans transcend biology*. Viking.
- Bostrom, N. (2014). *Superintelligence: Paths, dangers, strategies*. Oxford University Press.

- Chalmers, D. J. (2010). The singularity: A philosophical analysis. *Journal of Consciousness Studies, 17*(9–10), 7–65.
- Clark, A. (2003). *Natural-born cyborgs: Minds, technologies, and the future of human intelligence.* Oxford University Press.
- Haraway, D. (1991). A cyborg manifesto. In *Simians, cyborgs, and women: The reinvention of nature.* Routledge. (Original work published 1985).
- Kelly, K. (1994). *Out of control: The new biology of machines, social systems, and the economic world.* Basic Books.
- Floridi, L. (2014). *The fourth revolution: How the infosphere is reshaping human reality.* Oxford University Press.
- Farahany, N. A. (2023). *The battle for your brain: Defending the right to think freely in the age of neurotechnology.* St. Martin's Press.
- Kurzweil, R. (2005). *The singularity is near.* Viking.
- Yuste, R., & Goering, S. (2017). Neurotechnology and human rights. *Nature, 551*(7679), 159–163.

5.1.2 Space & Cosmology

- Hawking, S. (1988). *A brief history of time.* Bantam.
- Greene, B. (2004). *The fabric of the cosmos.* Vintage Books.
- Smolin, L. (2001). *Three roads to quantum gravity.* Basic Books.
- Penrose, R. (2004). *The road to reality.* Knopf.
- Sagan, C. (1980). *Cosmos.* Random House.
- Dyson, F. (1979). *Disturbing the universe.* Harper & Row.
- Tipler, F. J. (1995). *The physics of immortality.* Doubleday.
- Bohm, D. (1980). *Wholeness and the implicate order.* Routledge.
- Verlinde, E. (2011). On the origin of gravity. *Journal of High Energy Physics, 2011*(4), 29.
- Smolin, L. (2019). *Einstein's unfinished revolution.* Penguin Press.
- Rovelli, C. (2017). *Reality is not what it seems.* Riverhead Books.
- Hameroff, S., & Penrose, R. (2014). Consciousness in the universe. *Physics of Life Reviews, 11*(1), 39–78.
- Hubble, E. (2013). *The realm of the nebulae.* Yale. (Original work published 1936).

- Gamow, G. (1999). *The creation of the universe*. Dover. (Original work published 1948).
- Hawking, S. (1988). *A brief history of time*. Bantam.
- Hawking, S., & Mlodinow, L. (2010). *The grand design*. Bantam.
- Penrose, R. (2010). *Cycles of time*. Knopf.
- Greene, B. (2004). *The fabric of the cosmos*. Knopf.
- Tsiolkovsky, K. E. (2011). Exploration of outer space by means of rocket devices. NASA. (Original work published 1903).
- Goddard, R. H. (2004). A method of reaching extreme altitudes. NASA. (Original work published 1919).
- von Braun, W. (1952). *The Mars Project*. University of Illinois Press.
- Hawking, S. (1996). *The universe in a nutshell*. Bantam.
- Chaikin, A. (1994). *A man on the moon: The voyages of the Apollo astronauts*. Penguin.
- Logsdon, J. M. (2015). *After Apollo?: Richard Nixon and the American space program*. Palgrave Macmillan.
- O'Neill, G. K. (1976). *The high frontier: Human colonies in space*. William Morrow.
- Zubrin, R. (1996). *The case for Mars: The plan to settle the red planet and why we must*. Free Press.
- Crawford, I. A. (2016). The long-term scientific benefits of space exploration. *Futures, 82*, 77–86.
- White, F. (1987). *The overview effect: Space exploration and human evolution*. Houghton Mifflin.
- Schwartz, J. S. J. (2011). Our moral obligation to support space exploration. *Environmental Ethics, 33*(1), 67–88.
- Cockell, C. S. (2015). *Planetary protection, ethics, and the law*. Springer.
- Dyson, F. (2004). *Infinite in all directions*. Harper Perennial.
- Musk, E. (2017). Making humans a multiplanetary species. *New Space, 5*(2), 46–61.
- Kaku, M. (2018). *The future of humanity*. Doubleday.
- Tegmark, M. (2017). *Life 3.0: Being human in the age of artificial intelligence*. Knopf.
- Copernicus, N. (1992). *On the revolutions of the heavenly spheres*. Prometheus. (Original work published 1543).
- Galileo, G. (1989). *Sidereus nuncius*. University of Chicago Press. (Original work published 1610).
- Kepler, J. (1997). *Astronomia nova*. Cambridge University Press. (Original work published 1609).
- Hawking, S. (1988). *A brief history of time*. Bantam.
- Tyson, N. D. (2004). *Origins*. W. W. Norton.
- Carroll, S. (2016). *The big picture*. Dutton.

- Barrow, J. D., & Tipler, F. J. (1986). *The anthropic cosmological principle*. Oxford University Press.
- Kaku, M. (1994). *Hyperspace*. Oxford University Press.

5.1.3 Mathematics & Philosophy of Number

- Euclid. (1956). *The elements* (T. L. Heath, Trans.). Dover. (Original work published 300 BCE).
- Descartes, R. (1954). *The geometry*. Dover. (Original work published 1637).
- Newton, I. (1999). *The principia*. University of California Press. (Original work published 1687).
- Gödel, K. (1992). *On formally undecidable propositions*. Dover. (Original work published 1931).
- Hardy, G. H. (1992). *A mathematician's apology*. Cambridge University Press. (Original work published 1940).
- Lakatos, I. (1976). *Proofs and refutations*. Cambridge University Press.
- Penrose, R. (1989). *The emperor's new mind*. Oxford University Press.
- Cantor, G. (1955). *Contributions to the theory of transfinite numbers*. Dover. (Original work published 1883).
- Cohen, P. J. (1966). *Set theory and the continuum hypothesis*. Benjamin.
- Gödel, K. (1986). *On formally undecidable propositions*. Princeton. (Original work published 1931).
- Nagel, E., & Newman, J. (2001). *Gödel's proof*. NYU Press. (Original work published 1958).
- Lobachevsky, N. (2006). *Pangeometry*. Springer. (Original work published 1840).
- Riemann, B. (2004). *On the hypotheses which lie at the foundations of geometry*. Dover. (Original work published 1854).
- Mandelbrot, B. (1982). *The fractal geometry of nature*. W. H. Freeman.
- Gleick, J. (1987). *Chaos: Making a new science*. Viking.
- Ribenboim, P. (1991). *The book of prime number records*. Springer.
- Derbyshire, J. (2003). *Prime obsession*. Plume.
- Hardy, G. H., & Wright, E. M. (2008). *An introduction to the theory of numbers*. Oxford. (Original work published 1938).
- Turing, A. M. (2004). *On computable numbers*. In *The essential Turing*. Oxford. (Original work published 1936).

- Chaitin, G. J. (1987). *Algorithmic information theory*. Cambridge
- Wolfram, S. (2002). *A new kind of science*. Wolfram Media.

5.2 Technology & Consciousness Interfaces

- Clark, A. (2003). *Natural-born cyborgs: Minds, technologies, and the future of human intelligence*. Oxford University Press.
- Farahany, N. A. (2023). *The battle for your brain: Defending the right to think freely in the age of neurotechnology*. St. Martin's Press.
- Kurzweil, R. (2005). *The singularity is near*. Viking.
- Yuste, R., & Goering, S. (2017). Neurotechnology and human rights. *Nature, 551*(7679), 159–163.

5.3 The Turing Test, Biomechanics, and the Protohuman Future

5.3.1 Foundations of AI & Computation

- Turing, A. M. (1950). Computing machinery and intelligence. *Mind, 59*(236), 433–460.
- Turing, A. M. (2004). On computable numbers, with an application to the Entscheidungsproblem. In B. Jack Copeland (Ed.), *The essential Turing*. Oxford University Press. (Original work published 1936).
- Wiener, N. (1961). *Cybernetics: Or control and communication in the animal and the machine*. MIT Press. (Original work published 1948).
- McCarthy, J., Minsky, M., Rochester, N., & Shannon, C. E. (1955). A proposal for the Dartmouth Summer Research Project on Artificial Intelligence.

5.3.2 Models of Mind, Intelligence, and Consciousness

- Searle, J. R. (1980). Minds, brains, and programs. *Behavioral and Brain Sciences, 3*(3), 417–457.
- Dennett, D. C. (1991). *Consciousness explained*. Little, Brown.
- Kurzweil, R. (2005). *The singularity is near: When humans transcend biology*. Viking.
- Bostrom, N. (2014). *Superintelligence: Paths, dangers, strategies*. Oxford University Press.
- Chalmers, D. J. (2010). The singularity: A philosophical analysis. *Journal of Consciousness Studies, 17*(9–10), 7–65.

5.3.3 AI as External Appendage & Human Extension

- Clark, A. (2003). *Natural-born cyborgs: Minds, technologies, and the future of human intelligence.* Oxford University Press.
- Haraway, D. (1991). A cyborg manifesto. In *Simians, cyborgs, and women: The reinvention of nature.* Routledge. (Original work published 1985).
- Kelly, K. (1994). *Out of control: The new biology of machines, social systems, and the economic world.* Basic Books.
- Floridi, L. (2014). *The fourth revolution: How the infosphere is reshaping human reality.* Oxford University Press.

5.3.4 Biomechanics, Robotics, Synthetic Life & Bioengineering

- Brooks, R. A. (2002). *Flesh and machines: How robots will change us.* Vintage.
- Moravec, H. (1988). *Mind children: The future of robot and human intelligence.* Harvard University Press.
- Warwick, K. (2002). *I, cyborg.* University of Illinois Press.
- Venter, J. C. (2013). *Life at the speed of light: From the double helix to the dawn of digital life.* Viking.
- Church, G., & Regis, E. (2012). *Regenesis: How synthetic biology will reinvent nature and ourselves.* Basic Books.

5.3.5 Protohuman & Evolutionary Perspectives

- Leakey, R. (1994). *The origin of humankind.* Basic Books.
- Mithen, S. (1996). *The prehistory of the mind: The cognitive origins of art, religion and science.* Thames & Hudson.
- Donald, M. (1991). *Origins of the modern mind: Three stages in the evolution of culture and cognition.* Harvard University Press.
- Clark, A., & Chalmers, D. J. (1998). The extended mind. *Analysis, 58*(1), 7–19.

5.3.6 Speculative Futures & Posthuman Thought

- Kurzweil, R. (1999). *The age of spiritual machines.* Viking.

- Hayles, N. K. (1999). *How we became posthuman: Virtual bodies in cybernetics, literature, and informatics.* University of Chicago Press.
- Hanson, R. (2016). *The age of em: Work, love, and life when robots rule the Earth.* Oxford University Press.
- Tegmark, M. (2017). *Life 3.0: Being human in the age of artificial intelligence.* Knopf.

5.4 Mathematical Anomalies and Strange Foundations

5.4.1 Infinity & Set Theory

- Cantor, G. (1955). *Contributions to the theory of transfinite numbers.* Dover. (Original work published 1883).
- Cohen, P. J. (1966). *Set theory and the continuum hypothesis.* Benjamin.

5.4.2 Gödel, Incompleteness & Logic

- Gödel, K. (1986). *On formally undecidable propositions.* Princeton. (Original work published 1931).
- Nagel, E., & Newman, J. (2001). *Gödel's proof.* NYU Press. (Original work published 1958).

5.4.3 Geometry & Non-Euclidean Realities

- Lobachevsky, N. (2006). *Pangeometry.* Springer. (Original work published 1840).
- Riemann, B. (2004). *On the hypotheses which lie at the foundations of geometry.* Dover. (Original work published 1854).

5.4.4 Fractals, Chaos & Irregular Orders

- Mandelbrot, B. (1982). *The fractal geometry of nature.* W. H. Freeman.
- Gleick, J. (1987). *Chaos: Making a new science.* Viking.

5.4.5 Prime Numbers, Irrationals & Unsolved Problems

- Ribenboim, P. (1991). *The book of prime number records.* Springer.
- Derbyshire, J. (2003). *Prime obsession.* Plume.
- Hardy, G. H., & Wright, E. M. (2008). *An introduction to the theory of numbers.* Oxford. (Original work published 1938).

5.4.6 Computability & Paradoxical Machines

- Turing, A. M. (2004). *On computable numbers*. In *The essential Turing*. Oxford. (Original work published 1936).
- Chaitin, G. J. (1987). *Algorithmic information theory*. Cambridge.
- Wolfram, S. (2002). *A new kind of science*. Wolfram Media.

5.5 Anomalies in Physics and Measurable Defiance of Theory

5.5.1 Quantum & Measurement Paradoxes

- Einstein, A., Podolsky, B., & Rosen, N. (1935). Can quantum-mechanical description of physical reality be considered complete? *Physical Review, 47*(10), 777–780.
- Bell, J. S. (1964). On the Einstein-Podolsky-Rosen paradox. *Physics, 1*(3), 195–200.
- Aspect, A., Dalibard, J., & Roger, G. (1982). Experimental test of Bell's inequalities. *Physical Review Letters, 49*(25), 1804–1807.
- Wheeler, J. A. (1978). The "delayed-choice" experiment. In *Foundations of Quantum Theory*. Academic Press.

5.5.2 Cosmological Anomalies

- Rubin, V. C., & Ford, W. K. (1970). Rotation of the Andromeda Nebula. *Astrophysical Journal, 159*, 379–403.
- Perlmutter, S., et al. (1999). Measurements of Ω and Λ from supernovae. *Astrophysical Journal, 517*(2).
- Verlinde, E. (2011). On the origin of gravity and the laws of Newton. *Journal of High Energy Physics, 2011*(4), 29.

5.5.3 Time, Relativity & Energy Puzzles

- Hafele, J. C., & Keating, R. E. (1972). Around-the-world atomic clocks. *Science, 177*(4044), 166–168.
- Podkletnov, E. (1992). Weak gravitational shielding properties. *Physica C, 203*(3–4).
- Tajmar, M., et al. (2006). Experimental detection of the gravitomagnetic London moment. *AIP Conference Proceedings, 880*(1).

5.5.4 Cold Fusion & Energy Anomalies

- Fleischmann, M., & Pons, S. (1989). Electrochemically induced nuclear fusion of deuterium. *Journal of Electroanalytical Chemistry, 261*(2).
- Storms, E. (2007). *The science of low energy nuclear reaction*. World Scientific.

5.5.5 Serious Anomalies in Consciousness & Physics

- Jahn, R. G., & Dunne, B. J. (1987). *Margins of reality*. Harcourt.
- Radin, D., & Nelson, R. (1989). Evidence for consciousness-related anomalies. *Foundations of Physics, 19*(12).
- Sheldrake, R. (2012). *Science set free*. Deepak Chopra Books.

5.6 Astronomy and Astrophysics

5.6.1 Foundations of Scientific Astronomy

- Copernicus, N. (1992). *On the revolutions of the heavenly spheres*. Prometheus. (Original work published 1543).
- Galileo, G. (1989). *Sidereus nuncius*. University of Chicago Press. (Original work published 1610).
- Kepler, J. (1997). *Astronomia nova*. Cambridge University Press. (Original work published 1609).

5.6.2 Modern Astrophysics

- Hawking, S. (1988). *A brief history of time*. Bantam.
- Tyson, N. D. (2004). *Origins*. W. W. Norton.
- Carroll, S. (2016). *The big picture*. Dutton.
- Barrow, J. D., & Tipler, F. J. (1986). *The anthropic cosmological principle*. Oxford University Press.

5.6.3 Bridging to Metaphysics

- Barrow, J. D., & Tipler, F. J. (1986). *The anthropic cosmological principle*. Oxford University Press.
- Kaku, M. (1994). *Hyperspace*. Oxford University Press.

5.7 Gravity, Cosmology, and the Structure of the Universe

5.7.1 Gravity & Relativity

- Newton, I. (1999). *The Principia*. University of California Press. (Original work published 1687).
- Einstein, A. (2005). *Relativity*. Routledge. (Original work published 1916).
- Misner, C. W., Thorne, K. S., & Wheeler, J. A. (1973). *Gravitation*. W. H. Freeman.
- Thorne, K. S. (1994). *Black holes and time warps*. W. W. Norton.

5.7.2 Earth Rotation & Planetary Dynamics

- Lambeck, K. (1980). *The Earth's variable rotation*. Cambridge University Press.
- Gross, R. S. (2007). Earth rotation variations. *Treatise on Geophysics, 3*.
- Goldreich, P. (1966). History of the lunar orbit. *Reviews of Geophysics, 4*(4).
- Melchior, P. (1983). *The tides of the planet Earth*. Pergamon.

5.7.3 Cosmology & the Universe

- Hubble, E. (2013). *The realm of the nebulae*. Yale. (Original work published 1936).
- Gamow, G. (1999). *The creation of the universe*. Dover. (Original work published 1948).
- Hawking, S. (1988). *A brief history of time*. Bantam.
- Hawking, S., & Mlodinow, L. (2010). *The grand design*. Bantam.
- Penrose, R. (2010). *Cycles of time*. Knopf.
- Greene, B. (2004). *The fabric of the cosmos*. Knopf.

5.7.4 Planetary Composition & Astrophysics

- Lodders, K., & Fegley, B. (1998). *The planetary scientist's companion*. Oxford University Press.
- Basaltic Volcanism Study Project. (1981). *Basaltic volcanism on the terrestrial planets*. Pergamon.
- de Pater, I., & Lissauer, J. J. (2015). *Planetary sciences*. Cambridge University Press.
- Lang, K. R. (2011). *The Cambridge guide to the solar system*. Cambridge University Press.

5.7.5 Sound & Vibrations in Space

- NASA (2013). Symphonies of the planets [CD series]. NASA Voyager plasma wave data sonifications.
- Gurnett, D. A., & Kurth, W. S. (2005). Plasma waves and radiation. In *Introduction to Space Physics*. Cambridge University Press.
- Alexander, C. J., & Ruzmaikin, A. (2017). Music of the spheres. *Physics Today, 70*(7).

5.7.6 Cosmic Philosophy & Human Meaning

- Sagan, C. (1980). *Cosmos*. Random House.
- Tyson, N. D. (2004). *Origins*. W. W. Norton.
- Rees, M. (1999). *Just six numbers*. Basic Books.
- Smolin, L. (2006). *The trouble with physics*. Houghton Mifflin.

5.8 Light, Distance, and the Relativity of Time

5.8.1 The Speed of Light

- Maxwell, J. C. (1954). A dynamical theory of the electromagnetic field. *Philosophical Transactions of the Royal Society, 155*, 459–512. (Original work published 1865).
- Einstein, A. (1952). On the electrodynamics of moving bodies. In *The principle of relativity*. Dover. (Original work published 1905).
- Greene, B. (2004). *The fabric of the cosmos*. Knopf.
- Magueijo, J. (2003). *Faster than the speed of light: The story of a scientific speculation*. Perseus Publishing.

5.8.2 Galactic Distance & Cosmic Scale

- Hubble, E. (1929). A relation between distance and radial velocity among extra-galactic nebulae. *PNAS, 15*(3), 168–173.
- Sandage, A. (1995). The redshift-distance relation. In *The Deep Universe*. Springer.
- Freedman, W. L., & Madore, B. F. (2010). The Hubble constant. *Annual Review of Astronomy and Astrophysics, 48*, 673–710.
- Weinberg, S. (1993). *The first three minutes: A modern view of the origin of the universe*. Basic Books. (Original work published 1977).

5.8.3 Time Dilation & Relativity in Practice

- Hafele, J. C., & Keating, R. E. (1972). Around-the-world atomic clocks: Predicted relativistic time gains. *Science, 177*(4044), 166–168.
- Langevin, P. (1911). The evolution of space and time. *Scientia, 10*, 31–54.
- Misner, C. W., Thorne, K. S., & Wheeler, J. A. (1973). *Gravitation*. W. H. Freeman.

5.8.4 Experiments & Measurements

- Rossi, B., & Hall, D. B. (1941). Variation of the rate of decay of mesotrons with momentum. *Physical Review, 59*(3), 223–228.
- Bailey, J., et al. (1977). Measurements of relativistic time dilatation for positive and negative muons in a circular orbit. *Nature, 268*(5618), 301–305.
- Ashby, N. (2003). Relativity and the global positioning system. *Physics Today, 55*(5), 41–47.

5.8.5 Philosophical & Conceptual Reflections

- Minkowski, H. (1952). Space and time. In *The principle of relativity*. Dover. (Original work published 1908).
- Rietdijk, C. W. (1966). A rigorous proof of determinism derived from special relativity. *Philosophy of Science, 33*(4), 341–344.
- Gödel, K. (1949). An example of a new type of cosmological solution of Einstein's field equations. *Reviews of Modern Physics, 21*(3), 447–450.
- Thorne, K. S. (2014). *The science of Interstellar*. W. W. Norton.
- Barrow, J. D. (2001). *The book of time*. Pantheon.

5.9 Black Holes, Wormholes, and the Quantum-Cosmic Frontier

5.9.1 Black Holes & Singularities

- Schwarzschild, K. (1916). On the gravitational field of a point mass. *Sitzungsberichte der Königlich Preussischen Akademie der Wissenschaften*.
- Oppenheimer, J. R., & Snyder, H. (1939). On continued gravitational contraction. *Physical Review, 56*(5), 455–459.
- Hawking, S. W. (1974). Black hole explosions? *Nature, 248*(5443), 30–31.

- Thorne, K. S. (1994). *Black holes and time warps*. W. W. Norton
- Falcke, H., & Rezzolla, L. (2021). *Light in the darkness: Black holes, the universe, and us*. MIT Press.
- Tyson, N. D. (2002). *The sky is not the limit: Adventures of an urban astrophysicist*. Prometheus Books. (Original work published 2000).

5.9.2 Wormholes & Exotic Spacetime

- Einstein, A., & Rosen, N. (1935). The particle problem in the general theory of relativity. *Physical Review, 48*(1), 73–77.
- Morris, M. S., Thorne, K. S., & Yurtsever, U. (1988). Wormholes, time machines, and the weak energy condition. *Physical Review Letters, 61*(13), 1446–1449.
- Visser, M. (1995). *Lorentzian wormholes: From Einstein to Hawking*. AIP Press.
- Lobo, F. S. N. (2017). *Wormholes, warp drives and energy conditions*. Springer.

5.9.3 Dark Matter & Dark Energy

- Rubin, V. C., & Ford, W. K. (1970). Rotation of the Andromeda Nebula. *Astrophysical Journal, 159*, 379–403.
- Clowe, D., et al. (2006). A direct empirical proof of dark matter. *Astrophysical Journal Letters, 648*(2), L109–L113.
- Frieman, J. A., Turner, M. S., & Huterer, D. (2008). Dark energy and the accelerating universe. *Annual Review of Astronomy and Astrophysics, 46*, 385–432.
- Verlinde, E. (2011). On the origin of gravity and the laws of Newton. *Journal of High Energy Physics, 2011*(4), 29.
- Smolin, L. (2013). *Time reborn: From the crisis in physics to the future of the universe*. Houghton Mifflin Harcourt.

5.9.4 Quantum Entanglement & Nonlocality

- Einstein, A., Podolsky, B., & Rosen, N. (1935). Can quantum-mechanical description of reality be considered complete? *Physical Review, 47*(10), 777–780.
- Bell, J. S. (1964). On the Einstein Podolsky Rosen paradox. *Physics Physique Физика, 1*(3), 195–200.
- Aspect, A., Dalibard, J., & Roger, G. (1982). Experimental test of Bell's inequalities using time-

varying analyzers. *Physical Review Letters, 49*(25), 1804–1807.
- Bohm, D. (1952). A suggested interpretation of quantum theory in terms of "hidden variables." *Physical Review, 85*(2), 166–179.
- Maldacena, J., & Susskind, L. (2013). Cool horizons for entangled black holes. *Fortschritte der Physik, 61*(9), 781–811. (ER=EPR conjecture).

5.9.5 Philosophy & Cosmic Meaning

- Wheeler, J. A., & Zurek, W. H. (Eds.). (1983). *Quantum theory and measurement*. Princeton University Press.
- Barrow, J. D. (2002). *The constants of nature*. Vintage.
- Tegmark, M. (2014). *Our mathematical universe*. Knopf.
- Tyson, N. D., & Trefil, J. (2021). *Cosmic queries: StarTalk's guide to who we are, how we got here, and where we're going*. National Geographic.
- Kauffman, S. (2016). *Humanity in a creative universe*. Oxford University Press.

5.10 The Future of Space Exploration and Colonization

5.10.1 Historical Visionaries and Early Frameworks

- Tsiolkovsky, K. E. (2011). Exploration of outer space by means of rocket devices. NASA. (Original work published 1903).
- Goddard, R. H. (2004). A method of reaching extreme altitudes. NASA. (Original work published 1919).
- von Braun, W. (1952). *The Mars Project*. University of Illinois Press.

5.10.2 Modern Space Science and Exploration

- Hawking, S. (1996). *The universe in a nutshell*. Bantam.
- Chaikin, A. (1994). *A man on the moon: The voyages of the Apollo astronauts*. Penguin.
- Logsdon, J. M. (2015). *After Apollo?: Richard Nixon and the American space program*. Palgrave Macmillan.

5.10.3 Colonization and the Prospect of Settlement

- O'Neill, G. K. (1976). *The high frontier: Human colonies in space*. William Morrow.
- Zubrin, R. (1996). *The case for Mars: The plan to settle the red planet and why we must*. Free Press.

- Crawford, I. A. (2016). The long-term scientific benefits of space exploration. *Futures, 82*, 77–86.

5.10.4 Philosophical and Ethical Considerations

- White, F. (1987). *The overview effect: Space exploration and human evolution*. Houghton Mifflin.
- Schwartz, J. S. J. (2011). Our moral obligation to support space exploration. *Environmental Ethics, 33*(1), 67–88.
- Cockell, C. S. (2015). *Planetary protection, ethics, and the law*. Springer.

5.10.5 Speculative and Posthuman Futures

- Dyson, F. (2004). *Infinite in all directions*. Harper Perennial.
- Musk, E. (2017). Making humans a multiplanetary species. *New Space, 5*(2), 46–61.
- Kaku, M. (2018). *The future of humanity*. Doubleday.
- Tegmark, M. (2017). *Life 3.0: Being human in the age of artificial intelligence*. Knopf.

Biology, Medicine, and Health

6.1 Cellular Biology & Frontiers in Medicine

6.1.1 Cellular Biology

- Alberts, B., Johnson, A., Lewis, J., et al. (2015). *Molecular biology of the cell* (6th ed.). Garland Science.
- Lodish, H., Berk, A., Kaiser, C. A., et al. (2021). *Molecular cell biology* (9th ed.). W. H. Freeman.
- Watson, J. D., Baker, T. A., Bell, S. P., et al. (2014). *Molecular biology of the gene* (7th ed.). Pearson.
- Alberts, B., et al. (2014). *Essential cell biology* (4th ed.). Garland Science.

6.1.2 Frontiers in Medicine

- Mukherjee, S. (2010). *The emperor of all maladies*. Scribner.
- Mukherjee, S. (2016). *The gene*. Scribner.
- Topol, E. J. (2012). *The creative destruction of medicine*. Basic Books.
- Topol, E. J. (2019). *Deep medicine*. Basic Books.
- Hood, L., & Lovejoy, J. C. (2014). *A systems approach to disease and health*. Springer.

- Fauci, A. S., Kasper, D. L., Hauser, S. L., et al. (2018). *Harrison's principles of internal medicine* (20th ed.). McGraw-Hill.
- Weinberg, R. A. (2013). *The biology of cancer* (2nd ed.). Garland Science.
- De Grey, A. D. N. J., & Rae, M. (2007). *Ending aging*. St. Martin's Press.
- Venter, J. C., Glass, J. I., Hutchison, C. A., & Smith, H. O. (2010). Synthetic genome in a bacterial cell. *Science, 329*(5987), 52–56.
- De Grey, A. D. N. J., & Rae, M. (2007). *Ending aging*. St. Martin's Press.

6.2 Experimental Research Models Under Scrutiny

6.2.1 Neuroscience & Consciousness

- Tononi, G. (2008). Consciousness as integrated information. *Biological Bulletin, 215*(3), 216–242.
- Koch, C. (2019). *The feeling of life itself*. MIT Press.
- Hameroff, S., & Penrose, R. (2014). Consciousness in the universe. *Physics of Life Reviews, 11*(1), 39–78.

6.2.2 Physics & Cosmology

- Bohm, D. (1980). *Wholeness and the implicate order*. Routledge.
- Verlinde, E. (2011). On the origin of gravity. *Journal of High Energy Physics, 2011*(4), 29.
- Smolin, L. (2019). *Einstein's unfinished revolution*. Penguin Press.
- Rovelli, C. (2017). *Reality is not what it seems*. Riverhead Books.

6.2.3 Medicine & Biology

- Montagnier, L., Aïssa, J., Ferris, S., Montagnier, J.-L., & Lavallée, C. (2009). Electromagnetic signals from bacterial DNA. *Interdisciplinary Sciences, 1*(2), 81–90.
- Venter, J. C., Glass, J. I., Hutchison, C. A., & Smith, H. O. (2010). Synthetic genome in a bacterial cell. *Science, 329*(5987), 52–56.
- De Grey, A. D. N. J., & Rae, M. (2007). *Ending aging*. St. Martin's Press.

6.2.4 Psychology & Frontier Models

- Sheldrake, R. (2009). *Morphic resonance* (4th ed.). Park Street Press. (Original work published 1981).
- Persinger, M. A. (1983). Mystical experiences as temporal lobe artifacts. *Perceptual and Motor Skills, 57*(3), 1255–1262.

6.3 Evolution, Consciousness, and Radical Origins

6.3.1 Darwin & Classic Evolutionary Theory

- Darwin, C. (2003). *On the origin of species*. Penguin Classics. (Original work published 1859).
- Darwin, C. (2004). *The descent of man*. Penguin Classics. (Original work published 1871).
- Wallace, A. R. (2011). *The geographical distribution of animals*. Cambridge University Press. (Original work published 1876).
- Dawkins, R. (2006). *The selfish gene*. Oxford University Press. (Original work published 1976).

6.3.2 Critiques & Alternative Evolutionary Views

- Gould, S. J. (1989). *Wonderful life*. W. W. Norton.
- Eldredge, N., & Gould, S. J. (1972). Punctuated equilibria. Freeman.
- Behe, M. (1996). *Darwin's black box*. Free Press.
- Denton, M. (1985). *Evolution: A theory in crisis*. Adler & Adler.

6.3.3 Psychedelic Ape & Radical Consciousness Hypotheses

- McKenna, T. (1992). *Food of the gods*. Bantam.
- Strassman, R. (2001). *DMT: The spirit molecule*. Park Street Press.
- Carhart-Harris, R. L., & Friston, K. J. (2019). REBUS and the anarchic brain. *Pharmacological Reviews, 71*(3), 316–344.
- Nichols, D. E. (2016). Psychedelics. *Pharmacological Reviews, 68*(2), 264–355.

6.3.4 Philosophical Alternatives on Consciousness

- Chalmers, D. J. (1996). *The conscious mind*. Oxford University Press.
- Nagel, T. (2012). *Mind and cosmos*. Oxford University Press.

- Penrose, R. (1989). *The emperor's new mind*. Oxford University Press.
- Hameroff, S., & Penrose, R. (2014). Consciousness in the universe. *Physics of Life Reviews, 11*(1), 39–78.
- Kastrup, B. (2019). *The idea of the world*. Iff Books.

6.3.5 Dual Earth, Multiverse & Radical Cosmologies

- Talbot, M. (1991). *The holographic universe*. Harper Perennial.
- Greene, B. (1999). *The elegant universe*. W. W. Norton.
- Greene, B. (2011). *The hidden reality*. Knopf.
- Tegmark, M. (2014). *Our mathematical universe*. Knopf.
- Smolin, L. (1997). *The life of the cosmos*. Oxford University Press.

6.4 Life in the Deep Sea and Extreme Environments

6.4.1 Deep Sea Exploration & Discovery

- Ballard, R. D. (2000). *Exploring the deep*. National Geographic.
- Broad, W. J. (1997). *The universe below*. Simon & Schuster.
- Nouvian, C. (2007). *The deep*. University of Chicago Press.
- Thuesen, E. V. (2009). Bioluminescence in the ocean. *Oceanography, 22*(4), 124–139.

6.4.2 Unique Forms of Life

- Van Dover, C. L. (2000). *The ecology of deep-sea hydrothermal vents*. Princeton University Press.
- Tyler, P. A. (2003). *Ecosystems of the deep oceans*. Elsevier.
- Gage, J. D., & Tyler, P. A. (1991). *Deep-sea biology*. Cambridge University Press.
- Ramirez-Llodra, E., et al. (2010). Deep, diverse and definitely different. *Biogeosciences, 7*(9).

6.4.3 Extreme Adaptations & Survival

- Childress, J. J., & Seibel, B. A. (1998). Adaptations of animals to low oxygen. *Journal of Experimental Biology, 201*(8).
- Somero, G. N. (1992). Adaptations to high hydrostatic pressure. *Annual Review of Physiology, 54*.

- Jannasch, H. W., & Taylor, C. D. (1984). Deep-sea microbiology. *Annual Review of Microbiology, 38*.
- Madigan, M. T., et al. (2017). *Brock biology of microorganisms*. Pearson.

6.4.4 Bioluminescence, Communication & Behavior

- Haddock, S. H. D., et al. (2010). Bioluminescence in the sea. *Annual Review of Marine Science, 2*.
- Widder, E. A. (1999). Bioluminescence. *Scientific American, 281*(5).
- Morin, J. G. (1983). Coastal bioluminescence. *Bulletin of Marine Science, 33*(4).

6.4.5 Deep Sea & Human Imagination

- Verne, J. (1993). *Twenty thousand leagues under the seas*. Oxford. (Original work published 1870).
- Carson, R. (2021). *The sea around us*. Oxford. (Original work published 1951).
- Cousteau, J.-Y., & Dugan, J. (2004). *The silent world*. National Geographic. (Original work published 1953).
- Sweeney, A. M., et al. (2007). Squid lenses and natural design. *Science, 317*(5846).

6.5 Disease, Epidemics, Warfare, and Power

6.5.1 Disease & Epidemics

- McNeill, W. H. (1998). *Plagues and peoples*. Anchor Books. (Original work published 1976).
- Diamond, J. (1997). *Guns, germs, and steel*. W. W. Norton.
- Snowden, F. M. (2019). *Epidemics and society: From the Black Death to the present*. Yale University Press.
- Garrett, L. (1994). *The coming plague: Newly emerging diseases in a world out of balance*. Basic Books.
- Quammen, D. (2012). *Spillover: Animal infections and the next human pandemic*. W. W. Norton.

6.5.2 Modern & Biological Warfare

- Ellis, J. (1990). *The social history of the machine gun*. Johns Hopkins University Press.
- Harris, R., & Paxman, J. (2002). *A higher form of killing: The secret story of gas and germ warfare*. Random House. (Original work published 1982).

- Leitenberg, M., & Zilinskas, R. A. (2012). *The Soviet biological weapons program*. Harvard University Press.
- Wheelis, M. (1999). Biological warfare at the 1346 siege of Caffa. *Emerging Infectious Diseases, 8*(9).

6.5.3 Nuclear Technology & War

- Rhodes, R. (1986). *The making of the atomic bomb*. Simon & Schuster.
- Rhodes, R. (1995). *Dark sun: The making of the hydrogen bomb*. Simon & Schuster.
- Hersey, J. (2020). *Hiroshima*. Vintage International. (Original work published 1946).
- Sagan, S., & Waltz, K. (2002). *The spread of nuclear weapons: A debate renewed*. W. W. Norton.
- Schlosser, E. (2013). *Command and control: Nuclear weapons, the Damascus accident, and the illusion of safety*. Penguin Press.

6.5.4 Corporate Power & Government Structures

- Chomsky, N. (1999). *Profit over people: Neoliberalism and global order*. Seven Stories Press.
- Klein, N. (2007). *The shock doctrine: The rise of disaster capitalism*. Metropolitan Books.
- Stiglitz, J. E. (2002). *Globalization and its discontents*. W. W. Norton.
- Galbraith, J. K. (2007). *The new industrial state*. Princeton University Press. (Original work published 1967).
- Mills, C. W. (2000). *The power elite*. Oxford University Press. (Original work published 1956).
- Monbiot, G. (2000). *Captive state: The corporate takeover of Britain*. Macmillan.

6.5.5 Government, Secrecy & Surveillance

- Arendt, H. (1973). *The origins of totalitarianism*. Harcourt. (Original work published 1951).
- Orwell, G. (1949). *Nineteen eighty-four*. Secker & Warburg.
- Zuboff, S. (2019). *The age of surveillance capitalism*. PublicAffairs.
- Foucault, M. (1995). *Discipline and punish: The birth of the prison*. Vintage. (Original work published 1975).
- Ellsberg, D. (2002). *Secrets: A memoir of Vietnam and the Pentagon Papers*. Viking.

6.6 Catastrophes, Natural Disasters, and Global Crises

6.6.1 Natural Disasters in History

- Winchester, S. (2003). *Krakatoa: The day the world exploded*. HarperCollins.
- Dvorak, J. (2014). *Earthquake storm: The fascinating history and volatile future of the San Andreas Fault*. Pegasus Books.
- McGuire, B. (2005). *Global catastrophes: A very short introduction*. Oxford University Press.
- Bryant, E. (2005). *Tsunami: The underrated hazard*. Springer.
- O'Keefe, P., Westgate, K., & Wisner, B. (1976). Taking the naturalness out of natural disasters. *Nature, 260*(5552), 566–567.

6.6.2 Pandemics & Global Shocks

- Spinney, L. (2017). *Pale rider: The Spanish flu of 1918 and how it changed the world*. PublicAffairs.
- Honigsbaum, M. (2019). *The pandemic century: One hundred years of panic, hysteria, and hubris*. W. W. Norton.
- Osterholm, M. T., & Olshaker, M. (2017). *Deadliest enemy: Our war against killer germs*. Little, Brown.

6.6.3 Climate Change & Anthropocene Threats

- Kolbert, E. (2014). *The sixth extinction: An unnatural history*. Henry Holt.
- Wallace-Wells, D. (2019). *The uninhabitable Earth: Life after warming*. Tim Duggan Books.
- Lovelock, J. (2006). *The revenge of Gaia*. Basic Books.
- Steffen, W., Crutzen, P. J., & McNeill, J. R. (2007). The Anthropocene: Are humans now overwhelming the great forces of nature? *AMBIO, 36*(8), 614–621.

6.6.4 Asteroids, Cosmic Risks & Existential Threats

- Morrison, D. (1997). The impact hazard. In *Hazards due to comets and asteroids*. University of Arizona Press.
- Bostrom, N. (2002). Existential risks: Analyzing human extinction scenarios. *Journal of Evolution and Technology, 9*.
- Rees, M. (2003). *Our final century: Will the human race survive the twenty-first century?* Basic Books.

- Turchin, A., & Denkenberger, D. (2018). *Feeding everyone no matter what: Managing food security after global catastrophe*. Academic Press.

6.6.5 Resilience & Crisis Response

- Taleb, N. N. (2012). *Antifragile: Things that gain from disorder*. Random House.
- Diamond, J. (2005). *Collapse: How societies choose to fail or succeed*. Viking.
- Kelman, I. (2020). *Disaster by choice: How our actions turn natural hazards into catastrophes*. Oxford University Press.
- Tierney, K. (2014). *The social roots of risk: Producing disasters, promoting resilience*. Stanford University Press.

Cultural, Historical, and Artistic Expressions

7.1 Journalism, Film, and Forensics

7.1.1 Investigative Journalism & Narrative Nonfiction

- Kean, L. (2010). *UFOs: Generals, pilots, and government officials go on the record*. Crown. → High-credibility journalism giving voice to military and government officials on UFO encounters.
- Kean, L., Blumenthal, R., & Leslie, R. (2021). *UFOs: Generals, pilots, and government officials go on the record* (updated edition with New York Times coverage). Crown.
- Blum, H. (1990). *Out there: The government's secret quest for extraterrestrials*. Simon & Schuster.
- Hastings, R. (2010). *UFOs and nukes: Extraordinary encounters at nuclear weapons sites*. AuthorHouse.
- Colvin, M. (2018). *On the front line: The collected journalism of Marie Colvin*. HarperCollins. → Not metaphysical, but exemplifies investigative integrity, relevant to framing serious consciousness journalism.

7.1.2 Documentary & Film

- Stone, O. (Director). (1991). *JFK* [Film]. Warner Bros. → A cultural landmark in investigative conspiracy narrative, blending film, politics, and forensic reconstruction.
- Nolan, C. (Director). (2014). *Interstellar* [Film]. Paramount Pictures. → Popular but deeply researched

exploration of black holes, relativity, and consciousness as a cosmic force
- Strieber, W., & Strieber, A. (1996). *Communion* [Film]. New Line Cinema.
- Greer, S. M. (Director). (2017). *Unacknowledged* [Documentary]. A & A Productions.
- West, L. A. (Director). (2018). *Surviving death* [Netflix Docuseries]. → Explores reincarnation, mediumship, and near-death experiences with a mix of testimony and research.

7.1.3 Forensics, Evidence & Scientific Inquiry

- Sagan, C. (1996). *The demon-haunted world: Science as a candle in the dark*. Random House. → Classic skeptical work on science and pseudoscience; valuable counterweight for forensic thinking.
- Klass, P. J. (1983). *UFOs: The public deceived*. Prometheus Books. → Example of forensic skepticism, dissecting cases with technical analysis.
- Hynek, J. A. (1972). *The UFO experience: A scientific inquiry*. Ballantine Books. → Astrophysicist's forensic cataloging of UFO encounters, introducing the "close encounters" classification.
- Jacobs, D. M. (1992). *Secret life: Firsthand documented accounts of UFO abductions*. Simon & Schuster. → A historian's forensic-style documentation of abduction testimonies.
- Nickell, J. (2005). *Adventures in paranormal investigation*. University Press of Kentucky. → Forensic debunking from a professional investigator; useful as a skeptical methodological resource.
- Guiley, R. E. (2000). *The encyclopedia of ghosts and spirits*. Facts on File. → Compiles forensic-style case studies of paranormal phenomena worldwide.

7.2 Conspiracy, Power, and Alternative Histories

7.2.1 Foundational & Classic Works

- Marrs, J. (2003). *Crossfire: The plot that killed Kennedy*. Basic Books. (Original work published 1993). → Source for Oliver Stone's JFK; one of the most influential Kennedy assassination investigations.
- Marrs, J. (1995). *Rule by secrecy: The hidden history that connects the Trilateral Commission, the Freemasons, and the Great Pyramids*. HarperCollins.

- Marrs, J. (1997). *Alien agenda: Investigating the extraterrestrial presence among us*. Harper Paperbacks.
- Marrs, J. (2008). *The rise of the Fourth Reich: The secret societies that threaten to take over America*. Harper. → Explores the survival and transformation of Nazi ideology into postwar global networks.
- Cooper, W. (1991). *Behold a pale horse*. Light Technology Publishing. → A cornerstone of conspiracy literature, blending UFO disclosure, government secrecy, and New World Order claims.
- Icke, D. (1999). *The biggest secret: The book that will change the world*. Bridge of Love. → Controversial but influential in modern conspiracy subculture.

7.2.2 Media & Cultural Influence

- Jones, A. (2002–present). Infowars [Broadcasts & publications]. → Central figure in modern conspiracy media.
- Chomsky, N. (1997). *Media control: The spectacular achievements of propaganda*. Seven Stories Press. → Not "conspiracy" per se, but critical theory often absorbed into conspiracy frameworks.

7.2.3 Political & Historical Counter-Narratives

- Griffin, D. R. (2004). *The new Pearl Harbor: Disturbing questions about the Bush administration and 9/11*. Olive Branch Press.
- Talbot, D. (2007). *Brothers: The hidden history of the Kennedy years*. Free Press.
- Garrison, J. (1988). *On the trail of the assassins*. Sheridan Square Press. → Basis for Oliver Stone's JFK film.

7.2.4 Forensic & Investigative

- Hancock, G. (1995). *Fingerprints of the gods: The evidence of Earth's lost civilization*. Crown.
- Ventura, J. (2009). *American conspiracies: Lies, lies, and more dirty lies the government tells us*. Skyhorse.
- Bamford, J. (1982). *The puzzle palace: Inside the National Security Agency, America's most secret intelligence organization*. Penguin Books.

7.3 Sovereignty, Admiralty Law, and Alternative Human Rights

7.3.1 Foundational Legal-Esoteric Claims

- Black's Law Dictionary. (2019). *Definitions of the terms and phrases of American and English jurisprudence.* Thomson Reuters. (Original work published 1910).
- Spooner, L. (1870). *No treason: The Constitution of no authority.* Boston.

7.3.2 Admiralty / Maritime Law & Sovereignty

- Phelps, A. (2000). *Admiralty law and the birth certificate.* Independent Press.
- Williams, R. (2015). *The redemption manual.* Sovereignty Press.

7.3.3 Alternative Human Rights & Global Law

- United Nations. (1948). *Universal Declaration of Human Rights.* United Nations.
- International Covenant on Civil and Political Rights (ICCPR). (1966). United Nations.
- Zinn, H. (1971). *A people's history of the United States.* Harper & Row. (Original work published 1980).

7.3.4 Modern Sovereignty / Free Citizen Texts

- Guyer, J. (2012). *Common law vs. statutory law: Pathways to sovereignty.* Independent Press.
- Anonymous. (2010). *Meet your strawman.* Common Law Educational Foundation.
- Menard, R. (2002). *Handbook for free men.* ThinkFree.ca.

7.4 History, Literature, and Cultural Foundations

7.4.1 Classical History & Philosophy

- Herodotus. (2003). *The histories* (R. Waterfield, Trans.). Oxford University Press. (Original work published 440 BCE).
- Thucydides. (1996). *The Peloponnesian War* (R. Warner, Trans.). Penguin Classics. (Original work published 431 BCE).
- Plato. (2008). *The Republic* (R. Waterfield, Trans.). Oxford University Press. (Original work published 360 BCE).

- Aristotle. (1999). *Nicomachean ethics* (T. Irwin, Trans.). Hackett Publishing. (Original work published 350 BCE).

7.4.2 Sacred & Epic Literature

- Homer. (1996). *The Iliad* (R. Fagles, Trans.). Penguin Classics. (Original work published 8th c. BCE).
- Homer. (1997). *The Odyssey* (R. Fagles, Trans.). Penguin Classics. (Original work published 8th c. BCE).
- Virgil. (2006). *The Aeneid* (R. Fagles, Trans.). Penguin Classics. (Original work published 19 BCE).
- Dante Alighieri. (2003). *The Divine Comedy* (M. Musa, Trans.). Penguin Classics. (Original work published 1320).
- Milton, J. (2008). *Paradise Lost* (G. Teskey, Ed.). Norton Critical Edition. (Original work published 1667).

7.4.3 World Literature & Mysticism

- Rumi. (1997). *The essential Rumi* (C. Barks, Trans.). HarperOne. (Original work published 1207–1273).
- Goethe, J. W. von. (2001). *Faust* (W. Arndt, Trans.). Norton Critical Edition. (Original work published 1808).
- Dostoevsky, F. (1990). *The brothers Karamazov* (R. Pevear & L. Volokhonsky, Trans.). Farrar, Straus and Giroux. (Original work published 1880).
- Tolstoy, L. (2007). *War and peace* (R. Pevear & L. Volokhonsky, Trans.). Vintage Classics. (Original work published 1869).
- Shakespeare, W. (2004). *Hamlet*. Arden Shakespeare. (Original work published 1603).
- Shakespeare, W. (2010). *The tempest*. Arden Shakespeare. (Original work published 1611).

7.4.4 Modern History & Global Perspectives

- Toynbee, A. J. (1987). *A study of history* (12 vols.). Oxford University Press. (Original work published 1934–1961).
- Spengler, O. (1991). *The decline of the West*. Oxford University Press. (Original work published 1918).
- Zinn, H. (1980). *A people's history of the United States*. Harper & Row.
- Said, E. (1994). *Orientalism*. Vintage Books. (Original work published 1978).
- Harari, Y. N. (2014). *Sapiens: A brief history of humankind*. Harper.

- Diamond, J. (1997). *Guns, germs, and steel: The fates of human societies.* W. W. Norton.

7.5 Radical Movements in History

7.5.1 Political Revolutions & Social Upheaval

- Marx, K., & Engels, F. (2014). *The communist manifesto.* Verso. (Original work published 1848).
- Bakunin, M. (1990). *Statism and anarchy.* Cambridge University Press. (Original work published 1873).
- Goldman, E. (2003). *Anarchism and other essays.* Dover Publications. (Original work published 1910).
- Fanon, F. (2004). *The wretched of the earth.* Grove Press. (Original work published 1961).
- Debord, G. (1994). *The society of the spectacle.* Zone Books. (Original work published 1967).

7.5.2 Civil Rights & Liberation Movements

- Douglass, F. (1997). *Narrative of the life of Frederick Douglass, an American slave.* W. W. Norton. (Original work published 1845).
- King, M. L., Jr. (2010). *Why we can't wait.* Beacon Press. (Original work published 1963).
- Malcolm X, & Haley, A. (1992). *The autobiography of Malcolm X.* Ballantine Books. (Original work published 1965).
- Davis, A. (1990). *Women, race, & class.* Vintage Books. (Original work published 1981).
- Lorde, A. (2007). *Sister outsider.* Crossing Press. (Original work published 1984).

7.5.3 Artistic & Cultural Radicalism

- Breton, A. (1972). *Manifestoes of surrealism.* University of Michigan Press. (Original work published 1924).
- Artaud, A. (1958). *The theatre and its double.* Grove Press. (Original work published 1938).
- Benjamin, W. (1968). The work of art in the age of mechanical reproduction. Schocken Books. (Original work published 1936).
- Marcuse, H. (1991). *One-dimensional man.* Beacon Press. (Original work published 1964).

5.7.4 Global Radical Currents

- Guevara, C. (2003). *Guerrilla warfare*. Ocean Press. (Original work published 1960).
- Mao, Z. (2007). *On guerrilla warfare*. University of Illinois Press. (Original work published 1937).
- Luxemburg, R. (2003). *The accumulation of capital*. Routledge. (Original work published 1913).
- Gramsci, A. (1971). Selections from the prison notebooks. International Publishers. (Original work published 1929–1935).
- Zapatistas (EZLN). (2001). *Our word is our weapon*. Seven Stories Press. (Original work published 1994).

7.6 Illusion, Magic, and Games of Deception

7.6.1 Illusion & Stage Magic

- Houdini, H. (2011). *A magician among the spirits*. Harper & Brothers. (Original work published 1924).
- Maskelyne, J. N. (1999). *Sharps and flats*. Dover Publications. (Original work published 1896).
- Fitzkee, D. (2011). *The trick brain*. Magic Inc. (Original work published 1945).
- Jay, R. (1993). *Learned pigs and fireproof women*. Villard.

7.6.2 Card Magic & Sleight of Hand

- Erdnase, S. W. (1995). *The expert at the card table*. Dover Publications. (Original work published 1902).
- Vernon, D. (1995). *Revelations*. Magic Inc. (Original work published 1982).
- Tamariz, J. (2007). *The magic way*. Hermetic Press. (Original work published 1988).
- Ortiz, D. (1994). *Cardshark*. Kaufman & Company.

7.6.3 Card Counting & Gambling Strategies

- Thorp, E. O. (1998). *Beat the dealer*. Vintage Books. (Original work published 1962).
- Uston, K. (2001). *Million dollar blackjack*. HarperCollins. (Original work published 1981).
- Snyder, A. (1983). *Blackbelt in blackjack*. Cardoza Publishing.
- Scarne, J. (1981). *Scarne's complete guide to gambling*. Simon & Schuster. (Original work published 1961).

7.6.4 Cheating & Deception Case Studies

- Forte, S. (2004). *Casino game protection*. SLF Publishing.
- Diaz, J. (2010). *Cheating at poker and how to detect it*. Cardoza Publishing.
- Steinmeyer, J. (2003). *Hiding the elephant*. Carroll & Graf.

7.7 Music and the Philosophy of Sound

7.7.1 Classical Foundations

- Pythagoras (attributed). (1917). The harmony of the spheres. Classical reprint.
- Helmholtz, H. (1954). *On the sensations of tone*. Dover. (Original work published 1863).
- Schopenhauer, A. (1969). *The world as will and representation* (Vol. 1). Dover. (Original work published 1818).
- Nietzsche, F. (1993). *The birth of tragedy*. Penguin Classics. (Original work published 1872).

7.7.2 Classical Music & Genius

- Solomon, M. (1998). *Beethoven*. Schirmer.
- Taruskin, R. (2005). *The Oxford history of western music*. Oxford University Press.
- Rosen, C. (1997). *The classical style*. Norton. (Original work published 1971).

7.7.3 Modern Music & Culture

- Davis, M. (1990). *Miles: The autobiography*. Simon & Schuster.
- Guralnick, P. (1994). *Last train to Memphis*. Little, Brown.
- Frith, S. (1996). *Performing rites*. Harvard University Press.
- Reynolds, S. (2011). *Retromania*. Faber & Faber.

7.8 Classical and Modern Art

7.8.1 Classical & Renaissance Art

- Vasari, G. (1998). *Lives of the artists*. Oxford University Press. (Original work published 1550).

- Gombrich, E. H. (2000). *The story of art*. Phaidon. (Original work published 1950).
- Baxandall, M. (1988). *Painting and experience in fifteenth-century Italy*. Oxford University Press. (Original work published 1972).

7.8.2 Modern Art & Movements

- Hughes, R. (1991). *The shock of the new*. Thames & Hudson.
- Danto, A. C. (1997). *After the end of art*. Princeton University Press.
- Kuspit, D. (2004). *The end of art*. Cambridge University Press.

7.8.3 Contemporary & Critical Perspectives

- Berger, J. (2008). *Ways of seeing*. Penguin. (Original work published 1972).
- Foster, H., Krauss, R., Bois, Y.-A., & Buchloh, B. (2004). *Art since 1900*. Thames & Hudson.
- Bourriaud, N. (2002). *Relational aesthetics*. Les presses du réel. (Original work published 1998).

7.9 Religious & Spiritual Upheavals Beyond the West

7.9.1 Middle Eastern & Islamic Movements

- Schimmel, A. (1975). *Mystical dimensions of Islam*. UNC Press.
- Hodgson, M. G. S. (1974). *The venture of Islam* (3 vols.). University of Chicago Press.
- Rahman, F. (1982). *Islam and modernity*. University of Chicago Press.
- Nasr, S. H. (2007). *Islamic spirituality: Foundations*. Routledge.

7.9.2 Russian Orthodoxy & Eastern Christianity

- Lossky, V. (2002). *The mystical theology of the Eastern Church*. St. Vladimir's. (Original work published 1957).
- Meyendorff, J. (1981). *Byzantine theology*. Fordham University Press.
- Florovsky, G. (1974). *The ways of Russian theology*. Nordland.
- Ware, T. (1997). *The Orthodox Church*. Penguin. (Original work published 1964).

7.9.3 Indian & Asiatic Reform Movements

- Vivekananda, S. (1996). *Raja Yoga*. Ramakrishna-Vivekananda Center. (Original work published 1896).
- Aurobindo, S. (2000). *The life divine*. Lotus Press. (Original work published 1914).
- Gandhi, M. K. (2007). *An autobiography*. Beacon Press. (Original work published 1927).
- Radhakrishnan, S. (1994). *The Hindu view of life*. HarperCollins. (Original work published 1927).
- Prabhupada, A. C. B. S. (1983). *Bhagavad-gītā as it is*. Bhaktivedanta. (Original work published 1968).

7.9.4 Chinese & East Asian Currents

- Confucius. (1997). *The Analects* (D. C. Lau, Trans.). Penguin. (Original work published 1997).
- Zhuangzi. (2009). *Basic writings* (B. Watson, Trans.). Columbia University Press. (Original work published 2009).
- Maspero, H. (1981). *Taoism and Chinese religion*. University of Massachusetts Press.
- Suzuki, D. T. (1996). *Essays in Zen Buddhism*. Grove. (Original work published 1927).
- Fung, Y. (1997). *A history of Chinese philosophy*. Princeton. (Original work published 1948).

7.9.5 Tibetan Buddhism & Himalayan Currents

- Evans-Wentz, W. Y. (2000). *The Tibetan Book of the Dead*. Oxford University Press. (Original work published 1927).
- Lopez, D. S. (1998). *Prisoners of Shangri-La*. University of Chicago Press.
- Gyatso, J. (1998). *Apparitions of the self*. Princeton University Press.
- Powers, J. (2007). *Introduction to Tibetan Buddhism*. Snow Lion.

7.9.6 South American & Indigenous Currents

- Harner, M. (1990). *The way of the shaman*. HarperOne. (Original work published 1980).
- Narby, J. (1998). *The cosmic serpent*. Tarcher/Putnam.
- Luna, L. E., & Amaringo, P. (1991). *Ayahuasca visions*. North Atlantic Books.
- Viveiros de Castro, E. (2014). *Cannibal metaphysics*. Univocal. (Original work published 1998).

- Taussig, M. (1987). *Shamanism, colonialism, and the wild man*. University of Chicago Press.

7.9.7 Native American Spiritualities & Movements

- Deloria, V., Jr. (1992). *God is red*. Fulcrum.
- Deloria, V., Jr. (2006). *The world we used to live in*. Fulcrum.
- Brown, J. E. (1989). *The sacred pipe*. University of Oklahoma Press. (Original work published 1953).
- Lame Deer, J. F., & Erdoes, R. (1994). *Lame Deer, seeker of visions*. Washington Square Press. (Original work published 1972).
- Irwin, L. (1994). *The dream seekers*. University of Oklahoma Press.
- Mooney, J. (1991). *The ghost-dance religion*. University of Chicago Press. (Original work published 1896).
- Estes, N. (2019). *Our history is the future*. Verso.

7.10 Heroes for All the Wrong Reasons (and All the Right Ones Too)

- Spartacus (see Bradley, K. R. (1989). *Slavery and rebellion in the Roman world*. Indiana University Press).
- Robin Hood (Dobson, R. B., & Taylor, J. (1976). *Rymes of Robyn Hood*. Sutton Publishing).
- Stiles, T. J. (2002). *Jesse James: Last rebel of the Civil War*. Vintage.
- McQuilton, J. (2001). *The Kelly Outbreak*. Melbourne University Press.
- Anderson, J. L. (1997). *Che Guevara: A revolutionary life*. Grove.
- Reynolds, D. S. (2005). *John Brown, abolitionist*. Vintage.
- Goldman, E. (2003). *Anarchism and other essays*. Dover. (Original work published 1910).
- Ellmann, R. (1988). *Oscar Wilde*. Knopf.
- MacCarthy, F. (2002). *Byron: Life and legend*. Farrar, Straus & Giroux.
- Hauser, T. (1991). *Muhammad Ali: His life and times*. Simon & Schuster.
- Thompson, H. S. (1971). *Fear and loathing in Las Vegas*. Random House.
- Goethe, J. W. von. (2001). *Faust*. Norton. (Original work published 1808).

7.11 The Satanic Panic and Moral Hysteria

- Victor, J. S. (1993). *Satanic panic*. Open Court.

- Richardson, J. T., Best, J., & Bromley, D. G. (1991). *The satanism scare*. Aldine de Gruyter.
- Nathan, D., & Snedeker, M. (1995). *Satan's silence*. Basic Books.
- Lanning, K. V. (1992). Investigator's guide to allegations of "ritual" child abuse. FBI.
- Wright, L. (1994). *Remembering Satan*. Knopf.
- Frankfurter, D. (2006). *Evil incarnate*. Princeton University Press.
- de Young, M. (2004). *The day care ritual abuse moral panic*. McFarland.

7.12 Millennial Panics, Apocalypses, and Simulation Reality

7.12.1 Y2K

- Yourdon, E., & Yourdon, J. (1998). *Time bomb 2000*. Prentice Hall.
- Yardeni, Y. (1998). *The Y2K survival guide*. Wiley.

7.12.2 2012

- Jenkins, J. M. (1998). *Maya cosmogenesis 2012*. Bear & Company.
- Pinchbeck, D. (2006). *2012: The return of Quetzalcoatl*. Tarcher.
- Aveni, A. (2009). *The end of time*. University Press of Colorado.

7.12.3 Simulation & Holographic Reality

- Talbot, M. (1991). *The holographic universe*. Harper.
- Bostrom, N. (2003). Are you living in a computer simulation? *Philosophical Quarterly, 53*(211).
- Tegmark, M. (2014). *Our mathematical universe*. Knopf.
- Baudrillard, J. (1994). *Simulacra and simulation*. University of Michigan Press. (Original work published 1981).
- Chalmers, D. J. (2022). *Reality+*. W. W. Norton.

7.13 MK-Ultra, PsyOps, and Declassified Realities

- Marks, J. (1991). *The search for the "Manchurian Candidate"*. Norton. (Original work published 1979).
- Kinzer, S. (2019). *Poisoner in chief*. Henry Holt.
- Thomas, G. (1989). *Journey into madness*. Bantam.
- Ross, C. A. (2000). *Bluebird*. Manitou Communications.
- CIA. (1973). MKUltra documents (FOIA release).

- CIA. (1995). Stargate documents (declassified).
- U.S. Senate (1976). Church Committee Final Report. GPO.
- U.S. Senate (1983). Project MKULTRA hearings. GPO.
- McCoy, A. W. (2006). *A question of torture*. Metropolitan.
- Albarelli, H. P. (2009). *A terrible mistake*. Trine Day.

Psychedelics and Altered States

8.1 Psychedelics & Altered States

- Grof, S. (1975). *Realms of the human unconscious: Observations from LSD research*. Viking Press.
- MAPS (Multidisciplinary Association for Psychedelic Studies). (2021). Clinical studies on psilocybin and MDMA for therapeutic use. *MAPS Bulletin*.
- Pollan, M. (2018). *How to change your mind*. Penguin Press.
- Shulgin, A., & Shulgin, A. (1991). *PIHKAL: A chemical love story*. Transform Press.
- Shulgin, A., & Shulgin, A. (1997). *TIHKAL: The continuation*. Transform Press.
- Griffiths, R. R., et al. (2006). Psilocybin mystical experiences. *Psychopharmacology, 187*(3), 268–283.
- Griffiths, R. R., et al. (2016). Psilocybin reduces depression. *Journal of Psychopharmacology, 30*(12), 1181–1197.
- Johnson, M. W., Richards, W. A., & Griffiths, R. R. (2008). Human hallucinogen research: Guidelines. *Journal of Psychopharmacology, 22*(6), 603–620.
- Nichols, D. E. (2016). Psychedelics. *Pharmacological Reviews, 68*(2), 264–355.
- Pollan, M. (2018). *How to change your mind*. Penguin Press.
- DeAngelis, S. (2015). *Smoke signals*. Scribner.

8.2 Visionary, Channelled, and Alternative Cosmologies

8.2.1 Core Channelled & Occult Transmissions

- Crowley, A. (1976). *The book of the law (Liber AL vel Legis)*. Weiser Books. (Original work published 1904).
- Crowley, A. (1998). *The vision and the voice (Liber 418)*. Weiser Books. (Original work published 1911).

8.2.2 Additional Cosmic Channelled Works

- Fortune, D. (2001). *Psychic self-defense*. Weiser Books. (Original work published 1930).
- DuQuette, L. M. (2001). *Psychic self-defense and the mysteries of magic*. Weiser Books.
- Roberts, J. (1972). *Seth speaks*. Prentice-Hall.
- Roberts, J. (1974). *The nature of personal reality*. Prentice-Hall.
- Cayce, E. (1968). *Edgar Cayce on Atlantis*. Warner Books.
- Marciniak, B. (1992). *Bringers of the dawn*. Bear & Company.
- Marciniak, B. (1994). *Earth: Pleiadian keys to the living library*. Bear & Company.
- Knight, J. Z. (1987). *A state of mind: My story*. Warner Books.
- Hicks, E., & Hicks, J. (2004). *Ask and it is given*. Hay House.
- Royal, L. (1996). *Preparing for contact*. Granite Publishing.
- Deane, A. (1992). *Voyagers: The sleeping abductees*. Granite Publishing.
- The Arcturian teachings. Starborn Unlimited.
- Schucman, H. (1975). *A course in miracles*. Foundation for Inner Peace.
- The Urantia book. (1955). Urantia Foundation.
- Newbrough, J. B. (1882). *Oahspe: A new Bible*.

8.2.3 Contact, Disclosure & Alien Consciousness

- Greer, S. M. (2006). *Hidden truth – forbidden knowledge*. Crossing Point.
- Greer, S. M. (2014). *Unacknowledged*. A & A Printing.
- Strieber, W. (1987). *Communion*. Morrow.
- Vallée, J. (1991). *Passport to Magonia*. McGraw-Hill / Contemporary Books. (Original work published 1969).
- Vallée, J. (1990). *Confrontations*. Ballantine Books.
- Mack, J. E. (1994). *Abduction*. Scribner.
- Kean, L. (2010). *UFOs: Generals, pilots, and government officials go on the record*. Crown.

8.2.4 Psychedelic Pioneers

- Huxley, A. (1954). *The doors of perception*. Harper & Brothers.
- Leary, T., Metzner, R., & Alpert, R. (1964). *The psychedelic experience*. University Books.

- Metzner, R. (1998). *Hallucinogens and shamanism*. Harper & Row.
- McKenna, T. (1992). *Food of the gods*. Bantam.
- McKenna, T. (1993). *True hallucinations*. HarperCollins.
- Strassman, R. (2001). *DMT: The spirit molecule*. Park Street Press.
- Strassman, R., Wojtowicz, S., Luna, L. E., & Frecska, E. (2008). *Inner paths to outer space*. Park Street Press.
- Grof, S. (1975). *Realms of the human unconscious*. Viking Press.
- Grof, S. (1985). *Beyond the brain*. SUNY Press.
- Grof, S. (1975). *Realms of the human unconscious: Observations from LSD research*. Viking Press.

8.2.5 Ethnobotany & Plant Medicines

- Schultes, R. E., & Hofmann, A. (1992). *Plants of the gods*. Healing Arts Press.
- Rätsch, C. (2005). *The encyclopedia of psychoactive plants*. Park Street Press.
- Narby, J. (1998). *The cosmic serpent*. Tarcher/Putnam.
- Luna, L. E. (1986). *Vegetalismo*. Almqvist & Wiksell International.

8.2.6 Neurotheology & Consciousness Research

- Newberg, A., D'Aquili, E., & Rause, V. (2001). *Why God won't go away*. Ballantine Books.
- Persinger, M. A. (1983). Mystical experiences as temporal lobe artifacts. *Perceptual and Motor Skills*.
- Strassman, R. (2014). *DMT and the soul of prophecy*. Park Street Press.

8.2.7 Modern Clinical Psychedelic Science

- Carhart-Harris, R. L., & Goodwin, G. M. (2017). The therapeutic potential of psychedelic drugs. *Neuropsychopharmacology, 42*(11), 2105–2113.
- Griffiths, R. R., et al. (2018). Psilocybin produces substantial and sustained decreases in depression and anxiety. *Journal of Psychopharmacology, 32*(4), 437–450.
- Johnson, M. W., & Griffiths, R. R. (2017). Potential therapeutic effects of psilocybin. *Neurotherapeutics, 14*(3), 734–740.
- Nichols, D. E. (2018). Psychedelic neuroscience. *Progress in Brain Research, 242*, 1–22.

- Pollan, M. (2018). *How to change your mind.* Penguin Press.
- DeAngelis, S. (2015). *Smoke signals.* Scribner.

Social and Political Dynamics

9.1 Atrocity, Oppression, and the Dark History of Civilization

9.1.1 Genocide & Mass Violence

- Lemkin, R. (2005). *Axis rule in occupied Europe.* Carnegie Endowment. (Original work published 1944).
- Totten, S., Parsons, W. S., & Charny, I. W. (Eds.). (2004). *Century of genocide.* Routledge.
- Browning, C. R. (1992). *Ordinary men.* Harper Perennial.
- Hilberg, R. (2003). *The destruction of the European Jews.* Yale University Press. (Original work published 1961).
- Kiernan, B. (2007). *Blood and soil.* Yale University Press.

9.1.2 Torture & Inquisition

- Peters, E. (1988). *Inquisition.* University of California Press.
- Kamen, H. (1997). *The Spanish Inquisition.* Yale University Press.
- Lea, H. C. (1993). *A history of the Inquisition of the Middle Ages.* AMS Press. (Original work published 1888).
- Scarry, E. (1985). *The body in pain.* Oxford University Press.

9.1.3 Witch Trials & Persecution

- Kramer, H., & Sprenger, J. (2009). *Malleus Maleficarum.* Cambridge University Press. (Original work published 1487).
- Levack, B. P. (2015). *The witch-hunt in early modern Europe.* Routledge. (Original work published 1987).
- Briggs, R. (2002). *Witches and neighbors.* Wiley-Blackwell.

9.1.4 Plague & Disease

- Ziegler, P. (1998). *The Black Death.* Harper Perennial. (Original work published 1969).

- Herlihy, D. (1997). *The Black Death and the transformation of the West*. Harvard University Press.
- Kelly, J. (2005). *The great mortality*. Harper Perennial.

9.1.5 Crusades & Religious Atrocities

- Asbridge, T. (2010). *The crusades*. HarperCollins.
- Riley-Smith, J. (2005). *The crusades: A history*. Yale University Press.
- Madden, T. F. (2014). *The concise history of the crusades*. Rowman & Littlefield.

9.1.6 Atrocities of Antiquity

- Gibbon, E. (1994). *The history of the decline and fall of the Roman Empire*. Modern Library. (Original work published 1776–1789).
- Kyle, D. G. (2007). *Spectacles of death in ancient Rome*. Routledge.

9.2 Religious Revolutions: Protestantism and Beyond

9.2.1 Protestant Reformation & Counter-Reformation

- Luther, M. (1957). *Three treatises*. Fortress Press. (Original work published 1520).
- Calvin, J. (1960). *Institutes of the Christian religion*. Westminster Press. (Original work published 1536).
- Erasmus, D. (2003). *In praise of folly*. Yale University Press. (Original work published 1509).
- MacCulloch, D. (2003). *The Reformation: A history*. Penguin Books.
- Cameron, E. (2012). *The European Reformation*. Oxford University Press. (Original work published 1991).

9.2.2 Other Religious & Social Revolutions

- Weber, M. (2002). *The Protestant ethic and the spirit of capitalism*. Routledge. (Original work published 1905).
- Troeltsch, E. (1992). *The social teaching of the Christian churches*. Westminster John Knox. (Original work published 1912).
- Stark, R. (1996). *The rise of Christianity*. HarperOne.
- Jenkins, P. (2002). *The next Christendom*. Oxford University Press.

9.3 Modern Theories in Behavioral Science

9.3.1 Foundational Behavioral Science

- Skinner, B. F. (2014). *Science and human behavior*. B. F. Skinner Foundation. (Original work published 1953).
- Bandura, A. (1977). *Social learning theory*. Prentice Hall.
- Festinger, L. (1957). *A theory of cognitive dissonance*. Stanford University Press.
- Milgram, S. (1974). *Obedience to authority*. Harper & Row.
- Zimbardo, P. (2007). *The Lucifer effect*. Random House.

9.3.2 Behavioral Economics & Decision Science

- Kahneman, D. (2011). *Thinking, fast and slow*. Farrar, Straus and Giroux.
- Thaler, R. H., & Sunstein, C. R. (2008). *Nudge*. Yale University Press.
- Ariely, D. (2008). *Predictably irrational*. HarperCollins.
- Gigerenzer, G. (2007). *Gut feelings*. Viking.

9.3.3 Behavioral Game Theory & Strategy

- Schelling, T. C. (1980). *The strategy of conflict*. Harvard University Press. (Original work published 1960).
- Axelrod, R. (2006). *The evolution of cooperation*. Basic Books. (Original work published 1984).
- Camerer, C. F. (2003). *Behavioral game theory*. Princeton University Press.

9.3.4 Applied Behavioral Science

- Cialdini, R. B. (2006). *Influence*. Harper Business. (Original work published 1984).
- Fogg, B. J. (2003). *Persuasive technology*. Morgan Kaufmann.
- Gneezy, U., & List, J. A. (2013). *The why axis*. PublicAffairs.
- Duckworth, A. (2016). *Grit*. Scribner.

9.3.5 Emerging Frontiers

- Mischel, W. (2014). *The marshmallow test*. Little, Brown.
- Sapolsky, R. M. (2017). *Behave*. Penguin Press.

- Baumeister, R. F., & Tierney, J. (2011). *Willpower*. Penguin Press.
- Henrich, J. (2020). *The WEIRDest people in the world*. Farrar, Straus and Giroux.

9.4 Anthropology, Human Origins, and Prehistoric Life

9.4.1 Foundations of Anthropology

- Boas, F. (1966). *The mind of primitive man*. Free Press. (Original work published 1911).
- Malinowski, B. (2002). *Argonauts of the Western Pacific*. Routledge. (Original work published 1922).
- Lévi-Strauss, C. (1966). *The savage mind*. University of Chicago Press. (Original work published 1962).
- Geertz, C. (1973). *The interpretation of cultures*. Basic Books.
- Mead, M. (2001). *Coming of age in Samoa*. Perennial. (Original work published 1928).

9.4.2 Human Origins & Evolutionary Anthropology

- Johanson, D. C., & Edey, M. A. (1981). *Lucy*. Simon & Schuster.
- Tattersall, I. (1995). *The fossil trail*. Oxford University Press.
- Leakey, R. E., & Lewin, R. (1977). *Origins*. Dutton.
- Harari, Y. N. (2015). *Sapiens*. Harper. (Original work published 2011).
- Klein, R. G. (2009). *The human career*. University of Chicago Press.

9.4.3 Neanderthals & Hominid Relatives

- Finlayson, C. (2009). *The humans who went extinct*. Oxford University Press.
- Tattersall, I., & Schwartz, J. H. (2000). *Extinct humans*. Westview Press.
- Pääbo, S. (2014). *Neanderthal man*. Basic Books.
- Stringer, C., & Andrews, P. (2005). *The complete world of human evolution*. Thames & Hudson.

9.4.4 Dinosaurs & Prehistoric Life

- Bakker, R. T. (1986). *The dinosaur heresies*. William Morrow.
- Horner, J. R., & Gorman, J. (1988). *Digging dinosaurs*. Workman Publishing.

- Brusatte, S. L. (2018). *The rise and fall of the dinosaurs.* William Morrow.
- Gee, H. (2017). *Across the bridge.* University of Chicago Press.

9.4.5 Anthropology & Cultural Evolution

- Harris, M. (1979). *Cultural materialism.* Random House.
- Diamond, J. (1997). *Guns, germs, and steel.* W. W. Norton.
- Henrich, J. (2015). *The secret of our success.* Princeton University Press.

Spirituality and Science Integration

10.1 The Science of Spirituality

10.1.1 Foundational Science–Mysticism Dialogue

- Capra, F. (2000). *The Tao of physics.* Shambhala. (Original work published 1975).
- Zukav, G. (1979). *The dancing Wu Li masters.* HarperOne.
- Laszlo, E. (2004). *Science and the Akashic field.* Inner Traditions.
- Bohm, D. (1980). *Wholeness and the implicate order.* Routledge.
- Sheldrake, R. (2009). *A new science of life.* Icon Books. (Original work published 1981).

10.1.2 Neuroscience, Meditation & Consciousness

- Austin, J. H. (1998). *Zen and the brain.* MIT Press.
- Newberg, A., D'Aquili, E., & Rause, V. (2001). *Why God won't go away.* Ballantine Books.
- Davidson, R. J., & Goleman, D. (2017). *Altered traits.* Avery.
- Wallace, B. A. (2007). *Contemplative science.* Columbia University Press.

10.1.3 Physics, Cosmology & Consciousness

- Penrose, R. (1989). *The emperor's new mind.* Oxford University Press.
- Hameroff, S., & Penrose, R. (2014). Consciousness in the universe. *Physics of Life Reviews, 11*(1), 39–78.

- Goswami, A. (2001). *The self-aware universe*. Tarcher/Putnam. (Original work published 1993).
- Kafatos, M., & Nadeau, R. (2000). *The conscious universe*. Springer.

10.1.4 Integrative & Interdisciplinary

- Wilber, K. (2000). *A theory of everything*. Shambhala.
- Ferrer, J. N. (2002). *Revisioning transpersonal theory*. SUNY Press.
- Grof, S. (2000). *Psychology of the future*. SUNY Press.
- Tarnas, R. (2006). *Cosmos and psyche*. Viking.

10.2 Evolution, Consciousness, and Radical Origins

10.2.1 Darwin & Classic Evolutionary Theory

- Darwin, C. (2003). *On the origin of species*. Penguin Classics. (Original work published 1859).
- Darwin, C. (2004). *The descent of man*. Penguin Classics. (Original work published 1871).

10.2.2 Critiques & Alternative Evolutionary Views

- Gould, S. J. (1989). *Wonderful life*. W. W. Norton.
- Eldredge, N., & Gould, S. J. (1972). Punctuated equilibria. Freeman.

10.2.3 Psychedelic Ape & Radical Consciousness Hypotheses

- McKenna, T. (1992). *Food of the gods*. Bantam.
- Strassman, R. (2001). *DMT: The spirit molecule*. Park Street Press.

10.2.4 Philosophical Alternatives on Consciousness

- Chalmers, D. J. (1996). *The conscious mind*. Oxford University Press.
- Nagel, T. (2012). *Mind and cosmos*. Oxford University Press.

10.2.5 Dual Earth, Multiverse & Radical Cosmologies

- Talbot, M. (1991). *The holographic universe*. Harper Perennial.
- Greene, B. (1999). *The elegant universe*. W. W. Norton.

Aeronautics & Propulsion

11.1 Flight & Aerodynamics

11.1.1 Foundational Works

- Anderson, J. D. (2017). *Fundamentals of aerodynamics* (6th ed.). McGraw-Hill Education.
- Anderson, J. D. (2007). *Introduction to flight* (6th ed.). McGraw-Hill Education.

11.2 Propulsion & Rocketry

11.2.1 Core Propulsion Texts

- Sutton, G. P., & Biblarz, O. (2016). *Rocket propulsion elements* (9th ed.). Wiley.
- Hill, P. G., & Peterson, C. R. (1992). *Mechanics and thermodynamics of propulsion* (2nd ed.). Addison-Wesley.

11.2.2 Electric & Ion Propulsion

- Goebel, D. M., & Katz, I. (2008). *Fundamentals of electric propulsion: Ion and Hall thrusters*. Wiley.
- Jahn, R. G. (2006). *Physics of electric propulsion* (reprint ed.). Dover.

Waveform Physics & Electromagnetic Fields

12.1 Classical Electrodynamics

- Jackson, J. D. (1998). *Classical electrodynamics* (3rd ed.). Wiley.
- Stratton, J. A. (1941). *Electromagnetic theory*. McGraw-Hill.

12.2 Optics & Wave Phenomena

- Born, M., & Wolf, E. (1999). *Principles of optics* (7th ed.). Cambridge University Press.
- Hecht, E. (2017). *Optics* (5th ed.). Pearson.
- Zangwill, A. (2012). *Modern electrodynamics*. Cambridge University Press.

Radio, Microwave & Frequency Engineering

13.1 Microwave Theory & Antennas

- Pozar, D. M. (2012). *Microwave engineering* (4th ed.). Wiley.
- Balanis, C. A. (2016). *Antenna theory: Analysis and design* (4th ed.). Wiley.

13.2 Communication & Applied EMF

- Ramo, S., Whinnery, J. R., & Van Duzer, T. (1994). *Fields and waves in communication electronics* (3rd ed.). Wiley.
- Haykin, S. (2001). *Communication systems* (4th ed.). Wiley.
- Ulaby, F. T., Michielssen, E., & Ravaioli, U. (2014). *Fundamentals of applied electromagnetics* (7th ed.). Pearson.

Orbital Mechanics & Counter-Orbital Dynamics

14.1 Astrodynamics Foundations

- Bate, R. R., Mueller, D. D., & White, J. E. (1971). *Fundamentals of astrodynamics*. Dover.
- Vallado, D. A. (2013). *Fundamentals of astrodynamics and applications* (4th ed.). Microcosm Press.
- Prussing, J. E., & Conway, B. A. (2012). *Orbital mechanics* (2nd ed.). Oxford University Press.

14.2 Non-Keplerian Orbits & Dynamics

- Farquhar, R. W., & Kamel, A. A. (1973). Quasi-periodic orbits about the translunar libration point. *Celestial Mechanics, 7*(4), 458–473.
- McInnes, C. R. (1999). *Solar sailing: Technology, dynamics and mission applications*. Springer.
- Koon, W. S., Lo, M. W., Marsden, J. E., & Ross, S. D. (2011). *Dynamical systems, the three-body problem and space mission design* (rev. ed.). Marsden Books.

Unsolvable Mathematics & Foundational Limits

15.1 Logic & Incompleteness

- Gödel, K. (1931). Über formal unentscheidbare Sätze der Principia Mathematica und verwandter Systeme I. *Monatshefte für Mathematik und Physik, 38*, 173–198.
- Turing, A. M. (1936). On computable numbers, with an application to the Entscheidungsproblem. *Proceedings of the London Mathematical Society, 42*(2), 230–265.

15.2 Computability & Complexity

- Matiyasevich, Y. (1970). The Diophantine representation of enumerable sets. *Doklady Akademii Nauk SSSR, 191*(2), 279–282.
- Cook, S. A. (1971). The complexity of theorem-proving procedures. *Proceedings of the Third Annual ACM Symposium on Theory of Computing*, 151–158.
- Garey, M. R., & Johnson, D. S. (1979). *Computers and intractability: A guide to the theory of NP-completeness*. W. H. Freeman.

15.3 Information & Randomness

- Chaitin, G. J. (2005). *Meta math!: The quest for Omega*. Pantheon.

Light, Relativity & the Limits of Speed

16.1 Foundational Works

- Einstein, A. (1905). On the electrodynamics of moving bodies. *Annalen der Physik, 17*, 891–921.
- Michelson, A. A., & Morley, E. W. (1887). On the relative motion of the Earth and the luminiferous ether. *American Journal of Science, 34*(203), 333–345.

16.2 Relativity & Cosmology

- Rindler, W. (2006). *Relativity: Special, general, and cosmological* (2nd ed.). Oxford University Press.
- Peebles, P. J. E. (1993). *Principles of physical cosmology*. Princeton University Press.
- Ryden, B. (2017). *Introduction to cosmology* (2nd ed.). Cambridge University Press.

16.3 Constraints & Distance Measures

- Hogg, D. W. (1999). Distance measures in cosmology. (arXiv preprint; pedagogical review).

Experimental & Hypothetical Propulsion Systems

17.1 Established Propulsion Concepts

- Jahn, R. G. (2006). *Physics of electric propulsion* (reprint ed.). Dover.
- Goebel, D. M., & Katz, I. (2008). *Fundamentals of electric propulsion: Ion and Hall thrusters*. Wiley.

17.2 Advanced & Speculative Designs

- Millis, M. G., & Davis, E. W. (Eds.). (2009). *Frontiers of propulsion science*. AIAA.
- Dyson, G. (2002). *Project Orion: The true story of the atomic spaceship*. Henry Holt.
- Zubrin, R. (2011). *The case for Mars* (rev. ed.). Free Press.

Computer Programming, Binary & Systems Theory

18.1 Foundations of Computing

- Knuth, D. E. (1997–2011). *The art of computer programming* (Vols. 1–4). Addison-Wesley.
- Shannon, C. E. (1948). A mathematical theory of communication. *Bell System Technical Journal, 27*, 379–423; 623–656.

18.2 Information & Complexity

- Cover, T. M., & Thomas, J. A. (2006). *Elements of information theory* (2nd ed.). Wiley.
- Hopcroft, J. E., Motwani, R., & Ullman, J. D. (2001). *Introduction to automata theory, languages, and computation* (2nd ed.). Addison-Wesley.

18.3 Systems & New Paradigms

- Tanenbaum, A. S. (2012). *Structured computer organization* (6th ed.). Pearson.
- Wolfram, S. (2002). *A new kind of science*. Wolfram Media.

Sentience in Non-Humans

19.1 Animal Cognition & Awareness

- de Waal, F. (2016). *Are we smart enough to know how smart animals are?* W. W. Norton.
- Griffin, D. R. (2001). *Animal minds: Beyond cognition to consciousness* (rev. ed.). University of Chicago Press.

19.2 Evolutionary & Neurobiological Perspectives

- Feinberg, T. E., & Mallatt, J. (2016). *The ancient origins of consciousness: How the brain created experience.* MIT Press.
- Birch, J. (2022). The search for animal consciousness. *Noûs, 56*(1), 133–152.
- Browning, H., & Veit, W. (2023). The evolution of sentience. *Philosophy Compass, 18*(7), e12832.

Non-Carbon-Based Life & Exobiology

20.1 Astrobiology Foundations

- Lunine, J. I. (2013). *Astrobiology: A multidisciplinary approach* (2nd ed.). Pearson.
- Cockell, C. S. (2015). *Astrobiology: Understanding life in the universe.* Wiley-Blackwell.

20.2 Alternative Chemistries

- Cleland, C. E., & Chyba, C. F. (2002). Defining "life." *Origins of Life and Evolution of the Biosphere, 32*(4), 387–393.
- Bains, W. (2004). Many chemistries could be used to build living systems. *Astrobiology, 4*(2), 137–167.
- Schulze-Makuch, D., & Irwin, L. N. (2008). *Life in the universe: Expectations and constraints* (2nd ed.). Springer.

Planetary Consciousness & Gaia Theory

21.1 Gaia Hypothesis Foundations

- Lovelock, J. E. (1979). *Gaia: A new look at life on Earth.* Oxford University Press.
- Lovelock, J. E., & Margulis, L. (1974). Atmospheric homeostasis by and for the biosphere: The Gaia hypothesis. *Tellus, 26*(1–2), 2–10.

21.2 Developments & Extensions

- Lenton, T. M., & Latour, B. (2018). Gaia 2.0. *Science, 361*(6407), 1066–1068.
- Volk, T. (1998). *Gaia's body: Toward a physiology of Earth*. Copernicus.
- Margulis, L., & Sagan, D. (1995). *What is life?* Simon & Schuster.

All-Awareness vs. Self-Awareness

22.1 Philosophical Foundations

- Nagel, T. (1974). What is it like to be a bat? *The Philosophical Review, 83*(4), 435–450.
- Block, N. (1995). On a confusion about a function of consciousness. *Behavioral and Brain Sciences, 18*(2), 227–247.

22.2 Neuroscientific & Theoretical Approaches

- Damasio, A. (2010). *Self comes to mind: Constructing the conscious brain*. Pantheon.
- Tononi, G. (2008). Consciousness as integrated information: A provisional manifesto. *Biological Bulletin, 215*(3), 216–242.
- Metzinger, T. (2003). *Being no one: The self-model theory of subjectivity*. MIT Press.

Non-Linear Transmission & Information Theory

23.1 Nonlinear Media & Wave Dynamics

- Strogatz, S. H. (2015). *Nonlinear dynamics and chaos* (2nd ed.). Westview Press.
- Agrawal, G. P. (2019). *Nonlinear fiber optics* (6th ed.). Academic Press.
- Drazin, P. G., & Johnson, R. S. (1989). *Solitons: An introduction*. Cambridge University Press.

23.2 Information & Complexity

- Shannon, C. E. (1948). A mathematical theory of communication. *Bell System Technical Journal, 27*, 379–423; 623–656.
- Cover, T. M., & Thomas, J. A. (2006). *Elements of information theory* (2nd ed.). Wiley.

- Prigogine, I., & Stengers, I. (1984). *Order out of chaos: Man's new dialogue with nature*. Bantam.

Particle Physics & the Higgs Boson

24.1 Foundational Papers

- Higgs, P. W. (1964). Broken symmetries and the masses of gauge bosons. *Physical Review Letters, 13*(16), 508–509.
- Englert, F., & Brout, R. (1964). Broken symmetry and the mass of gauge vector mesons. *Physical Review Letters, 13*(9), 321–323.
- Guralnik, G. S., Hagen, C. R., & Kibble, T. W. B. (1964). Global conservation laws and massless particles. *Physical Review Letters, 13*(20), 585–587.

24.2 LHC Discoveries

- Aad, G., et al. [ATLAS Collaboration]. (2012). Observation of a new particle in the search for the Standard Model Higgs boson with the ATLAS detector at the LHC. *Physics Letters B, 716*(1), 1–29.
- Chatrchyan, S., et al. [CMS Collaboration]. (2012). Observation of a new boson at a mass of 125 GeV with the CMS experiment at the LHC. *Physics Letters B, 716*(1), 30–61.
- Ellis, J. (2012). The Higgs boson explained. *Nature Physics, 8*(6), 421–423.

The Large Hadron Collider & High-Energy Experiments

25.1 LHC Machine & Infrastructure

- Evans, L., & Bryant, P. (2008). LHC machine. *Journal of Instrumentation, 3*(08), S08001.

25.2 Major Experiments

- ATLAS Collaboration. (2008). The ATLAS experiment at the CERN Large Hadron Collider. *Journal of Instrumentation, 3*(08), S08003.
- CMS Collaboration. (2008). The CMS experiment at the CERN LHC. *Journal of Instrumentation, 3*(08), S08004.
- Aamodt, K., et al. [ALICE Collaboration]. (2008). The ALICE experiment at the CERN LHC. *Journal of Instrumentation, 3*(08), S08002.

25.3 Combined Results

- ATLAS & CMS Collaborations. (2015). Combined measurement of the Higgs boson mass in pp collisions at $\sqrt{s}$ = 7 and 8 TeV. *Physical Review Letters, 114*(19), 191803.

Micro and Macro Information Systems

26.1 Systems Theory & Complexity

- Von Bertalanffy, L. (1968). *General system theory*. George Braziller.
- Simon, H. A. (1996). *The sciences of the artificial* (3rd ed.). MIT Press.
- Mitchell, M. (2009). *Complexity: A guided tour*. Oxford University Press.

26.2 Information Across Scales

- Gell-Mann, M. (1994). *The quark and the jaguar*. W. H. Freeman.
- Barabási, A.-L. (2002). *Linked: The new science of networks*. Perseus.
- Deutsch, D. (2011). *The beginning of infinity*. Viking.

Anti-Gravity & Alternative Gravity Theories

27.1 Conventional Gravitation

- Einstein, A. (1916). The foundation of the general theory of relativity. *Annalen der Physik, 49*, 769–822.
- Misner, C. W., Thorne, K. S., & Wheeler, J. A. (1973). *Gravitation*. W. H. Freeman.

27.2 Anti-Gravity & Hypothetical Concepts

- Forward, R. L. (1996). *Indistinguishable from magic*. Baen.
- Woodward, J. F. (2013). *Making starships and stargates: The science of interstellar transport and absurdly benign wormholes*. Springer.
- Hajdukovic, D. (2011). Is dark matter an illusion created by the gravitational polarization of the quantum vacuum? *Astrophysics and Space Science, 334*(2), 215–218.

Dark Matter & Its Alternatives

28.1 Dark Matter Foundations

- Bertone, G., Hooper, D., & Silk, J. (2005). Particle dark matter: Evidence, candidates and constraints. *Physics Reports, 405*(5–6), 279–390.
- Feng, J. L. (2010). Dark matter candidates from particle physics and methods of detection. *Annual Review of Astronomy and Astrophysics, 48*, 495–545.

28.2 Dark Matter Critiques & Alternatives

- Milgrom, M. (1983). A modification of the Newtonian dynamics as a possible alternative to the hidden mass hypothesis. *Astrophysical Journal, 270*, 365–370.
- Moffat, J. W. (2006). Scalar–tensor–vector gravity theory. *Journal of Cosmology and Astroparticle Physics, 2006*(03), 004.
- Kroupa, P. (2012). The dark matter crisis: Falsification of the current standard model of cosmology. *Publications of the Astronomical Society of Australia, 29*(4), 395–433.

Universe Within a Black Hole Theory

29.1 Black Hole Cosmology

- Pathria, R. K. (1972). The universe as a black hole. *Nature, 240*(5379), 298–299.
- Easson, D. A., & Brandenberger, R. H. (2001). Universe generation from black hole interiors. *Journal of High Energy Physics, 2001*(06), 024.

29.2 Modern Interpretations

- Popławski, N. J. (2010). Cosmology with torsion: An alternative to cosmic inflation. *Physics Letters B, 694*(3), 181–185.
- Smolin, L. (1997). *The life of the cosmos*. Oxford University Press.

Quantum Entanglement

30.1 Foundations

- Einstein, A., Podolsky, B., & Rosen, N. (1935). Can quantum-mechanical description of physical reality be considered complete? *Physical Review, 47*(10), 777–780.

- Bell, J. S. (1964). On the Einstein Podolsky Rosen paradox. *Physics Physique Физика, 1*(3), 195–200.

30.2 Experimental Confirmations

- Aspect, A., Dalibard, J., & Roger, G. (1982). Experimental test of Bell's inequalities using time-varying analyzers. *Physical Review Letters, 49*(25), 1804–1807.
- Zeilinger, A. (2010). *Dance of the photons: From Einstein to quantum teleportation.* Farrar, Straus and Giroux.

30.3 Interpretations

- Bohm, D. (1980). *Wholeness and the implicate order.* Routledge.
- Vedral, V. (2018). *Decoding reality: The universe as quantum information.* Oxford University Press.

Time Travel Theory

31.1 Relativity & Closed Timelike Curves

- Gödel, K. (1949). An example of a new type of cosmological solutions of Einstein's field equations of gravitation. *Reviews of Modern Physics, 21*(3), 447–450.
- Tipler, F. J. (1974). Rotating cylinders and the possibility of global causality violation. *Physical Review D, 9*(8), 2203–2206.

31.2 Wormholes & Exotic Spacetimes

- Morris, M. S., Thorne, K. S., & Yurtsever, U. (1988). Wormholes, time machines, and the weak energy condition. *Physical Review Letters, 61*(13), 1446–1449.
- Visser, M. (1995). *Lorentzian wormholes: From Einstein to Hawking.* Springer.

31.3 Contemporary Possibilities

- Everett, H. (1957). "Relative state" formulation of quantum mechanics. *Reviews of Modern Physics, 29*(3), 454–462.
- Deutsch, D. (1991). Quantum mechanics near closed timelike lines. *Physical Review D, 44*(10), 3197–3217.

Time Travel Possibility in Popular & Scientific Discourse

32.1 Popular Science Explorations

- Wells, H. G. (2002). *The time machine*. Modern Library. (Original work published 1895).
- Thorne, K. S. (1994). *Black holes and time warps: Einstein's outrageous legacy*. W. W. Norton.
- Kaku, M. (2008). *Physics of the impossible*. Doubleday.

32.2 Critical Perspectives

- Novikov, I. D. (1998). *The river of time*. Cambridge University Press.
- Lewis, D. (1976). The paradoxes of time travel. *American Philosophical Quarterly, 13*(2), 145–152.

33. Classical Medical Canons

33.1 Chinese Medicine

- Huangdi Neijing (Yellow Emperor's Inner Classic). (2011). *Huang Di Nei Jing Su Wen: An annotated translation of Huang Di's Inner Classic – Basic questions*. University of California Press.
- Huangfu Mi. (c. 3rd century CE). *Zhen Jiu Jia Yi Jing (Systematic classic of acupuncture and moxibustion)*.
- Zhang Zhongjing. (c. 200 CE). *Shang Han Lun (Treatise on cold damage and miscellaneous diseases)*.
- Li Shizhen. (2003). *Ben Cao Gang Mu (Compendium of materia medica)*. Foreign Languages Press. (Original work published 1596).

33.2 Ayurvedic Medicine

- Charaka. (2003). *Charaka Samhita* (P. Sharma, Trans.). Chaukhambha Orientalia.
- Sushruta. (2001). *Sushruta Samhita* (K. K. Bhishagratna, Trans.). Chowkhamba Sanskrit Series.
- Vagbhata. (1995). *Ashtanga Hridayam* (K. R. Srikantha Murthy, Trans.). Chaukhambha Krishnadas Academy.

33.3 Greco-Roman Medicine

- Hippocrates. (2005). *Hippocratic writings* (G. E. R. Lloyd, Ed.). Penguin Classics.

- Galen. (2006). *On the natural faculties* (A. J. Brock, Trans.). Loeb Classical Library.

33.4 Islamic & Persian Medicine

- Avicenna (Ibn Sina). (1999). *The canon of medicine (al-Qanun fi al-Tibb)* (L. E. Goodman, Ed. & Trans.). Oxford University Press.
- al-Razi (Rhazes). (2009). *Kitab al-Hawi (The comprehensive book on medicine)*. Routledge.

33.5 Tibetan Medicine

- Gyüshi (Four Tantras). (1995). (Tsarong, D., Trans.). Library of Tibetan Works and Archives.

33.6 Other Cultural Canons

- Ebers Papyrus. (1937). *The Ebers Papyrus: A new English translation*. Geoffrey Bles.
- Codex de la Cruz-Badiano. (1991). *An Aztec herbal: The classic codex of 1552*. Dover Publications.
- Otsuka, K. (2010). *A textbook of Kampo: Japanese traditional medicine*. Elsevier.

34. Folk & Esoteric Healing Traditions

34.1 African Diaspora Traditions

- Anderson, J. T. (2005). *Conjure in African American society*. University of North Carolina Press.
- Hyatt, H. M. (1970). *Hoodoo – Conjuration – Witchcraft – Rootwork* (Vols. 1–5). Alma Egan Hyatt Foundation.
- Métraux, A. (1959). *Voodoo in Haiti*. Pantheon Books.

34.2 Crystal Healing

- Hall, J. (2003). *The crystal bible*. Walking Stick Press.
- Melody. (1991). *Love is in the earth: A kaleidoscope of crystals*. Earth Love Publishing.

34.3 Herbalism & Aromatherapy

- Grieve, M. (1971). *A modern herbal*. Dover Publications.
- Duke, J. A. (2002). *Handbook of medicinal herbs* (2nd ed.). CRC Press.

- Tisserand, R., & Young, R. (2013). *Essential oil safety* (2nd ed.). Churchill Livingstone.

34.4 Shamanism & Indigenous Healing

- Harner, M. (1990). *The way of the shaman*. HarperOne.
- Eliade, M. (1964). *Shamanism: Archaic techniques of ecstasy*. Princeton University Press.
- Cajete, G. (2000). *Native science: Natural laws of interdependence*. Clear Light Publishers.

35. Somatic, Physiological, and Modern Integrative Practices

35.1 Sensory Deprivation & Floatation

- Lilly, J. C. (1977). *The deep self: Profound relaxation and the tank isolation technique*. Simon & Schuster.
- Kjellgren, A., & Westman, J. (2014). Beneficial effects of sensory isolation in flotation tanks as preventive health-care intervention – a randomized controlled pilot trial. *BMC Complementary and Alternative Medicine, 14*(1), 1–12.

35.2 Cold Exposure & the Wim Hof Method

- Hof, W. (2019). *The Wim Hof method: Activate your full human potential*. Sounds True.
- Hof, W., & Rosales, J. (2015). *Becoming the iceman*. ManKind Publishing.
- Kox, M., et al. (2014). Voluntary activation of the sympathetic nervous system and attenuation of the innate immune response in humans. *PNAS, 111*(20), 7379–7384.

35.3 Breathwork & Mind-Body Practices

- Grof, S. (1988). *The adventure of self-discovery*. SUNY Press.
- Nestor, J. (2020). *Breath: The new science of a lost art*. Riverhead Books.
- Benson, H. (1975). *The relaxation response*. William Morrow.
- Kabat-Zinn, J. (1990). *Full catastrophe living*. Delta.

35.4 Heat, Sweat, and Fasting

- Hannuksela, M. L., & Ellahham, S. (2001). Benefits and risks of sauna bathing. *The American Journal of Medicine, 110*(2), 118–126.
- Eliade, M. (1964). *Shamanism: Archaic techniques of ecstasy*. Princeton University Press.

36. The Vertical Frontier: Mountains, Mines, and the Limits of Endurance

36.1 Summits: Aspiration and the Sacred Heights

- Hillary, E. (1955). *High adventure*. Oxford University Press.
- Messner, R. (2014). *The crystal horizon: Everest – The first solo ascent*. Mountaineers Books.
- Bonatti, W. (2001). *The mountains of my life*. Modern Library.
- Terray, L. (2001). *Conquistadors of the useless*. Mountaineers Books.
- Diemberger, K. (1989). *Summits and secrets*. Mountaineers Books.
- Herzog, M. (1997). *Annapurna*. Modern Library.
- Reinhard, J. (1993). *The ice maiden*. National Geographic.
- Reinhard, J., & Ceruti, M. C. (2010). *Sacred mountains, sacred rocks*. Cotsen Institute of Archaeology Press.
- Simpson, J. (2004). *Touching the void*. Harper Perennial.
- Terris, D. (2013). *Aconcagua*. Mountaineers Books.

36.2 Yosemite Counterculture & Rock Revolution

- Robbins, R. (1992). *Advanced rockcraft*. Sierra Club Books.
- Harding, W. (1975). *Downward bound*. Mountain N' Air Books.
- Roper, S. (2004). *Camp 4*. Mountaineers Books.
- Long, J. (1998). *How to rock climb!*. Falcon Guides.
- Child, G. (1994). *Postcards from the ledge*. Stackpole Books.

36.3 Edge Figures of the Heights

- Honnold, A. (2017). *Alone on the wall*. W.W. Norton.
- Rosen, E. (2018). *Free solo* [Documentary film]. National Geographic.

- Osman, D. (1991–1998). *Masters of stone* [Film series]. Sender Films.
- Potter, D. (2014). *The mountain within*. Insight Editions.

36.4 Depths: Descent into Earth and Sea

- Collinson, P. (2003). *The international history of mining engineering*. Routledge.
- Verne, J. (2008). *Journey to the center of the earth*. Modern Library.
- Mayol, J. (1983). *Homo Delphinus: The dolphin within man*. Idelson-Gnocchi.
- Nery, G. (2014). *One breath: Freediving, death, and the quest to shatter human limits*. Harper.
- Beebe, W. (2004). *Half mile down*. Dover Publications.
- Cousteau, J. Y., & Dumas, F. (1953). *The silent world*. National Geographic.
- Exley, S. (1994). *Caverns measureless to man*. Cave Books.
- Taylor, V., & Taylor, R. (2000). *Blue meridian: The search for the great white shark*. Harper Perennial.
- Godfrey, A. (2010). *Sharkman*. HarperCollins.

36.5 Extremes: Polar Frontiers, Sky, and Innovation

- Shackleton, E. (1999). *South*. Penguin Classics.
- Amundsen, R. (2010). *The south pole*. Cambridge University Press.
- Baumgartner, F. (2012). *Mission to the edge of space*. National Geographic.
- Kittinger, J. (1960). *The long, lonely leap*. U.S. Air Force.
- Clarke, A. C. (2001). *Profiles of the future*. Orion.

37. Beasts of Burden and Power

37.1 Horse: Engine of Mobility and Empire

- Clutton-Brock, J. (1992). *Horse power: A history of the horse and the donkey in human societies*. Harvard University Press.
- Levine, M. A., Renfrew, C., & Boyle, K. (2003). *Prehistoric steppe adaptation and the horse*. McDonald Institute.
- Di Cosmo, N. (2002). *Ancient China and its enemies*. Cambridge University Press.

37.2 Camel: Master of Deserts and Trade

- Bulliet, R. W. (1990). *The camel and the wheel*. Harvard University Press.
- Al-Jallad, A. (2020). *The religion and rituals of the nomads of pre-Islamic Arabia*. Brill.
- Fagan, B. (2011). *Elixir: A history of water and humankind*. Bloomsbury.

37.3 Elephant: War, Awe, and Sacredness

- Trautmann, T. R. (2015). *Elephants and kings: An environmental history*. University of Chicago Press.
- Kistler, J. M. (2007). *War elephants*. University of Nebraska Press.
- Lair, R. C. (1997). *Gone astray*. FAO.

37.4 Dog: The First Ally

- Serpell, J. (1995). *The domestic dog*. Cambridge University Press.
- Morey, D. F. (2010). *Dogs: Domestication and the development of a social bond*. Cambridge University Press.
- Clutton-Brock, J. (1995). *Origins of the dog*. Yale University Press.

37.5 Falconry and the Sky Hunters

- Cummins, J. (1988). *The hound and the hawk*. Weidenfeld & Nicolson.
- Epstein, H. (2011). The origin of falconry. *Journal of the History of Biology*. (Original work published 1943).
- Macdonald, H. (2006). *Falcon*. Reaktion Books.
- Fadlallah, R. (2017). *Falconry in the Middle East*. AuthorHouse.
- Dixon, J. (2008). *Falcons and falconry in history*. Hancock House.

37.6 Resource and Economy Animals

- Sherratt, A. (1981). Plough and pastoralism: Aspects of the secondary products revolution. In *Pattern of the past*. Cambridge University Press.
- Crane, E. (1999). *The world history of beekeeping and honey hunting*. Routledge.

- Seeley, T. D. (2010). *Honeybee democracy*. Princeton University Press.
- Kuhn, D. (1988). *Silk and religion*. Oxford University Press.
- Zhao, F. (2015). *Chinese silks*. Yale University Press.
- Diamond, J. (1999). *Guns, germs, and steel*. W.W. Norton.

38. Machines of Motion: From Horses to Ford

- Ford, H. (1988). *My life and work*. Dover Publications. (Original work published 1922).
- Hounshell, D. A. (1984). *From the American system to mass production, 1800–1932*. Johns Hopkins University Press.
- Sorensen, C. E. (1956). *My forty years with Ford*. Norton.
- Chandler, A. D. (1977). *The visible hand: The managerial revolution in American business*. Harvard University Press.
- Flink, J. J. (1988). *The automobile age*. MIT Press.
- Norton, P. D. (2008). *Fighting traffic*. MIT Press.
- Mom, G. (2014). *Atlantic automobilism*. Berghahn Books.

39. Alien Mirrors: Creatures That Redefine Life

39.1 Octopus and Cephalopods

- Godfrey-Smith, P. (2016). *Other minds: The octopus, the sea, and the deep origins of consciousness*. Farrar, Straus and Giroux.
- Hanlon, R. T., & Messenger, J. B. (2018). *Cephalopod behaviour*. Cambridge University Press.
- Montgomery, S. (2015). *The soul of an octopus*. Atria Books.
- Wells, M. J. (1978). *Octopus: Physiology and behaviour of an advanced invertebrate*. Chapman & Hall.

39.2 Spiders

- Foelix, R. F. (2011). *Biology of spiders* (3rd ed.). Oxford University Press.
- Witt, P. N., Reed, C. F., & Peakall, D. B. (1968). *A spider's web: Problems in regulatory biology*. Springer.
- Shear, W. A. (1986). *Spiders: Webs, behavior, and evolution*. Stanford University Press.

- Preston-Mafham, K., & Preston-Mafham, R. (1993). *The natural history of spiders*. MIT Press.

39.3 Tardigrades

- Nelson, D. R. (2002). Current status of the Tardigrada: Evolution and ecology. *Integrative and Comparative Biology, 42*(3), 652–659.
- Møbjerg, N., et al. (2011). Survival in extreme environments — adaptations in tardigrades. *Journal of Zoology, 293*(1), 1–8.
- Jönsson, K. I. (2007). Tardigrades as a model for astrobiology. *Acta Astronautica, 60*(4–7), 136–140.
- Bertolani, R., et al. (2014). *Tardigrada: A handbook for the study of the phylum*. Cambridge Scholars Publishing.

40. Animal Art

40.1 Animals as Artists

- Morris, D. (1962). *The biology of art*. Aldine.
- Anderson, J. R. (2011). Animal innovation and creativity: Insights from animal art. *Animal Cognition, 14*(1), 141–147.

40.2 Prehistoric and Indigenous Animal Depictions

- Clottes, J. (2008). *Cave art*. Phaidon.
- Lewis-Williams, D. (2002). *The mind in the cave: Consciousness and the origins of art*. Thames & Hudson.
- Bahn, P. G., & Vertut, J. (1997). *Journey through the Ice Age*. University of California Press.
- Curtis, G. (2006). *The cave painters*. Anchor.

40.3 Animals as Sacred Symbols in Art

- Cirlot, J. E. (2001). *A dictionary of symbols*. Routledge. (Original work published 1962).
- Chevalier, J., & Gheerbrant, A. (1996). *A dictionary of symbols*. Blackwell.
- Ovid. (2004). *Metamorphoses* (A. D. Melville, Trans.). Oxford University Press.
- Campbell, J. (1988). *The power of myth*. Doubleday.

40.4 Modern Animal-Inspired Art

- Berger, J. (2009). *Why look at animals?*. Penguin.
- Beuys, J. (1984). *I like America and America likes me* [Performance documentation].
- Hirst, D. (1991). *The physical impossibility of death in the mind of someone living* [Shark installation]. Tate Modern.

41. Mammals of the Sea: Intelligence, Song, and Myth

41.1 Whales

- Payne, R. (1995). *Among whales*. Scribner.
- Whitehead, H. (2003). *Sperm whales: Social evolution in the ocean*. University of Chicago Press.
- Earle, S. (1995). *Sea change: A message of the oceans*. Ballantine Books.
- Slijper, E. J. (1979). *Whales*. Cornell University Press.
- Hoare, P. (2009). *Leviathan: Or, the whale*. HarperCollins.

41.2 Dolphins and Porpoises

- Lilly, J. C. (1961). *Man and dolphin*. Doubleday.
- Lilly, J. C. (1978). *Communication between man and dolphin: The possibilities of talking with other species*. Crown Publishers.
- Herman, L. M. (2010). What laboratory research has told us about dolphin cognition. *International Journal of Comparative Psychology, 23*(3), 310–330.
- Ridgway, S. H. (Ed.). (1987). *Handbook of marine mammals* (Vol. 1). Academic Press.

41.3 Orca: Apex Predator and Ocean Sovereign

- Ford, J. K. B. (2009). *Killer whales: The natural history and genealogy of Orcinus orca in British Columbia and Washington State*. UBC Press.
- Neiwert, D. (2015). *Of orcas and men: What killer whales can teach us*. Overlook Press.
- Whitehead, H. (2003). *Sperm whales: Social evolution in the ocean*. University of Chicago Press. (comparative cetacean social structure; useful context).
- Barrett-Lennard, L. G. (2000). Population structure and mating patterns of killer whales as revealed by DNA

- analysis. *Proceedings of the Royal Society B, 267*(1454), 259–265.
- Foote, A. D., et al. (2016). Genome-culture coevolution promotes rapid divergence of killer whale ecotypes. *Nature Communications, 7*, 11693.

41.4 Cuttlefish: Nature's Neural Visionaries (incl. Huberman)

- Hanlon, R. T., & Messenger, J. B. (2018). *Cephalopod behaviour* (2nd ed.). Cambridge University Press.
- Godfrey-Smith, P. (2016). *Other minds: The octopus, the sea, and the deep origins of consciousness*. Farrar, Straus and Giroux. (essential cephalopod cognition context).
- Wardill, T. J., et al. (2015). Neural control of rapid adaptive camouflage in cephalopods. *Philosophical Transactions of the Royal Society B, 371*(1704), 20150267.
- Mather, J. A., Anderson, R. C., & Wood, J. B. (2010). *Octopus: The ocean's intelligent invertebrate*. Timber Press. (cross-reference for ceph sensory/cognitive ecology).
- Huberman, A. / Huberman Lab (UC San Diego): Experimental work using cuttlefish to study vision and prey capture dynamics; binocular/eye-cover manipulation illustrating stereopsis-dependent strike accuracy; high-speed imaging and electrophysiology discussed across Huberman's talks/interviews and lab materials (pair with Hanlon & Messenger for technical depth).
- Feord, R., et al. (2020). Cuttlefish use stereopsis to judge distance. *Science Advances, 6*(12), eaay6033. (the "tiny 3D glasses" depth-perception study).

42. Massage Therapy & Bodywork

42.1 General Massage Therapy Texts

- Biel, A. (2019). *Trail guide to the body: A hands-on guide to locating muscles, bones and more* (6th ed.). Books of Discovery.
- Fritz, S., & Paholsky, M. J. (2020). *Mosby's fundamentals of therapeutic massage* (7th ed.). Elsevier.
- Beck, M. F. (2016). *Theory & practice of therapeutic massage* (6th ed.). Cengage Learning.
- Riggs, A. (2002). *Deep tissue massage: A visual guide to techniques*. North Atlantic Books.

- Davies, C., & Davies, A. (2015). *The trigger point therapy workbook: Your self-treatment guide for pain relief* (3rd ed.). New Harbinger Publications.
- Juhan, D. (2003). *Job's body: A handbook for bodywork* (3rd ed.). Station Hill Press.
- Foreman, J. (2014). *A nation in pain: Healing our biggest health problem.* Oxford University Press.
- Hargrove, T. R. (2014). *A guide to better movement: The science and practice of moving with more skill and less pain.* Better Movement.
- Doidge, N. (2007). *The brain that changes itself: Stories of personal triumph from the frontiers of brain science.* Viking.
- Jackson, M. (2002). *Pain: The science of suffering.* Columbia University Press.
- Capellini, S., & Van Welden, M. (2010). *Massage for dummies* (2nd ed.). For Dummies.
- Lidell, L., Thomas, S., Porter, S., & Jones, C. (2001). *The book of massage: The complete step-by-step guide to Eastern and Western techniques* (rev. ed.). Fireside.

42.2 Rolfing (Structural Integration)

- Rolf, I. P. (1989). *Rolfing: Reestablishing the natural alignment and structural integration of the human body for vitality and well-being* (rev. ed.). Healing Arts Press.
- Rolf, I. P. (1990). *Rolfing and physical reality.* Healing Arts Press.
- Bond, M. (1993). *Balancing your body: A self-help approach to Rolfing movement.* Healing Arts Press.
- Schultz, R. L., & Feitis, R. (1996). *The endless web: Fascial anatomy and physical reality.* North Atlantic Books.
- Maitland, J. (1995). *Spacious body: Explorations in somatic ontology.* North Atlantic Books.
- Jacobson, E. (2011). *Structural integration and energy medicine: A handbook of advanced bodywork.* Healing Arts Press.

42.3 Bowen Therapy

- Pennington, G. (2013). *A textbook of Bowen technique: A comprehensive guide to the practice of Bowen therapy.* Graham Pennington.
- Wilks, J. (2014). *Using the Bowen technique to address complex and common conditions.* Singing Dragon.
- Wilks, J. (2007). *Understanding the Bowen technique.* First Stone Publishing.

- Baker, J. (2001). *The Bowen technique*. Corpus Publishing.
- Baker, J. (2013). *Bowen unravelled: A journey into the fascial understanding of the Bowen technique*. North Atlantic Books.
- Whittaker, P. (2007). *Principles of Bowen technique*. Paul Whittaker.

42.4 Lomi Lomi

- Chai, M. R. (compiler). (2005). *Na Mo'olelo Lomilomi: The traditions of Hawaiian massage and healing*. Bishop Museum Press.
- Kahalewai, N. S. (2004). *Hawaiian lomilomi: Big island massage*. Mutual Publishing.
- Jim, H. U., & Arledge, G. (2007). *Wise secrets of aloha: Learn and live the sacred art of lomilomi*. Weiser Books.
- Allen, A. (2000). *The art of Hawaiian lomi lomi*. Self-published.
- Chalmers, R. (2001). *Lomi lomi: Hawaiian massage*. R. Chalmers.
- McKinnon, M. (2016). *Lomi lomi: A practitioner's manual*. Self-published.

42.5 Craniosacral Therapy

- Upledger, J. E. (2001). *Craniosacral therapy* (rev. ed.). North Atlantic Books.
- Upledger, J. E., & Vredevoogd, J. D. (1983). *Craniosacral therapy*. Eastland Press.
- Shea, M. J. (2007). *Biodynamic craniosacral therapy* (Vol. 1). North Atlantic Books.
- Kern, M. (2001). *Wisdom in the body: The craniosacral approach to essential health*. North Atlantic Books.
- Milne, H. (1995). *The heart of listening: A visionary approach to craniosacral work* (Vol. 1). North Atlantic Books.
- Manheim, C. (2001). *The myofascial release manual* (3rd ed.). Slack Incorporated. (Related, as often combined).

42.6 Myofascial Release

- Barnes, J. F. (1990). *Myofascial release: The search for excellence—A comprehensive evaluatory and treatment approach*. John F. Barnes.
- Duncan, R. (2014). *A therapist's guide to myofascial release*. Human Kinetics.

- Manheim, C. (2008). *The myofascial release manual* (4th ed.). Slack Incorporated.
- Earls, J., & Myers, T. (2010). *Fascial release for structural balance*. North Atlantic Books.
- Chaitow, L. (2013). *Fascial dysfunction: Manual therapy approaches*. Handspring Publishing.
- Schleip, R., Findley, T. W., Chaitow, L., & Huijing, P. A. (Eds.). (2012). *Fascia: The tensional network of the human body*. Churchill Livingstone.

42.7 Thai Massage

- Salguero, C. P. (2007). *The encyclopedia of Thai massage: A complete guide to traditional Thai massage therapy and acupressure* (2nd ed.). Findhorn Press.
- Chow, K. T. (2002). *Thai yoga massage: A dynamic therapy for physical well-being and spiritual energy*. Healing Arts Press.
- Mercati, M. (1998). *Thai massage: A step-by-step guide to traditional techniques*. Sterling Publishing.
- Gold, R. (2007). *Thai massage: A traditional medical technique* (2nd ed.). Mosby.
- Asokananda, H. (1990). *The art of traditional Thai massage*. Editions Duang Kamol.
- Balaskas, L., & Macfarlane, A. (2000). *Nuad bo'rarn: Traditional Thai massage*. Findhorn Press.

42.8 Shiatsu

- Beresford-Cooke, C. (2011). *Shiatsu theory and practice* (3rd ed.). Singing Dragon.
- Lundberg, P. (2003). *The book of shiatsu: A complete guide to using hand pressure and gentle manipulation to improve your health, vitality and stamina*. Gaia Books.
- Namikoshi, T. (1974). *Shiatsu therapy: Theory and practice*. Japan Publications.
- Jarmey, C., & Mojay, G. (1999). *Shiatsu: The complete guide*. Thorsons.
- Ohashi, W. (1976). *Do-it-yourself shiatsu: How to perform the ancient Japanese art of acupressure*. Dutton.
- Masunaga, S., & Ohashi, W. (1977). *Zen shiatsu: How to harmonize yin and yang for better health*. Japan Publications.

42.9 Tui Na & Qi-Based Massage Systems

- Pritchard, S. (2015). *Tui na: A manual of Chinese massage therapy*. Singing Dragon.

- Bisio, T., & Butler, F. (2007). *Zheng gu tui na: A Chinese medical massage textbook*. Zheng Gu Tui Na.
- Xiangcai, X. (2002). *Chinese tui na massage: The essential guide to treating injuries, improving health & balancing qi*. YMAA Publication Center.
- Mercati, M. (2018). *The tui na manual: Chinese massage to awaken body and mind*. Healing Arts Press.
- Thomas, S. (1994). *The handbook of Chinese massage: Tui na techniques to awaken body and mind*. Healing Arts Press.
- Yang, J. (2005). *Qigong massage: Fundamental techniques for health and relaxation* (2nd ed.). YMAA Publication Center.
- Kaneko, D. T. (2010). *Shiatsu anma therapy: DoAnn's short & long forms*. Kaneko Healing Arts.
- Chia, M., & Wei, W. U. (2013). *Chi nei ching: Muscle, tendon, and meridian massage*. Destiny Books.

References

Ader, R. (2007). *Psychoneuroimmunology* (4th ed.). Academic Press.

Ali, W. (2001). *The Clash of Fundamentalism: Crusades, Jihads and Modernity.* Verso.

Baldwin, A. L., & Trent, N. L. (2017). A randomized controlled trial of Reiki for women undergoing breast biopsy. *Holistic Nursing Practice, 31*(2), 80–89. https://doi.org/10.1097/HNP.0000000000000196

Baldwin, A. L., Vitale, A., Brownell, E., & De Stefano, G. (2020). The effects of Reiki on human physiology. *Journal of Alternative and Complementary Medicine, 26*(8), 695–702. https://doi.org/10.1089/acm.2019.0410

Beard, D. J., Rees, J. L., Cook, J. A., Rombach, I., Cooper, C., Merritt, N., ... Gray, A. M. (2018). Arthroscopic subacromial decompression for subacromial shoulder pain (CSAW): A multicentre, pragmatic, parallel group, placebo-controlled, three-group, randomised surgical trial. *The Lancet, 391*(10118), 329–338. https://doi.org/10.1016/S0140-6736(17)32457-1

Benedetti, F. (2008). *Placebo effects: Understanding the mechanisms in health and disease.* Oxford University Press.

Benson, H., & Friedman, R. (1996). Harnessing the power of the placebo effect and renaming it "remembered wellness." *Annual Review of Medicine, 47*(1), 193–199. https://doi.org/10.1146/annurev.med.47.1.193

Boehme, R., van Ettinger-Veenstra, H., Sundström, T., & Larsson, E. M. (2014). Enhanced hippocampal–prefrontal connectivity during rest in major depressive disorder. *Frontiers in Psychiatry, 5*, 34. https://doi.org/10.3389/fpsyt.2014.00034

Boyce, W. E., & DiPrima, R. C. (2017). *Elementary differential equations and boundary value problems (11th ed.).* Wiley.

Buchbinder, R., Osborne, R. H., Ebeling, P. R., Wark, J. D., Mitchell, P., Wriedt, C., ... Esmail, R. (2009). A randomized trial of vertebroplasty for painful osteoporotic vertebral fractures. *New England Journal of Medicine, 361*(6), 557–568. https://doi.org/10.1056/NEJMoa0900429

Cannon, A. J. (1901–1907). Spectral classification work at Harvard College Observatory [Observational data and classification plates]. *Harvard College Observatory Archives.*

Cannon, D. (2011). *The convoluted universe: Book four.* Ozark Mountain Publishing.

Capra, F. (1975). *The Tao of physics.* Shambhala.

Chalmers, D. J. (1996). The conscious mind: In search of a fundamental theory. *Oxford University Press.*

Cleary, T. (1993). *The flower ornament scripture: A translation of the Avatamsaka Sutra.* Shambhala.

Coan, J. A., Schaefer, H. S., & Davidson, R. J. (2006). Lending a hand: Social regulation of the neural response to threat. *Psychological Science, 17*(12), 1032–1039. https://doi.org/10.1111/j.1467-9280.2006.01832.x

Confucius. (1997). *Analects* (A. Waley, Trans.). Vintage.

Crowley, A. (1929/1997). *Magick in theory and practice.* Dover Publications. (Original work published 1929)

Davidson, R. J., Kabat-Zinn, J., Schumacher, J., Rosenkranz, M., Muller, D., Santorelli, S. F., ... Sheridan, J. F. (2003). Alterations in brain and immune function produced by mindfulness meditation. *Psychosomatic Medicine, 65*(4), 564–570. https://doi.org/10.1097/01.PSY.0000077505.67574.E3

Decety, J. (1996). The neurophysiological basis of motor imagery. *Behavioural Brain Research, 77*(1–2), 45–52. https://doi.org/10.1016/0166-4328(95)00225-1

Diego, M. A., & Field, T. (2009). Moderate pressure massage elicits a parasympathetic nervous system response. *International Journal of Neuroscience, 119*(5), 630–638. https://doi.org/10.1080/00207450802329605

Doniger, W. (Trans.). (1981). *The Rig Veda: An anthology.* Penguin Classics.

Dumas, G., Nadel, J., Soussignan, R., Martinerie, J., & Garnero, L. (2010). Inter-brain synchronization during social interaction. *PLoS ONE, 5*(8), e12166. https://doi.org/10.1371/journal.pone.0012166

Dyson, F. W., Eddington, A. S., & Davidson, C. (1920). A determination of the deflection of light by the Sun's gravitational field, from observations made at the total eclipse of 29 May 1919. Philosophical Transactions of the Royal Society A: *Mathematical, Physical and Engineering Sciences, 220*(571–581), 291–333. https://doi.org/10.1098/rsta.1920.0009

Einstein, A. (1916/2005). *The foundation of the general theory of relativity.* In H. A. Lorentz, A. Einstein, H. Minkowski, & H. Weyl, The principle of relativity (pp. 111–164). Dover Publications. (Original work published 1916)

Field, T. (2016). Massage therapy research review. *Complementary Therapies in Clinical Practice, 24*, 19–31. https://doi.org/10.1016/j.ctcp.2016.04.005

Feynman, R. P., Leighton, R. B., & Sands, M. (1963). *The Feynman lectures on physics, Vol. 1.* Addison-Wesley.

Gaia Collaboration, Prusti, T., de Bruijne, J. H. J., Brown, A. G. A., Vallenari, A., Babusiaux, C., ... Bailer-Jones, C. A. L. (2016). The Gaia mission. *Astronomy & Astrophysics, 595*, A1. https://doi.org/10.1051/0004-6361/201629272

Garcia-Argibay, M., Santed, M. A., & Reales, J. M. (2019). Efficacy of binaural auditory beats in cognition, anxiety, and pain perception: A meta-analysis. *Psychological Research, 83*(2), 357–372. https://doi.org/10.1007/s00426-017-0946-8

Goyal, M., Singh, S., Sibinga, E. M. S., Gould, N. F., Rowland-Seymour, A., Sharma, R., ... Haythornthwaite, J. A. (2014). Meditation programs for psychological stress and well-being: A systematic review and meta-analysis. *JAMA Internal Medicine, 174*(3), 357–368. https://doi.org/10.1001/jamainternmed.2013.13018

Guth, A. H. (1997). *The inflationary universe: The quest for a new theory of cosmic origins*. Perseus Books.

Hamblin, M. R. (2017). Mechanisms and applications of the anti-inflammatory effects of photobiomodulation. *AIMS Biophysics, 4*(3), 337–361. https://doi.org/10.3934/biophy.2017.3.337

Hankey, A. (2005). The scientific value of Ayurveda. *Journal of Alternative and Complementary Medicine, 11*(2), 221–225. https://doi.org/10.1089/acm.2005.11.221

Hawking, S. (1988). *A brief history of time: From the big bang to black holes*. Bantam.

Hecht, J. (2016). *Laser pioneers*. Academic Press.

Horvath, A. O., & Symonds, B. D. (1991). Relation between working alliance and outcome in psychotherapy: A meta-analysis. *Journal of Counseling Psychology, 38*(2), 139–149. https://doi.org/10.1037/0022-0167.38.2.139

Huijing, P. A. (2009). Epimuscular myofascial force transmission: A historical review and implications for new research. *Journal of Biomechanics, 42*(1), 9–21. https://doi.org/10.1016/j.jbiomech.2008.09.027

Kaplan, R. (2000). *The nothing that is: A natural history of zero*. Oxford University Press.

Kallmes, D. F., Comstock, B. A., Heagerty, P. J., Turner, J. A., Wilson, D. J., Diamond, T. H., ... Gray, L. A. (2009). A randomized trial of vertebroplasty for osteoporotic spinal fractures. *New England Journal of Medicine, 361*(6), 569–579. https://doi.org/10.1056/NEJMoa0900563

Kaptchuk, T. J. (2000). *The web that has no weaver: Understanding Chinese medicine*. McGraw-Hill.

Konvalinka, I., Xygalatas, D., Bulbulia, J., Schjoedt, U., Jegindo, E.-M., Wallot, S., ... Roepstorff, A. (2011). Synchronized arousal between performers and related spectators in a fire-walking ritual. *Proceedings of the National Academy of Sciences, 108*(20), 8514–8519. https://doi.org/10.1073/pnas.1016955108

Laozi. (2003). *Tao Te Ching* (D. C. Lau, Trans.). Penguin Books. (Original work published ca. 4th century BCE)

Lane, J. D., Kasian, S. J., Owens, J. E., & Marsh, G. R. (1998). Binaural auditory beats affect vigilance performance and mood. *Physiology & Behavior, 63*(2), 249–252. https://doi.org/10.1016/S0031-9384(97)00436-8

Langevin, H. M., Cornbrooks, C. J., & Taatjes, D. J. (2005). *Fibroblasts form a body-wide cellular network. Histochemistry and Cell Biology, 122*(1), 7–15. https://doi.org/10.1007/s00418-004-0670-y

Leavitt, H. S. (1912). Periods of 25 variable stars in the Small Magellanic Cloud. *Harvard College Observatory Circular, 173*, 1–3.

Levänen, S., Jousmäki, V., & Hari, R. (1998). Vibration-induced auditory-cortex activation in a congenitally deaf adult. *Current Biology, 8*(15), 869–872. https://doi.org/10.1016/S0960-9822(98)70327-2

Lutz, A., Greischar, L. L., Rawlings, N. B., Ricard, M., & Davidson, R. J. (2004). Long-term meditators self-induce high-amplitude gamma synchrony during mental practice. *Proceedings of the National Academy of Sciences, 101*(46), 16369–16373. https://doi.org/10.1073/pnas.0407401101

McCraty, R., Atkinson, M., Tomasino, D., & Bradley, R. T. (2009). The coherent heart: Heart–brain interactions, psychophysiological coherence, and the emergence of system-wide order. *Integral Review, 5*(2), 10–115.

Moseley, J. B., O'Malley, K., Petersen, N. J., Menke, T. J., Brody, B. A., Kuykendall, D. H., ... Wray, N. P. (2002). A controlled trial of arthroscopic surgery for osteoarthritis of the knee. *New England Journal of Medicine, 347*(2), 81–88. https://doi.org/10.1056/NEJMoa013259

Nasr, S. H. (2015). *Islam and the plight of modern man*. Kazi Publications.

Newton, I. (1687). *Philosophiæ Naturalis Principia Mathematica*. Jussu Societatis Regiæ.

O'Regan, B., & Hirshberg, C. (1993). *Spontaneous remission: An annotated bibliography*. Institute of Noetic Sciences.

Ogilvie, M. B. (2000). *Women in science: Antiquity through the nineteenth century (2nd ed.)*. MIT Press.

Palumbo, R. V., Marraccini, M. E., Weyandt, L. L., Wilder-Smith, O., McGee, H. A., Liu, S., & Goodwin, M. S. (2017). Interpersonal autonomic physiology: A systematic review of the literature. *Personality and Social Psychology Review, 21*(2), 99–141. https://doi.org/10.1177/1088868316628405

Patwardhan, B. (2014). Ayurveda and integrative medicine: Riding a tiger. *Journal of Ayurveda and Integrative Medicine, 5*(1), 1–2. https://doi.org/10.4103/0975-9476.128848

Payne, C. H. (1925). *Stellar atmospheres: A contribution to the observational study of high temperature in the reversing layers of stars* (Doctoral dissertation, Radcliffe College). Harvard University Press.

Peper, E., & Ancoli, S. (1979). A biofeedback and electromyographic study of voluntary control of skin temperature. *Biofeedback and Self-Regulation, 4*(1), 1–9. https://doi.org/10.1007/BF00998906

Penrose, R. (1994). *Shadows of the mind: A search for the missing science of consciousness*. Oxford University Press.

Popp, F. A. (1992). Biophoton emission: Experimental background and theoretical approaches. *Modern Physics Letters B, 6*(21), 1269–1296. https://doi.org/10.1142/S0217984992001309

Punkanen, M., & Ala-Ruona, E. (2012). Contemporary vibroacoustic therapy: Perspectives on clinical practice, research, and training. *Music and Medicine, 4*(3), 128–135. https://doi.org/10.1177/1943862112445324

Rand, W. (2019). *The Reiki touch: Complete handbook.* Sounds True.

Russell, H. N. (1929). On the composition of the Sun's atmosphere. *Astrophysical Journal, 70*(1), 11–82. https://doi.org/10.1086/143197

Schedlowski, M., Enck, P., Rief, W., & Bingel, U. (2015). Placebo responses in medicine: Mechanisms and clinical implications. *Philosophical Transactions of the Royal Society B: Biological Sciences, 370*(1677), 20140108. https://doi.org/10.1098/rstb.2014.0108

Schleip, R. (2003). Fascial plasticity: A new neurobiological explanation, Part 1. *Journal of Bodywork and Movement Therapies, 7*(1), 11–19. https://doi.org/10.1016/S1360-8592(02)00067-0

Schleip, R., Findley, T. W., Chaitow, L., & Huijing, P. A. (2012). *Fascia: The tensional network of the human body.* Churchill Livingstone.

Seife, C. (2000). *Zero: The biography of a dangerous idea.* Viking.

Seto, A., Kusaka, C., Nakazato, S., Sato, T., Hisamitsu, T., & Takeshige, C. (1992). Detection of extraordinary large bio-magnetic field strength from human hand during external Qi emission. *Acupuncture & Electro-Therapeutics Research, 17*(1), 75–94. https://doi.org/10.3727/036012992816356486

Silver, F. H., Freeman, J. W., & DeVore, D. (2001). Viscoelastic properties of human skin and processed dermis. *Skin Research and Technology, 7*(1), 18–23. https://doi.org/10.1034/j.1600-0846.2001.007001018.x

Smithsonian Magazine. (2025, March). A century ago, Cecilia Payne-Gaposchkin showed us what stars are made of. *Smithsonian Magazine.*

Stecco, C., Pavan, P., Porzionato, A., Macchi, V., Lancerotto, L., & De Caro, R. (2011). Mechanisms of pain in myofascial pain syndrome: A histological study. *European Journal of Pain, 15*(1), 55–62. https://doi.org/10.1016/j.ejpain.2010.05.009

Takata, H. (1981). *Reiki: Hawayo Takata's story.* Office of Hawayo Takata.

Tang, Y. Y., Hölzel, B. K., & Posner, M. I. (2015). The neuroscience of mindfulness meditation. *Nature Reviews Neuroscience, 16*(4), 213–225. https://doi.org/10.1038/nrn3916

Thorne, K. S. (1994). *Black holes and time warps: Einstein's outrageous legacy.* W. W. Norton & Company.

Thrane, S., & Cohen, S. M. (2014). Effect of Reiki therapy on pain and anxiety in adults: An in-depth literature review of randomized trials with effect size calculations. *Pain Management Nursing, 15*(4), 897–908. https://doi.org/10.1016/j.pmn.2013.07.008

Usui, M. (2003). *The original Reiki handbook of Dr. Mikao Usui* (F. Petter, Trans.). Lotus Press. (Original work published 1990)

van der Kolk, B. A. (2014). *The body keeps the score: Brain, mind, and body in the healing of trauma.* Viking.

Wahbeh, H., Calabrese, C., & Zwickey, H. (2007). Binaural beat technology in humans: A pilot study to assess psychologic and physiologic effects. *Journal of Alternative and Complementary Medicine, 13*(1), 25–32. https://doi.org/10.1089/acm.2006.6201

Watts, A. (1974). *Cloud-hidden, whereabouts unknown: A mountain journal.* Vintage Books.

Watts, A. (1996). *The book: On the taboo against knowing who you are.* Vintage Books. (Original work published 1969)

Weerapong, P., Hume, P. A., & Kolt, G. S. (2005). The mechanisms of massage and effects on performance, muscle recovery, and injury prevention. *Sports Medicine, 35*(3), 235–256. https://doi.org/10.2165/00007256-200535030-00004

Weiss, R. (1972). *Electromagnetically coupled broadband gravitational antenna.* Massachusetts Institute of Technology.

Winkelman, M. (2010). *Shamanism: A biopsychosocial paradigm of consciousness and healing.* Praeger.

Zubieta, J. K., Bueller, J. A., Jackson, L. R., Scott, D. J., Xu, Y., Koeppe, R. A., & Nichols, T. E. (2005). Placebo effects mediated by endogenous opioid activity on µ-opioid receptors. *Journal of Neuroscience, 25*(34), 7754–7762. https://doi.org/10.1523/JNEUROSCI.0439-05.2005

Glossary of Terms

Preface to the Glossary

Language is not neutral. Every term we use carries the weight of its tradition, its worldview, and its limits. The purpose of this glossary is twofold:

1. To offer **traditional definitions** as they are understood in medicine, science, philosophy, and metaphysical traditions.
2. To provide **modified, integrative definitions** that reframe those terms within the alchemical framework of this book.

In some cases, new compound terms — here called **"superphrases"** — are introduced. These are scholarly-sounding yet integrative constructs that blend empirical rigor with metaphysical openness, designed to bridge skeptic and practitioner alike.

Allopathic Medicine

- *Traditional:* The dominant system of Western medicine, focused on diagnosing and treating disease primarily with drugs, surgery, and radiation.
- *Modified:* A powerful but partial framework. Allopathy excels at acute and structural intervention but often excludes consciousness, energy, and context. In an integrative model, it is one tool among many, not the whole toolbox.

Ancillary Measure

- *Traditional:* An indirect or secondary measure used in research when the phenomenon itself cannot be directly observed (e.g., biomarkers as proxies for stress).
- *Modified:* A bridge concept. Ancillary measures are how science can engage healing phenomena now — heart rate variability, oxytocin, cortisol shifts — without claiming they exhaust the whole.

Attunement

- *Traditional:* Emotional resonance between people, often described in psychology as the felt sense of being understood and in physiology as autonomic synchrony.
- *Modified:* More than empathy. Attunement is the mechanism and metaphor of healing itself: resonance across consciousness fields, measurable in physiology yet lived as presence.

Ayurveda

- *Traditional:* An ancient Indian system of medicine emphasizing balance across body, mind, spirit, and the five koshas (layers of being). Treatments include diet, herbs, massage, yoga, and meditation.
- *Modified:* A coherent whole-person health model that anticipates modern integrative frameworks. Ayurveda articulates multiple "bodies" of health that parallel modern stress biology and psychosomatic medicine.

Biofield

- *Traditional:* A hypothesized organizing field of energy and information around and within the body, not yet formally recognized by mainstream science.
- *Modified:* The experiential correlate of measurable subtle phenomena — magnetic emissions, electrical skin conductance, infrared heat. The biofield is both metaphor and candidate mechanism.

Bodywork

- *Traditional:* A broad category of hands-on therapies (massage, myofascial release, structural integration) designed to improve physical function.
- *Modified:* Bodywork is not only musculoskeletal manipulation but a mode of consciousness–body interaction. It often overlaps with energy work when presence and intention are central.

Chakra

- *Traditional:* Centers of subtle energy in Indian and yogic traditions, often aligned with endocrine glands and psychological functions.
- *Modified:* Functional metaphors for regulatory nodes in consciousness–body systems, potentially correlating with measurable bioelectric or magnetic phenomena.

Consciousness

- *Traditional:* Awareness or subjective experience, often treated in neuroscience as an emergent property of brain activity.
- *Modified:* The zero point, the field of potential itself. Not a product but the substrate of experience. Consciousness emits polarities, sustains oscillations, and integrates them back into awareness.

EEG (Electroencephalogram)

- *Traditional:* A measurement system that records brainwave activity through scalp electrodes.
- *Modified:* A tool for mapping correlates of consciousness. Captures oscillations but not the essence of awareness — an ancillary measure of a deeper field.

EKG (Electrocardiogram)

- *Traditional:* A measurement of the heart's electrical activity.
- *Modified:* Beyond cardiac rhythm, an ancillary measure of coherence, resonance, and relational entrainment.

Empirical

- *Traditional:* Knowledge derived from observation, experiment, and repeatable measurement.
- *Modified:* Expanded to include both direct and ancillary measures. "Empirical Plus" accepts correlational data (e.g., entrainment, placebo) as legitimate evidence of consciousness–physiology interaction.

Energy Work

- *Traditional:* A broad term for healing modalities that manipulate or engage subtle energies (Reiki, qi gong, therapeutic touch).
- *Modified:* Energy work describes practices rooted in attunement, intention, and resonance. It is not opposed to bodywork but completes it by engaging the subtle field of the person.

Gravity

- *Traditional:* A fundamental physical force of attraction between masses.
- *Modified:* The classic example of an "impossible measured" — known by outcomes (falling apples, orbiting planets) long before mechanisms were understood. A precedent for how healing should be treated.

Ineffable

- Traditional: Refers to realities, experiences, or insights that cannot be fully expressed in language, and even art. The concept acknowledges that some dimensions of consciousness or spirituality transcend description.
- Limitation: Labeling something "ineffable" can risk shutting down inquiry, placing it beyond dialogue or investigation. What is called ineffable may instead be what current language, science, or culture has not yet learned to articulate.
- Integrative Alternative: Treating the ineffable as a horizon rather than a barrier invites humility and curiosity. It challenges us to expand our metaphors, symbols, and scientific models to approach — even if never fully capture — what lies beyond words.

Lightworker

- *Traditional:* A New Age term for someone who channels or works with healing light or higher vibrations to assist others.
- *Modified:* A cultural label for intuitive healers who view their role as bringing consciousness, compassion, and subtle energy into the healing space.

Materialism

- *Traditional:* The doctrine that matter is the fundamental substance in nature, and all phenomena (including consciousness) arise from material interactions.
- *Modified:* A useful but narrowing worldview. Materialism explains much but not all; it falters where phenomena exceed physical reduction.

Metaphysics

- *Traditional:* The branch of philosophy dealing with first principles and ultimate reality, beyond physical phenomena.
- *Modified:* In practice, the symbolic grammar cultures use to articulate what science cannot yet measure. Not opposed to empiricism but complementary to it.

Newest Mathematical Models

- *Traditional:* Contemporary frameworks in mathematics such as chaos theory, complexity theory, fractals, information theory, and holographic models of reality. Each challenges classical linear, deterministic assumptions.
- *Modified:* Together these models provide formal languages for describing consciousness as field-like, relational, and emergent. They suggest reality is not reducible to parts, but patterned, self-organizing, and deeply interwoven — an ontology much closer to metaphysics than to classical materialism.

Ontology

- *Traditional:* The branch of philosophy dealing with the nature of being.
- *Modified:* The ground of questions that matter and energy alone cannot answer. In this framework, consciousness is treated as the primary ontology.

Philosophy

- *Traditional:* The systematic study of knowledge, reality, and existence.
- *Modified:* The intellectual ancestor of both science and metaphysics, and still their interpreter. Philosophy names the questions that science cannot measure but must face.

Placebo Effect

- *Traditional:* Symptom improvement arising from expectation, belief, or context rather than the active properties of a treatment.
- *Modified:* Proof of the mind–body bridge. Placebo is not "nothing," but evidence of consciousness influencing physiology. Reiki and other energy practices amplify and direct this capacity.

Prana / Qi / Ki

- *Traditional:* Life force or vital energy in Vedic, Chinese, and Japanese traditions.
- *Modified:* Symbolic languages for the same substrate science encounters as bioelectricity, biomagnetism, and entrainment fields. Different dialects of the same principle.

Quantum Physics

- *Traditional:* The branch of physics that describes the behavior of matter and energy at atomic and subatomic scales, characterized by uncertainty, probability, and wave-particle duality.
- *Modified:* The first empirical system to admit that observation alters outcome — effectively placing consciousness inside the equations. Quantum entanglement, superposition, and collapse echo metaphysical claims of non-locality and intentionality.

Reductionism

- **Value:** A method of inquiry that isolates and analyzes parts to understand mechanisms. It provides clarity, precision, and measurable outcomes, making it indispensable in science and medicine.
- **Limitation:** When adopted as a worldview rather than a tool, reductionism risks fragmenting reality, ignoring the relationships, contexts, and emergent properties that cannot be reduced to components alone.
- **Integrative Alternative:** Healing and consciousness studies benefit from complementing reductionist analysis with systems thinking, emergence, and relational fields — perspectives that honor both the parts and the whole.

Reiki

- *Traditional:* A Japanese healing system developed by Mikao Usui in the early 20th century, using hands-on or near-body techniques to channel universal life energy (*ki*).
- *Modified:* A modern codification of ancient energy practices. Reiki exemplifies how presence, intention, and symbol can be formalized into a system that bridges East–West models of healing.

Resonance

- *Traditional:* A physical phenomenon where a system vibrates at greater amplitude when frequencies align.
- *Modified:* The shared heartbeat of physics and metaphysics. Resonance is literal in waveforms, symbolic in relationships, and clinical in healing encounters.

Skeptic

- *Traditional:* One who questions or doubts accepted claims without sufficient evidence.
- *Modified:* An essential partner in inquiry, but incomplete when doubt becomes dogma. True skepticism demands openness to disproof *and* to unexpected confirmation.

Symbol vs. Signal

- *Traditional:* Symbols are metaphoric representations; signals are measurable physical phenomena.
- *Modified:* In healing, symbols are proto-scientific vocabularies awaiting translation into signals. Reiki symbols, chakras, sacraments — each can be honored as symbol and explored as potential signal.

Synchronicity

- *Traditional:* Coined by Carl Jung to describe meaningful coincidences with no apparent causal connection.
- *Modified:* A possible expression of pattern-recognition across consciousness fields. Synchronicity may act as an ancillary measure of consciousness–environment interaction.

Vibration

- *Traditional:* Oscillatory movement around an equilibrium point, a physical phenomenon.
- *Modified:* The universal metaphor of healing traditions and the universal fact of physics. Consciousness itself may be described as vibration: zero emitting oscillations into polarity and returning to baseline.

Vibroacoustic Therapy (VAT)

- *Traditional:* A therapeutic modality that uses low-frequency sound vibrations delivered through a table, chair, or mat to relax the body and improve health outcomes.
- *Modified:* A clinical bridge between metaphysics and medicine. VAT demonstrates that vibration is both symbol and signal: ancient metaphor rendered in modern technology.

Superphrases: Bridging Empirical and Metaphysical Language

While classical terms ground the conversation, new integrative language can expand it. "Superphrases" combine traditional scholarly terms into research-ready frameworks that acknowledge science's methods while embedding them in a larger context. These serve as conceptual tools sthat use familiar language in integrative combinations.

Logical Reduction Ancillary Measurement System (LRAMS)

Accepts reductionist tools but reframes them as partial. Uses ancillary measures (e.g., HRV, cortisol) to study consciousness–body interactions now, while admitting the substrate of consciousness is larger than its proxies.

Empirical Correlate Expansion Model (ECEM)

Expands empiricism by validating correlational markers of healing (outcomes, biomarkers) as legitimate evidence. ECEM acknowledges these correlates as footholds into the study of consciousness without pretending they exhaust the field.

Consciousness Baseline Oscillation Framework (CBOF)

Frames consciousness mathematically as zero (baseline), emitting polarities (+/–) into oscillations (waves). Provides a bridge between metaphysics (Brahman, vibration) and physics (wave-particle duality) in a shared ontology.

Integrative Resonance Measurement Paradigm (IRMP)

Treats resonance as the universal bridge across disciplines: measurable in physics (waves), biology (entrainment, HRV), and metaphysics (vibration, ki, prana). IRMP positions resonance as both symbol and signal of healing.

Synchronicity Integration Protocol (SIP)

Acknowledges synchronicity as more than coincidence: a potential expression of pattern recognition across consciousness fields. SIP proposes structured documentation of synchronicities in clinical and research settings as data points, treating them as ancillary measures of the consciousness–environment interface.

Appendix - Dr. Hunt -Thesis and Dissertation Scholarly Review

Appendix A

PARAPSYCHOLOGY REDISCOVERED

Hunt, M. (2023). *Parapsychology rediscovered* (Doctoral dissertation, University of Sedona).

Scholarly Overview of *Parapsychology Rediscovered*

Michael Hunt's dissertation, *Parapsychology Rediscovered* (2025), examines the relationship between psychology and parapsychology, advancing the view that both disciplines address different but interconnected aspects of human consciousness. At its core, the work emphasizes the nonlocality of consciousness—the idea that consciousness cannot be reduced to physical mechanisms alone—and proposes that parapsychology offers a vital additional lens through which psychology may better understand mind, behavior, and human experience.

Structure of the Dissertation

The dissertation is divided into five primary sections: introduction, psychology literature review, parapsychology literature review, discussion, and conclusion.

- **Introduction** – Establishes the problem of disciplinary separation, noting that while psychology is recognized as a mainstream science of behavior and mind, parapsychology has often been dismissed as pseudoscience. Hunt identifies early issues in parapsychological research, including fraud, difficulty replicating results, and reliance on subjective reports, as factors that shaped its reputation. At the same time, he positions parapsychology as a rediscovery of forgotten dimensions of human consciousness, particularly nonlocal and anomalous experiences.
- **Psychology Literature Review** – Surveys traditional psychological theories that grapple with unseen or unmeasurable aspects of mind. Jung's concepts of the collective unconscious and archetypes are central here,

alongside discussions of behaviorism, prosocial behavior, instinct, learning, and cognition. These perspectives provide a foundation for integrating parapsychology into the broader psychological framework.
- **Parapsychology Literature Review** – Explores key terms and ideas in psi research, including extrasensory perception (ESP), psychokinesis (PK), precognition, and telepathy. Drawing on authors such as Wills Harman, Kevin Brewer, and Brendan O'Regan, Hunt outlines both the possibilities and the methodological challenges of parapsychology. Special attention is given to "paraphysics," a conceptual language for theorizing paranormal processes in ways that parallel scientific models.
- **Discussion** – Focuses on clinical applications, particularly the role of parapsychology in psychotherapy. Drawing from works like *Perspectives of Clinical Parapsychology* (2012) and Kelley's *Clinical Parapsychology: Extrasensory Exceptional Experiences* (2015), this section highlights how anomalous experiences—such as synchronicity, out-of-body experiences, or near-death experiences—can be understood in therapeutic contexts without automatically being pathologized. Cultural frameworks and archetypal imagery are emphasized as interpretive tools.
- **Conclusion** – Summarizes the dissertation's central claim that psychology and parapsychology are not opposing but complementary lenses. The recognition of consciousness as nonlocal underscores the value of expanding psychology beyond empirical behavior and cognition into experiential and symbolic domains.

Central Themes

Three major themes emerge throughout the dissertation:

1. **Nonlocality of consciousness** – Consciousness is described as a phenomenon that cannot be fully explained through neurological activity alone. It is instead expressed through archetypes, images, symbolic experiences, and anomalous events that transcend local physical explanation.
2. **Parapsychology as a complementary lens** – Parapsychology is presented not as a rival to psychology but as an essential perspective that investigates anomalous, extrasensory, and culturally embedded experiences. These studies, while difficult to replicate,

enrich the understanding of human consciousness when viewed alongside established psychological theories.

3. **Reputation and historical challenges** – The work acknowledges that parapsychology acquired a poor reputation due to fraudulent séances, unrepeatable experiments, and sensationalized claims in its early history. Hunt treats these not as reasons to dismiss the field but as historical barriers that must be recognized if parapsychology is to find renewed legitimacy.

Contribution

The dissertation's contribution lies in re-framing parapsychology as a rediscovery rather than an innovation. By situating anomalous experiences within the framework of psychology, it bridges two fields that have long been treated as separate. Its emphasis on nonlocality of consciousness provides a conceptual anchor, while its clinical discussion highlights the importance of not pathologizing patients who report extrasensory experiences.

Summary

Parapsychology Rediscovered presents a comprehensive synthesis of psychology and parapsychology, arguing that both fields are concerned with the same fundamental subject: the human mind. By addressing nonlocality, integrating archetypal theory, and acknowledging the challenges of parapsychological research, Hunt positions parapsychology as a valuable lens for modern psychology. The dissertation underscores that experiences often dismissed as anomalous or extraordinary may hold important clues to the nature of consciousness and the future of psychological science.

Appendix B

THE SOUND OF SPIRITUAL SELF-REALIZATION

Hunt, M. (2022). The sound of spiritual self-realization (Master's thesis, University of Metaphysics).

Scholarly Overview of *The Sound of Spiritual Self-Realization*

Michael Hunt's master's thesis, *The Sound of Spiritual Self-Realization* (2022), investigates the relationship between sound-based therapies, meditation, and the broader metaphysical question of consciousness. The work situates vibroacoustic therapy (VAT) and brainwave entrainment as scientifically measurable practices that can alter physiological states, while contrasting these approaches with meditation, which is described as the most enduring path toward true spiritual realization. The thesis integrates empirical neuroscience, psychology, metaphysical philosophy, and parapsychology to frame a holistic account of consciousness, its measurable correlates, and its non-measurable depths.

Structure of the Thesis

The thesis is organized into four main sections: introduction, review of literature, discussion, and conclusion.

- **Introduction** – Establishes the problem of how consciousness may be altered through intentional or induced practices. It defines "mind" in metaphysical terms, distinguishing it from the physical brain, and sets out the thesis aim: to explore how sound-based healing techniques, while effective in altering brain states, differ fundamentally from meditation in their capacity to achieve spiritual self-realization.
- **Review of Literature** – Provides extensive coverage of electroencephalogram (EEG) science, brainwave classifications, and research into meditation. It draws upon authorities such as Paul Nunez on EEG neurophysics, William Tatum on brainwave states, and Claire Braboszcz and colleagues on meditation-related gamma wave activity. This section also covers vibroacoustic therapy, brainwave entrainment, and binaural beats as explored by researchers including Olav Skille, Christine Beauchene, Ezzatollah Ahmadi, and Tianbao Zhuang. Parallel discussions include Jung's

- theories of archetypes and the unconscious, metaphysical definitions of consciousness, and reflections on self-awareness and metacognition.
- **Discussion** – Explores the limits and potentials of both meditation and vibroacoustic therapy. Meditation is portrayed as an intentional practice that not only alters brain states but may also restructure neural morphology and deepen introspection, allowing access to unconscious content. Vibroacoustic therapy and binaural beats, by contrast, are described as external stimuli that passively synchronize brainwaves, with demonstrable benefits for focus, memory, and anxiety reduction, though without altering the deeper contents of mind or consciousness itself. The section also distinguishes between self-awareness, defined as metacognition and reflective thought, and spiritual self-realization, described as a transformative recognition of consciousness beyond brain function.
- **Conclusion** – Summarizes the findings that VAT and meditation both facilitate altered brain states but serve different purposes. While VAT may aid cognitive performance and relaxation, meditation remains unique as a path toward spiritual self-realization because of its introspective and transformative qualities. The thesis closes by affirming that consciousness transcends brain activity, and realization of this truth requires personal introspection, not solely physiological intervention.

Central Themes

Several recurring themes unify the thesis:

1. **Consciousness and Brain Waves** – Consciousness is not identical with the brain, though brainwave activity provides measurable correlates. EEG technology demonstrates states such as alpha, beta, theta, delta, and gamma waves, yet these represent physiological conditions rather than the full scope of mind.
2. **Meditation vs. Vibroacoustic Therapy** – Both practices can alter brain states, but meditation is intentional and introspective, potentially reshaping mental content, while vibroacoustic therapy is externally induced and supports brain function without altering unconscious structures.
3. **Self-Awareness vs. Spiritual Self-Realization** – Self-awareness is linked to psychological processes of reflection and social comparison, while realization

involves a deeper recognition of consciousness as distinct from physical brain activity.
4. **Metaphysics and Parapsychology** – The thesis positions metaphysics as the study of realities beyond physics and psychology, while parapsychology examines mental powers outside conventional explanation. Both frameworks are employed to underscore the nonlocal and unquantifiable nature of consciousness.
5. **The Question of Spirit or Soul** – Although the thesis does not require belief in a soul to discuss consciousness, it acknowledges that metaphysical inquiry into self-realization often involves considerations of universal consciousness, spirit, or higher awareness.

Contribution

The thesis contributes to metaphysical science by offering a synthesis of neuroscience, psychology, and metaphysics that underscores the limits of physiological approaches to consciousness. It highlights the measurable effects of vibroacoustic therapy on brainwave synchronization while affirming that spiritual realization is primarily achieved through meditation and introspection. By distinguishing between awareness and realization, the thesis provides a framework for understanding consciousness not only as a scientific phenomenon but also as a deeply personal and spiritual pursuit.

Summary

The Sound of Spiritual Self-Realization presents a multi-disciplinary exploration of consciousness, bridging empirical EEG research, psychological theory, and metaphysical reflection. While vibroacoustic therapy demonstrates the potential of sound to alter brain states, meditation stands out as the primary method for accessing deeper layers of mind and achieving spiritual self-realization. Ultimately, Hunt's thesis concludes that while science may continue to map the physiological correlates of consciousness, the discovery of its true nature remains an introspective and metaphysical journey.

Author Education & Credentials

I completed my undergraduate studies at Capella University and earned both my Master's and PhD through the University of Sedona and the International Metaphysical Ministry, under the direction of Dr. Leon Masters. My early foundation in emergency medicine came through the Paramedic Program at Santa Rosa Junior College in California, and I later expanded into integrative care as a Licensed Massage Therapist in Washington State, a Reiki Master, and a licensed hypnotherapist. I founded Reiki Massage Metaphysical Healing Service in Olympia, WA in Nov, 2023.

My work is fueled by a profound interest in energy-based therapeutic systems, intention, meditation, and practices such as Shiatsu and Tui Na. I see these not as alternatives but as pieces of a unified, yet largely unexplored, model of non-dogmatic expansion in healing. If medicine is truly a "practice," then we must allow ourselves to practice more radically: to test new models, explore new vocabularies, and embrace approaches that science is only beginning to measure. The science is here, but the work should not wait on science—and the world should not wait on science either.

The Hidden Chapter:

A Candidate for the Most Valuable Information I Have Ever Received

From Knowing to Gnosis

> *To my Daughter—this single chapter holds the book I wished to write for you: all there is to know about magic.*
>
> *Love Dad*

I once drove north through the golden hills of Mendocino County to The City of Ten Thousand Buddhas in Ukiah, California. A seminary campus which is open to the public. Peacocks walking around the campus openly as if part of the crowd. Deer, just grazing in the grass near the visitor center. I stepped into the main temple. It was cavernous—rows of empty meditation mats stretched across the polished floor, and the ceiling lifted into a hush that swallowed even my own footsteps.

Curiosity carried me farther in. I chose a mat at random and sat. A minute later, soft robes whispered at my shoulder. A monk stood beside me, face open, voice almost playful.

"You're sitting on a meditation mat," he said.

"Yes," I answered.

"You're not meditating."

The words landed like an anvil—so clean, so perfect in its accuracy that I couldn't even register whether it was meant as a slight. It was too sharp, too concise, as if the whole of my struggle had been distilled into a single strike. Offense dissolved before it could form, replaced by a strange awe at the sheer mastery of the delivery. I laughed, caught between recognition and discomfort, and admitted the truth: I had tried meditation many times and failed spectacularly. Silence, and stillness of the mind seemed inaccessible.

He shook his head. "That's because you're doing it wrong," he said, not unkindly. "If you are trying to quiet your mind, you will fail every time. Consciousness is pure thought. That is its nature. You can't turn it off."

He let the words hang there, then continued: "But you can change your relationship to it. Imagine yourself as an observer, or a listener. Notice that even when you don't participate, your thoughts continue. They go on by themselves. And when you truly see this, something important happens: you discover you are not your mind."

He knelt to be level with me, as if we were conspiring together. "Meditation is not the forced silencing of thoughts," he said. "It is the recognition of the one who notices."

Then he gave me a practice so simple it seemed to fall within the category of the impossible. "Close your eyes," he said. "Tell yourself you will think of only one thing. Choose anything—a white dot, the color green, the feeling of your breath at the tip of your nose. Hold just that."

He paused, already smiling at the outcome he knew would follow. "Even advanced meditators forget. The mind starts to wander. Stories appear. Errands, memories, sermons, catastrophes. Then, suddenly, you remember what you were doing. 'Oh yes—one thing.' At that moment, open your eyes and ask: *"What happened between those two points?"*

With a certain emphasis he stated, "It does not matter *what* happened. Your mind may have embroidered a revelation or simply checked whether you locked the door. The content isn't the lesson. The lesson is that your thoughts are stronger than your will. You commanded, 'Just one thing,' and the mind did what minds do—it took over."

He sat back on his heels. "Now ask the more difficult question: *How often does this happen in your daily life?* How often does the mind run the show while you believe you are choosing?" He tapped his chest lightly. "Meditation shows you that you are not your mind. You are not your thoughts. You are the awareness that notices them—something deeper, quieter, and not compelled, that which you truly are. Always keep that eye on your mind." (of course this spawned immediate thoughts about ancient Egyptian symbols that closely mimic structures within the brain, such as the eye of Horus)... I digress.

The temple around us felt even larger. I realized I had been measuring progress by the wrong instrument—by the absence of thought—when the real measure was the intimacy of attention, the reliability of turning toward the one who notices. He hadn't offered me a technique so much as a redefinition.

I tried it there on the mat. Eyes closed, I chose a single point—the simplest shade of green. Within seconds the mind did what it does: it collected memories of a coat, a forest, a logo, a hospital sign, and then it drafted a to-do list for Monday. When the remembering came—*Oh right, just green*—I opened my eyes as instructed and asked myself, *What happened between those two points?* The answer came back as a collage of images and impulses, none of which I had chosen. I laughed quietly.

On the way out I stopped at the threshold and turned back to the mats, suddenly grateful for their emptiness. Also, in some sense, the feeling as if the entire encounter was a gift. The emptiness of the temple, the lone student who approached to offer a lesson. It is as if the whole event was orchestrated. Perhaps that is one version of synchronicity.

The empty mats were not an invitation to conquer thought but to witness it. The practice I carried away from Ukiah was almost scandalously direct: do not try to switch off the mind. Sit, choose one thing, notice the wandering, and then—without blame—notice the one who noticed. Contemplate that piece of oneself, recognize it is oneself, work within that place, outside of chaos of the mind, and within the silence found there. Repeat. Repeat. Repeat.

Years later, I still think of that afternoon as one of the most valuable lessons I have ever received. It did not make the mind quieter overnight. It made *me* less fooled by it. And that small shift—away from wrestling thoughts and toward recognizing awareness—changed the way I approach healing, teaching, and my own life. The mind keeps doing what minds do. Awareness keeps noticing. Somewhere in that simple relationship, freedom begins.

> *"The first condition of success in Magic is therefore the ability to control thought; to still the mind, to concentrate it upon a single idea."* **(Crowley,** *Magick in Theory and Practice,* **1929/1997, Ch. I)**

"The master has failed more times than the student has tried."

> *— Anonymous proverb*

www.ingramcontent.com/pod-product-compliance
Lightning Source LLC
Chambersburg PA
CBHW051620010526
44119CB00009B/216